THE ART OF My Father's Dragon

Written by Ramin Zahed

Foreword by Bonnie Curtis and Julie Lynn

Abrams, New York

Contents

Foreword
7

Charting an Unpredictable Journey
11

CHARACTERS
41

LOCATIONS
115

Anatomy of a Scene:
The Crocodile River Crossing
216

Final Words
221

Acknowledgments
222

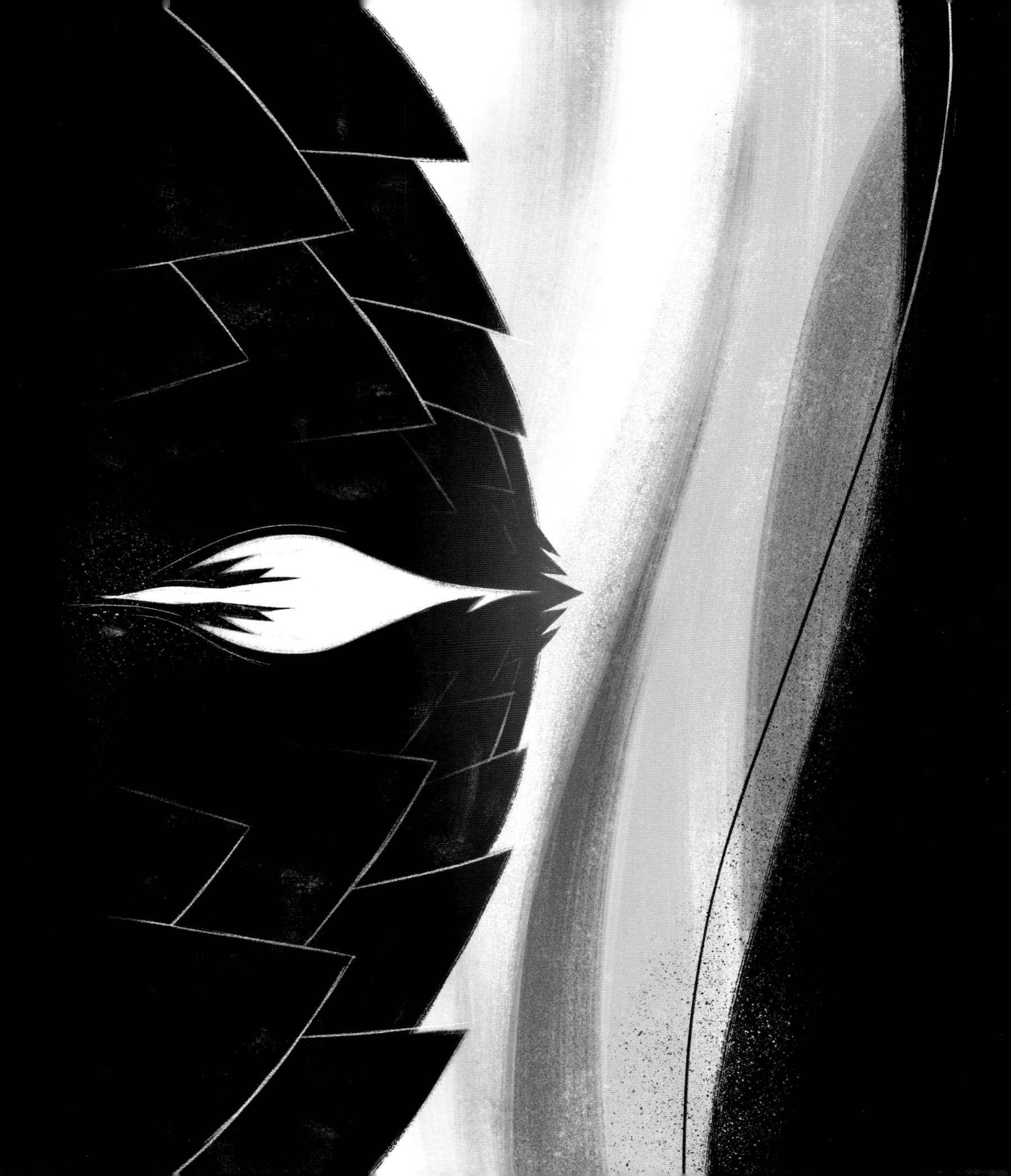

Foreword

By Bonnie Curtis and Julie Lynn

More than a dozen years ago, Julie optioned Ruth Stiles Gannett's *My Father's Dragon* with writers Meg LeFauve and John Morgan. Together we opened our hearts to what this wonderful book could become and started to think about how to develop its story for cinema. The book had been Julie's husband's favorite as a child . . . and all three of us had shared it with our own children.

When we partnered at Mockingbird Pictures, Bonnie joined that merry band. Not long after we set the project up with Cartoon Saloon and Netflix, we lost John to cancer. His spirit and his voice are firmly established in the film, but he is missed every day.

We feel so blessed to have Cartoon Saloon as our animation home—everyone there has been extraordinary. Meg and Julie clearly remember the moment when we asked ourselves, "Who do we most want to bring the film to life?" Just as Meg was saying out loud, "Whoever is that studio that made *The Secret of Kells*" . . . Julie flipped up her notebook to show Meg that she had written down . . . *The Secret of Kells*! We had just completed our film *Albert Nobbs* when Julie traveled to show it at the Dublin International Film Festival and asked our colleague Alan Moloney at Parallel Films to introduce us to Cartoon Saloon. Nora and Julie met in a hotel lobby. Halfway through the conversation, Julie realized that Nora was pitching her on Cartoon Saloon . . . and she was able to say, "No, no, no . . . we came to convince *you* . . . Let's start making it!" Together with Tomm Moore and Paul Young, the whole group (Nora, Meg, John, and us) pitched the project in Hollywood and chose Netflix as our studio, which turned out to be a happy and fruitful collaboration.

We strongly believe that no group of animators in the world is making more beautiful art than Cartoon Saloon. There is something about their hand-drawn, unique style that is extraordinarily intimate and emotional. Its bespoke nature cannot be duplicated by the larger studios working principally in 3-D. Nora herself is the best match imaginable for the material. Elmer and Boris are two youngsters figuring out how to overcome the obstacles in their lives. As a mother herself to two boys, Nora understands their strengths, their vulnerabilities, and their humor. A sense of wonder too often confined to the young among us stays very much alive in Nora. She is the perfect interpreter for our film.

We are fascinated by the boy who goes off in search of something outside himself, only to realize that he has everything he needs inside his own "backpack" (what a metaphor)! The book that inspires our film ends with Elmer freeing the dragon, but for our movie that is just the launching point—what movie-makers call "the inciting incident"—for a story about friendship. About how honesty, authenticity, wit, and vulnerability can help us become our best selves. What Nora and Meg have done so beautifully is illustrate this journey with two regular boys . . . one of whom just happens to be a dragon.

We warned Ruth early on that the movie would diverge quite dramatically from the book that has inspired it. She asked us to hold on to one important thing: that Elmer's decisions are his to make—when to go, whom to stand up for, when to return. Ruth wrote the book in 1948, when that was a big statement—for a boy to have personal agency, something she felt was

PAGE 1 Early concept art by Rosa Ballester Cabo

PAGES 2-3 Early concept for mushroom path by Ciarán Duffy

PAGES 4-5 Concept art by Lily Bernard

OPPOSITE Production scene illustration for Elmer's dream by Áine Mc Guinness

OPPOSITE Concept art from 2016 by Nora Twomey

ABOVE Early concept art exploring a flat, theater stage style by Lily Bernard

underrepresented in children's literature. The book has never yet gone out of print and has been published in many, many languages and countries.

Nora Twomey. We stand in awe of her! In the early days she voiced every one of the characters for the animatics—with hilarious and moving differences—and drew templates with her magic pen. She is inside every frame of this film, along with her incredible artistic team. We have watched her direct the entire team of artists, as well as the voice performers, with immense talent and grace.

The vibrant world that Nora and Cartoon Saloon and our LA-based sound and colour teams have created is exquisite. Please enjoy the stunning images in these pages, which offer a glimpse of the meticulous, creative craftsmanship that has occurred over these many years in service to the story of *My Father's Dragon*.

We hope that the audience feels the journey of these characters as we do, taking home the knowledge that Boris and Elmer have chosen to make a true friendship, therein "finding their fire" . . . as we hope you all may do.

Bonnie Curtis and **Julie Lynn**'s Mockingbird Pictures productions include award-winning festival favorites *Albert Nobbs*, *5 to 7*, and *To the Bone*—as well as studio fare including *Life*, *Terminator: Dark Fate*, and the upcoming *Heart of Stone*. Before joining Mockingbird, Ms. Curtis worked for fifteen years with Steven Spielberg, on movies including *Schindler's List*, *Saving Private Ryan*, and *Minority Report*. Prior to Ms. Curtis joining the company, Ms. Lynn produced independent films under the Mockingbird banner including *Nine Lives*, *Mother and Child*, and *The Jane Austen Book Club*. *My Father's Dragon* is Mockingbird's first feature in animation.

Charting an Unpredictable Journey

OPPOSITE Concept artwork, inspired by children's imaginations, by Rosa Ballester Cabo

Ever since author Ruth Stiles Gannett's charming children's book *My Father's Dragon* was first published in 1948, young readers have enjoyed its wildly imaginative story about the friendship between a young boy and a dragon on an undiscovered island. The Newbery Medal–winning book, which is part of an acclaimed trilogy by the author and is illustrated by Gannett's stepmother, Ruth Chrisman Gannett, is the source of inspiration for the new movie produced by Ireland's beloved studio Cartoon Saloon and Netflix and directed by studio co-founder and Oscar©-nominated director Nora Twomey (*The Breadwinner*).

The journey to bring young Elmer Elevator and Boris the dragon to the silver screen began after Cartoon Saloon's Paul Young and Twomey's first meeting with Julie Lynn of Mockingbird Pictures (acclaimed producers of live-action fare such as *Albert Nobbs* and *Terminator: Dark Fate*) in a hotel in Dublin in 2012. "Soon after that, we began creating some concept pieces with the artists at Cartoon Saloon and thinking about how to explore the themes from the book in a cinematic way," recalls Twomey. The project entered its development period; for animated films this process can take anything from a year to a decade or beyond, and is usually done alongside other projects.

Around this time, Twomey, who had co-directed *The Secret of Kells* and had been head of story on Tomm Moore's Oscar-nominated 2014 movie *Song of the Sea*, also took on the widely loved 2017 feature *The Breadwinner* as her next project. This film raised its full budget first and so would become Twomey's next production. She would serve as *The Breadwinner*'s director. "I had young kids at that point, so it took a while before I felt ready for *My Father's Dragon* to enter production. But through the years, we were picking up Ruth's book and doing colourful and imaginative-visual explorations of Nevergreen and Wild Island. While the concept art was underway, writers Meg LeFauve (*Inside Out*, *The Good Dinosaur*) and John Morgan were creating an outline and treatment for the film. Twomey recalls; "Later, when John's illness became apparent, he helped Meg, Julie, Bonnie, Paul, and me pitch the film around Hollywood. I'll always remember the passion John had for this film, the world he could evoke with his beautiful storyteller's voice, and the love he had for Elmer and Boris. Everyone in the room with him could feel it too."

My Father's Dragon became one of the first feature animated films picked up by Netflix. John Morgan passed away in early 2016, several months before Twomey herself was diagnosed with cancer. Meg would go on to write the script in several drafts, each one clarifying Elmer's arc and enriching his emotional journey. Twomey recovered fully, and it wasn't until she wrapped up the publicity run for *The Breadwinner* in 2018 that she and the team at the Kilkenny-based studio were able to devote their full attention to *My Father's Dragon*. The film, which is Cartoon Saloon's fifth animated feature, following *The Secret of Kells* (2009), *Song of the Sea* (2015), *The Breadwinner* (2018), and *WolfWalkers* (2020), went through a series of narrative changes during its initial phases.

As Twomey explains, "I started working on the animatic in 2018, and we completed the first rough pass in a couple of months with Giovanna Ferarri, my head of story; a tiny, agile storyboard team; and editors Richie Cody and Darren Holmes. At that time, I was still searching for what the film was ultimately about. We had built the script around the theme of trust—the trust between the boy and his mum; a trust that had

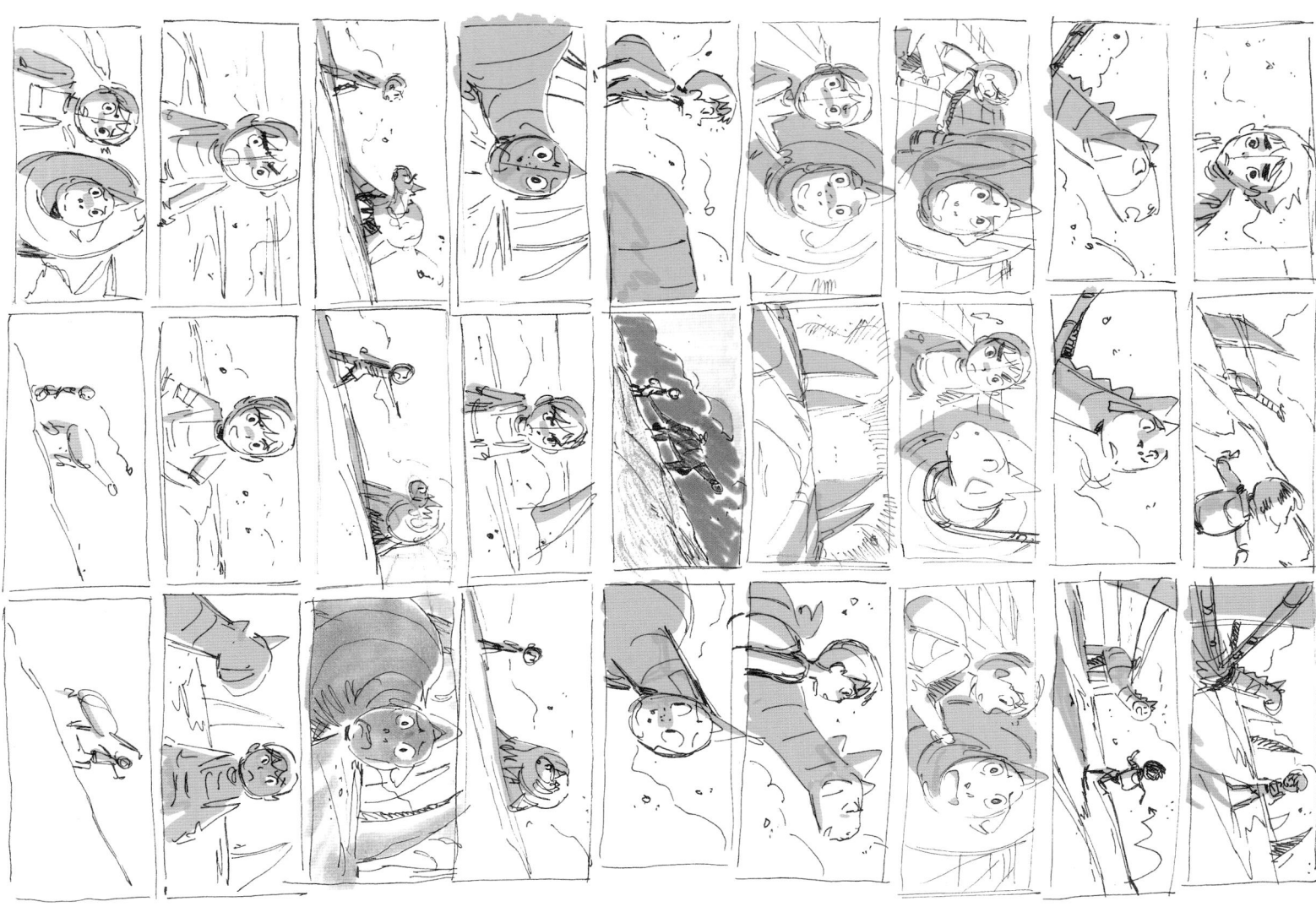

been broken. But something about that idea didn't quite seem right to me instinctually, probably because of what I'd gone through recently—the journey this project had taken, an innocence that had been lost. It took a number of animatic passes for me to connect with the heart of the story. Eventually, I realized the heart of the film is that Elmer and Boris are afraid of the challenges they face yet find strength in their friendship together. The film is an exploration of fear; for each character it manifests in different ways, and each deals with it in different ways. Trust is a thematic element, but not the core theme. By confiding their fears, Elmer and Boris find strength in each other's compassion, and that becomes bigger than their fear itself."

The director remembers reading the book to her sons, who were quite young when she first embarked on the journey. "I felt immediately that Ruth was such a fantastic storyteller," she notes. "She always keeps the reader right beside Elmer, never running ahead of him, never moralizing, never telling them what they should think. I also understood how Elmer's mom wanted to protect him from something huge that is going on in their lives; in a different way, my children understood that, too. I felt very privileged to be able to watch my children play and observed how they escaped into their own imaginations to try to make sense of the world around them. Ultimately your children go on without you, so for Elmer to find his 'Wild Island survival tools' without his mum felt important to me. He's coming of age, he's figuring things out for himself."

To dig deeper into the source, Twomey traveled to the town of Trumansburg in Upstate New York to meet with Gannett in person. "Ruth was ninety-six when I met her in her very colourful family home, surrounded by nature. It was late summer, and runner beans grew in her vegetable garden, butterflies flitted around the wildflower borders. Ruth made fresh bread, and I ate it with her, along with soup made by her daughter Louise and blueberry pie with berries freshly picked from the garden. Ruth had raised seven daughters in that much-loved yellow house with her husband, Peter," says the director. "Not only that, but she had played an active role in the local community and helped young children with the local school's literacy program down through the years.

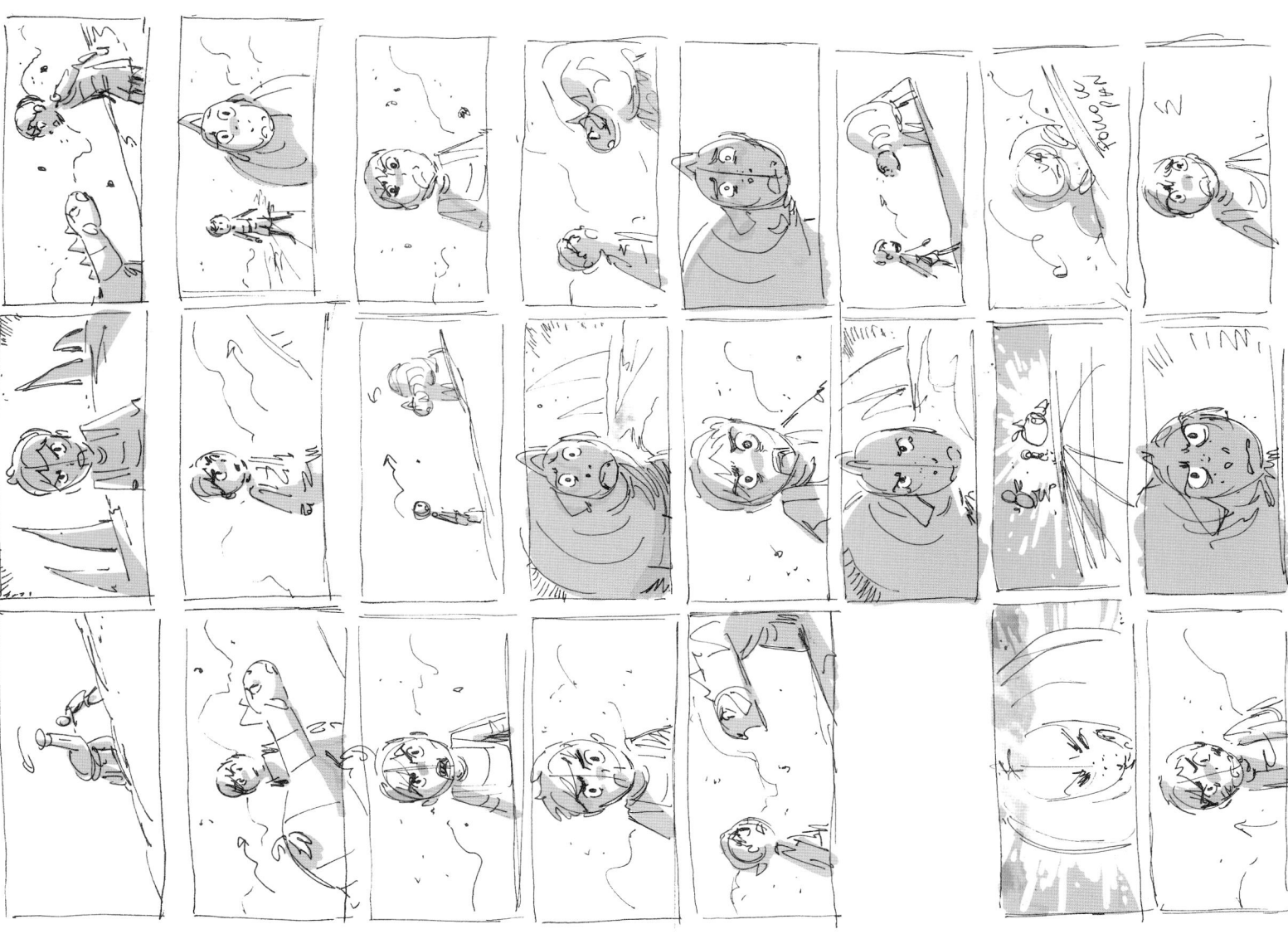

She was incredibly inspiring, and I wanted to take some of her passion, intelligence, and love of life and include as much of it as I could in the film."

Of course, like many animation professionals, Twomey and her talented team at Cartoon Saloon had to adapt to the brave, new world of working remotely during the height of the COVID-19 pandemic. *"The Breadwinner* had its own set of challenges and difficulties, but this movie had another level of obstacles, with everyone working from home, actors recording pick-ups in their bedroom closets (to dampen sound reverberance), and none of us knowing whether we could get together again in one month, one year, or ever," recalls Twomey. "However, on the bright side, the challenges of a pandemic production necessitated documenting everything on a much bigger level, since we had to prepare many share-screen visual slideshows, documents, and references for each sequence of the film to ensure we were communicating fully, and that nothing fell between cracks."

Twomey says the immersive quality of Elmer's world both in Nevergreen city and on Wild Island played a big role in the overall visual narrative. "We wanted to place the audience inside the friendship between Boris and Elmer," she notes. "In a way, *My Father's Dragon* is a buddy film between the boy and the dragon, but it's also very much about vulnerability and generosity. It's not about having the biggest muscles, but having the biggest heart. There's a lot of self-awareness and bravery in the admission of fear, at any age. That's something that I'm really happy that we got onto the screen."

The director also points out that working with Netflix executives Melissa Cobb, Gregg Taylor, and Lara Breay allowed the film's creative team to develop and polish the central themes of the movie extensively, and made sure these themes echoed throughout the story organically. "If there was a story resolution problem, we always tracked the source to the beginning," she says. "When you have problems in the third act, it's always essential to revisit the setup. For me, it was very instinctual. For example, there are scenes in the movie where Boris reveals this deep shame about not being 'dragon enough.'

THIS SPREAD Storyboard panels by Federico Chericoni

And later on, Elmer knows by empowering Boris, by giving him confidence, he may lose him. Elmer has to be utterly selfless when he says to Boris, 'Go do what you need to do, and I'll be here for you when you get back.' We kept refining their emotional arcs so that we could earn these important moments."

Cartoon Saloon co-founder Tomm Moore, who is also one of *My Father's Dragon*'s producers, notes, "I think it's a joy to see how Nora brought something deeply personal and authentic to the story, and yet she remained inclusive of all her collaborators and the source material. To me, this project is a master class in the subtle and difficult art of adaptation. The movie's scope and ambition on every level are way above anything else we have attempted, and it really shows on-screen. To my mind, this film is an expression of the style we evolved over all these years, but with production values dialed up to the maximum."

Twomey hopes that audiences will recognize a little bit of their own experiences and lives reflected back at them when they watch *My Father's Dragon* with their families. "We hope that they are taken away on an adventure, but it's also important that they feel the heart and truth of the story," she concludes. "Ruth believed in young people like Elmer when she first wrote him into existence in 1948; she never underestimated or devalued children. That's timeless and universal. If we've seen anything recently, it is the power of children and how they can use their voices to help us all make changes for the better. *My Father's Dragon*, like all stories, is intended as a companion, one that walks us through the tough times and challenges in our lives to remind us that we're not alone, whatever our age."

Departmental Snapshots

DIRECTING

When the cast and crew of *My Father's Dragon* talk about their experiences on the movie, they often mention Nora Twomey's gifts of empathy, compassion, and clarity of vision. The film's assistant director, Louise Bagnall, who is best known for directing the Oscar-nominated short *Late Afternoon* and has also worked on the studio's *Song of the Sea*, *The Breadwinner*, and *WolfWalkers*, says, "She's very perceptive and doesn't rush things; she's very careful when she makes decisions. That reflects in her directing style and the choices she makes for her characters. She also likes to listen to everyone and is open to everyone's ideas and contributions; she observes her own kids and is eager to bring the same realness to the characters and is always keen on finding the truth in each one of them."

"Nora understood thoroughly why every single thing in her film exists and what each moment, action, line, or glance achieved in the greater narrative," says assistant director Mark Mullery. "Nora has a sense of exactly how a sequence or a shot will come together coupled with an openness to having other voices introduce a depth she might not yet have discovered, but knows her team are capable of."

Bagnall points out that the ambition and scope of *My Father's Dragon* were quite different from the other Cartoon Saloon movies. "We have all the different characters and the many locations, so the scale and range of the film is larger than previous projects. However, the friendship at the heart of this story is pretty real—even though it's between a giant striped dragon and a young boy."

One of the key challenges for the director and her three assistant directors was figuring out the logistics for this massive project, especially since the production faced the many difficulties of working remotely in early 2020, right after the preproduction stage and the completion of the animatics. "On top of the movie being one of the biggest projects we had worked on at Cartoon Saloon, we also had to adapt to the new world where everyone had to work from home," says Bagnall. "We needed to keep people connected to each other. Everyone was brilliant and they were all working very hard, but we started to see cracks appearing in the system and had to work twice as hard to make sure everyone was communicating."

Assistant director Fabian Erlinghäuser mentions that the scale of the movie was twice as large as anything

ABOVE This art by Tomm Moore was the first image that got Boris close to the book design but also allowed for the expressiveness of animation.

that he had worked on. While part of the animation and cleanup was handled by FOST studio in France, the majority of the production was handled in-house, by up to 180 people at Cartoon Saloon at the height of the project. "It was a huge number for us, but if you compare it to a big Hollywood studio movie like *The Lion King*, we still had fewer people working on it," he notes.

"It was something that we hadn't done in previous features," says Bagnall. "Just figuring out the logistics of trying to find time for Nora to actually review all the work from all the departments in her calendar every day was a challenge. It was important for us to keep the openness that we like in our studio between the director and the team members all throughout the project, despite the restrictions of the pandemic."

Erlinghäuser believes another wrinkle was that the studio encourages its talent to spread their wings and explore other positions on different projects. "Some of the people that I had worked with on previous projects had gone on to work in different departments, so we often had to recast key roles," says the Cartoon Saloon veteran, who has worked as an animator, animation supervisor, and animation director on the studio's four previous movies and TV shows. "But one of the main priorities for me is that we still want to preserve that original spark that made a scene great in the first place, despite the fact that it might go through many hands. There's a chance that a scene that was funny in the storyboard or animatic stage might lose its spark after it has gone through seven or eight departments. So, just shepherding a scene all the way to the finish line is the greatest achievement I could wish for."

Bagnall also points out that while the storyline and setting of the movie are quite different from Cartoon Saloon's previous efforts, it has a lot in common with them in terms of general creative direction and distinctive characters. "I think what drives the team at the studio is not the specifics of the stories, but the point of view: The big goal for us is to find a way to tell a story that means something to somebody, especially to give kids feelings of empowerment and connection."

Twomey herself says she hopes audiences will see a little bit of themselves reflected on the big screen. "I certainly do as a filmmaker," she notes. "I mean, all we can do is scratch the surface of ourselves and try to reflect something real that connects us to the audience."

THE SCREENPLAY

The early treatment for the movie was first fleshed out by the team of John Morgan and Pixar veteran Meg LeFauve, using the original 1948 book as a source of inspiration. The duo worked together on the project and turned in at least twenty versions of the treatment before Morgan passed away in March 2016.

LeFauve, who is best known for writing the screenplays for *Inside Out* and *The Good Dinosaur*, says she loved the book as a young girl. "I loved a child who had answers to any problem in his backpack! And I loved the idea of freeing a dragon and wondered, what if that dragon became your friend? I found out that my then-writing partner, John Morgan, also loved the book. At the time I had never done animation, and honestly, it was a long shot I could get it made. But we optioned the rights and got the most amazing producers and then took it to Cartoon Saloon. It was like winning the lottery when Nora [Twomey] wanted to do it.

The acclaimed screenwriter says she likes to think of any film as a long road, and the best part for her was the people who were traveling with her. "John Morgan was such a creative force and inspiration as we formed the story, and it was a dream come true when Nora came on board and made it her own," she says. "Everyone throughout the process cared so deeply for Elmer and Boris the dragon—and what we could say with this movie; that sometimes we can't control what happens to us: We can't fix it, or make it like it was before, but as long as we are willing to be in the struggle, connect to friends, and believe in each other, we will be okay, and maybe even have a wonderful adventure.

Translating the book's relatively short plot to a full-length feature had its challenges; instead of directly adapting the book, the filmmakers took inspiration from its characters and themes and developed a narrative from that. "The original book is a lovely story that we had to expand and dig into in the source material," says LeFauve. "We very much wanted to keep to the spirit and fun of the book while at the same time deepening and expanding the story. The book ends with Elmer freeing the dragon, and we knew we wanted the main relationship of the film to be between Elmer and the dragon. The next challenge was that the book is episodic, while we needed a story with rising action and stakes that took Elmer on an adventure through the island and within himself . . . John, Nora, and I spent years creating many versions of the adapted story. Once the story went into storyboards, it evolved again as the stunning art, artists, and actors brought the story to life."

Every creative project comes with its challenges, says the acclaimed screenwriter. "It's part of the process—to push ourselves to find the best possible and most authentic story," adds LeFauve. "As creatives and artists, we choose to go on a journey with our character, to take on the challenges and evolve ourselves, to embrace the adventure. When we first optioned the book I sat down with our producer, Julie Lynn, and she asked me, 'Who in our wildest dreams would be our animation partner on this film?' We both had the same answer—Cartoon Saloon. So, that's why I consider myself the luckiest writer in the world to have the chance to work with Nora and the artists at the studio. Their artistry is breathtaking, their storytelling so emotional, and their process is so inclusive."

STORYBOARD AND ANIMATICS

After wrapping up *The Breadwinner*, Nora Twomey was able to devote her complete attention to the project in 2018. Once the script was ready for animatic in late 2018, it entered a phase of rapid, rough storyboards to get the essential film onto the screen as early as possible. On any animated film, you can expect narrative changes; as animation is such a visual medium, a paragraph of description can become a few minutes of adventure. The story lives and breathes; a cut here, an expansion there.

Giovanna Ferrari, who was both the head of story and the animation director on the movie, recalls that the script had a very solid core and that the characters and the friendship between Boris and Elmer were very vibrant and convincing from the beginning.

"We actually did the first draft of the animatic quickly in three months," says Ferrari, who had also worked on *Song of the Sea*, *The Breadwinner*, and *Wolfwalkers*. "We did a quick beat board and established the sensibility.

OPPOSITE Storyboards by Giovanna Ferrari. This was one of the many passes of the tiger sequence, exploring the tigers leaving the camouflage of their environment to close in on Elmer and Boris.

We did a first pass from September to December, and then realized there were a lot of things that we could let go and focus on what was at the heart of the movie." Often, a first-pass animatic is bloated. The story and editing team had to start cutting away anything that Elmer didn't need.

Ferrari points out that one of the biggest challenges of her job was the fact that her duties as head of story and animation director on the project overlapped. "We were supposed to be done with the storyboards by the time we began the animation process, but things were changing, as they often do," she recalls. "The movie is also so lively and there was so much action going on, and I had to make sure the early poses did not get lost in translation and made it to the final animation stage."

"We all felt free to express ideas, spitball, and brainstorm," says Ferrari. "You felt this freedom to go as far as you wanted with your crazy ideas, and then maybe bring them back down to something more grounded. I felt that we could play with the story and characters until everything really clicked. I know that there are some story rooms where you feel judged and maybe not really free. But Nora has this talent in creating a very safe space for herself and her team to play and have fun. That brings out the best in everyone."

In terms of the actual story, Ferrari says the realism in certain aspects of the characters and their interactions with each other also made the experience quite different from anything else she had worked on. "As a single parent, I felt the same pressures that the mother feels in the movie," she shares. "I also had to relocate with my kid on my own from Italy to Ireland, so I know how it feels for the child and the parent to be uprooted. I think it's important that the movie expresses these difficult situations and features these flawed characters without any exaggerations or fake tropes. It also confronts the way boys have to deal with fear and how they're not allowed to express it."

The film's storyline also allows Elmer to empower his friend to do something great. "I believe that the classical 'hero's journey' has lost its reason to exist," concludes Ferrari. "I think the whole world and this entire historical moment we're living in are telling us that perhaps we don't need a hero. We need people who can empower others. Be brave enough to go to a hard place and do something magical and amazing. I think that's how Nora works too. She took this immigrant from Italy and empowered me to confront something as scary as being the head of story and director of animation. That's something I learned from her, and I think we have to teach that to our children, too."

ART DIRECTION

Like all of Cartoon Saloon's movies, *My Father's Dragon* follows a very distinctive aesthetic, reflected in both its meticulous art direction and its stylized character and background designs. However, since the movie was inspired by an existing picture book, the creative team used the source material as a starting point, taking inspiration from the character design and colours, as well as the lush environments, from the original illustrations by Ruth Chrisman Gannett. The team also used children's drawings to inform Elmer's world from a child's perspective.

The film's art director, Áine Mc Guinness, who has worked on movies such as *The Breadwinner* and *Late Afternoon* and TV shows such as *Dorg Van Dango* and *The Amazing World of Gumball*, recalls that in one of their earliest discussions with Nora Twomey, "the director expressed that this was a film about faces. So the most important thing, from an art direction perspective, was to honor the characters' emotional journey and remember that the story is always key." With this in mind, the character designs leaned toward the more simplified and naïvist, but when they start to move were very much rooted in a realistic approach to acting, volume, and gravity. Expressions needed to be believable and naturalistic.

"We took the same approach with the world that the characters inhabit," explains Mc Guinness. "The design language for the environments was largely inspired by the illustrative work of production designer Rosa Ballester Cabo. Taking her playful, charming approach to design and adding more depth and volume, we emerged with a visual style that was a mix between naivism and semirealism. We intentionally avoided compositions that

ABOVE Explorations of subtle head-tilts by Alessandro Toccacelli as part of the design process for animation

OPPOSITE Early concept art by Rosa Ballester Cabo

framed the characters too perfectly. Instead, more emphasis was placed on creating an immersive and believable world for Elmer.

"Lighting was one of our boldest compositional tools, staging the world with strong values and compositions that enhanced the story and the action. We often went quite bold in order to guide the viewer's eye to the focal point of the shot. The values needed to be clear and strong so that the movie could essentially work in black-and-white, heavily inspired by film noir aesthetics.

"Each location in the film has its own unique colour palette. For example, the film opens with warm, golden light, which is something we revisit throughout the film as a representation of home and safety. In contrast, the palette in Nevergreen shifts to colder, less saturated blues. As we descend into Elmer's imagination on Wild Island, we use much bolder colour profiles, intentionally chosen to reflect the emotional journey of our characters and the mood of each particular sequence of the film."

Assistant art director Emilie Bach Nielsen also points out that one of the reasons she loved working on the movie was the fact that they were encouraged to take more subtle risks and to explore quieter moments and gentle aesthetics. "In the beginning of the job, I worked closely with our production designer, Rosa Ballester Cabo," she says. "It's close to what the real world looks like. Yet, on the other hand, you can feel the influences of movies like *The Wizard of Oz* and *The Night of the Hunter*, two classics that we went back to for inspiration. The backgrounds and the character designs are flat, but when the characters move and act, they have a lot of subtlety and volume to them. As a rule, we wanted the world to feel very immersive."

Nielsen further explains that the characters' designs could be childlike and naivist, but when they were put in their space and allowed to live in the world, the combination had a more realistic feel to it. "This is something that was different from what we did in *WolfWalkers*, where the world of the characters catered to each one of the central figures. In *My Father's Dragon*, we dramatically lit the stage for the characters, but we don't cradle them. Everything is more chaotic, because the focus is on Elmer and Boris's journey. We don't want the world to be easy for them."

She also says it was quite interesting to explore the way each one of the movie's locations could be especially colour-coded to reflect a certain mood or feeling. "We have the initial contrast between the real world versus the fantasy world of Wild Island," Nielsen offers. "The fantasy world of Wild Island is a lot more vibrant and expressive. Then, in the city of Nevergreen, because we see it through Elmer's eyes, everything feels desaturated and drab, because that's how the main character feels about it initially. We also use a lot of colours to differentiate each one of the many different locations on the island. They each have their unique flavor so that the audience can easily distinguish them from one another."

For the assistant art director, what really elevates this movie from many other family movies is its subtlety and dreamlike quality. "It's more about an inner conflict than outside actions," she recalls. "It has some slower moments that I really appreciated and was able to contribute to in terms of art and design. We don't go full-on squash and stretch and really focused on the gentle, human qualities and movements. I love that we got to experiment with the bold style and the overlays as well."

ABOVE A colour key showing the moment Elmer's imagination begins to run away with him, as explored by assistant art director Emilie Bach Nielsen

OPPOSITE Colour script by Ciarán Duffy, Marti Furgber Morales, Alice Dieudonné, and Emilie Bach Nielsen

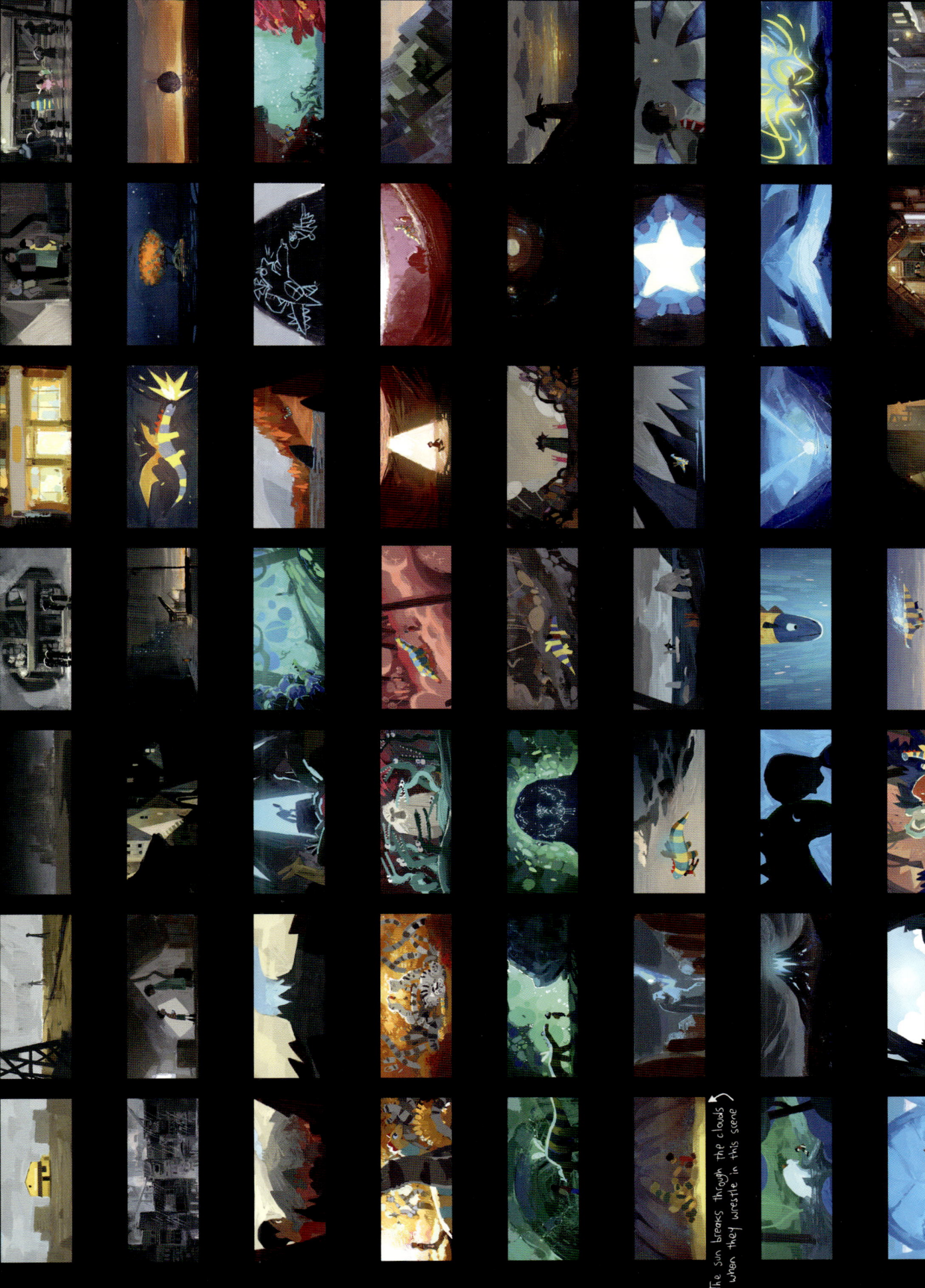

CHARACTER AND BACKGROUND DESIGNS

Rosa Ballester Cabo (*Song of the Sea*, *The Breadwinner*), who worked as both production designer and character designer on the movie, remembers receiving an email with the PDF file of the original book from Nora Twomey about ten years ago. "She asked me if I could do some concept work for Elmer, Boris, the cat, and a bird (which never made it into the final film!)," she remembers. "Then in 2016, I was contacted again when there was a treatment for the movie, but still no script. I was asked to create some illustrations with characters and their locations so I could demonstrate my idea for the general style of the movie. Then, when the movie got the greenlight in 2018, I really started to work on it."

"I liked how each location and each world is done slightly differently," she notes. "The shapes in the city are dull and boring, while the island is crazy, colourful, and vibrant. Things were constantly evolving and changing. One thing I loved about it was that I hardly had any notes or restrictions initially. They just let me be free, so I thought of the whole project as a gift. I could really have the freedom to create this book from a young boy's point of view of a boy and a dragon. I have young kids of my own, and when I see them draw, it amazes me because they approach everything in such a fresh way. So, I wanted to approach this job in the same way."

To stay away from past ideas and learned habits, Ballester Cabo tried to draw as loosely and freely as possible, even going as far as using her left hand even though she's right-handed. "Sometimes, you can get some weird and unusual shapes when you do it with your left hand," she admits. "Other times, I would distort some of the animal characters. I'd grab the head or the tail and make them bigger or longer."

Lead character designer Esther Morales Sanchez mentions that one of the key points they tried to convey was that the main character was always in real danger, although the island is seen as quite a fantastic place. "We wanted to show that Elmer could get hurt if he fell or that the animals could actually eat him," she says. "It was really important to keep that in mind in the design process—he's a real kid and that gravity is always pulling him down. We had to feel the weight of his body. Sometimes in the designs, you can make things too pushed or cartoony, but here this was the first project where we had to combine a stylized design with a realistic feel."

She also brings up the fact that the design team had more of a hard time zeroing in on the visuals for Elmer than for Boris the dragon. "We had a clear idea for Boris with the stripes and the colours because we wanted to be faithful to the original version seen in the book, but for Elmer, we had more freedom. We went back and forth with different versions, because he needed to look relatable for a kid who is watching the movie today, but we didn't want to go with just a generic young boy."

For Boris, the designers had to opt for fewer stripes on the dragon's body to make life a bit easier for the animators. "He is still a very young dragon, so his facial expressions were very important," says Sanchez. "The fact that he could walk on all four legs and then stand on his two hind legs like a big bear and use his arms was very important. He is a dragon, but he's not an animal from the island. He's more relatable that way."

The film's background supervisor, Eduardo Damasceno, who joined the team in the fall of 2019, says he was captivated by the storyline because things don't

ABOVE
1 Poses by Elle Power, Vir Prieto Calvo, and Rebecca Gautrey

2 Poses by Elle Power, Vir Prieto Calvo, Rebecca Gautrey, Maria Blowers, and Valerie Bousquie

necessarily happen the way you expect them to. "Nora told us that she wanted to duplicate the feel of a soundstage from a 1940s movie set, and to try to find that delicate balance between how to paint something that is realistic while also very stylized," he says.

Damasceno also points out that unlike Cartoon Saloon's *WolfWalkers*, this feature didn't require as much attention to real-life natural habitats and research into physical world locations. "Nora wanted the visuals to look more like a movie set, so we looked at some classic noir movies," he recalls. "We also referred to the Italian neorealist movie *Bicycle Thieves* (1948) to get ideas for the way we wanted to depict the clouds in the sky."

The veteran background designer says he worked with about two hundred "colour script" swatches (palettes showing shades of colour) to map out the colour schemes of the movie. He also mentions that they had regular reviews of the flora and fauna with the director and the art director. "As the months went by, I had a clear grasp of what they wanted to see in the background designs, which were painted digitally," he says. "We did paint a lot of the textures traditionally with gouache, because one of the rules was that we didn't want too much of a watercolour look to the brushstrokes. We wanted things to look solid and to connect with the animation and the idea that the danger in this world is real. Elmer is not just strolling through a painting. I think using gouache textures helped that a lot, and then a lot of the artists were able to translate that to digital images using Photoshop."

One of the most challenging backgrounds was conceived for the sequence where Elmer sees the Wild Island summit for the first time. "We would see this location many times in the movie, so they wanted to make sure it was done correctly," he notes. "Part of the challenge was figuring out the right balance for the amount of texture and brushwork that we wanted to see on-screen. This was a specific one that took a long time to get right. We wanted something that didn't look like a painting, but we also wanted to show the hand of the artist. We wanted that little bit of wobbliness and uncertainty. When we got there, I think we could see the team soar, and it became quite exciting to assign the backgrounds and enjoy what they would come up with."

CHARACTER POSING

Since making *The Secret of Kells*, Cartoon Saloon has taken Layout Character Posing a step further than most animation productions, ensuring the character models have a grace that complements the scene composition in a cinematic way. This requires great skill, and Sandra Andersen was tasked with this department, as well as the design and model sheets that come before it, based on production designer Rosa Ballester Cabo's character concepts.

Model sheets were extra important on *My Father's Dragon*, with animators working remotely (there was a team of animators and clean animators working in FOST Studio in Paris, as well); they were used as communication tools between artists.

Sandra Andersen, who had the task of supervising the character designs and model sheets and posing for the pictures, joined the team in November 2019. "What I do is take all the concepts, designs, and base images for the characters and break them down and construct them to make them animatable. Of course, every movie has its own different visual language and sensibility. You can't just jump into a project and do everything the way you always do. *My Father's Dragon* has a different style from the other Cartoon Saloon movies. The graphic choices and the way we drew the characters was a bit different this time."

Andersen says the posing for the movie followed an overall elegant, warm, and soft pattern—even the poses used for Saiwa, the large gorilla who is the leader of the Wild Island animals. "I think some of the choices were even less dimensional than what we usually do. It was really important for the creative lead to stay true to that look, although it's quite difficult to move characters like that in animation."

Among the many details Andersen had to keep an eye on was how to make sure the characters' design details

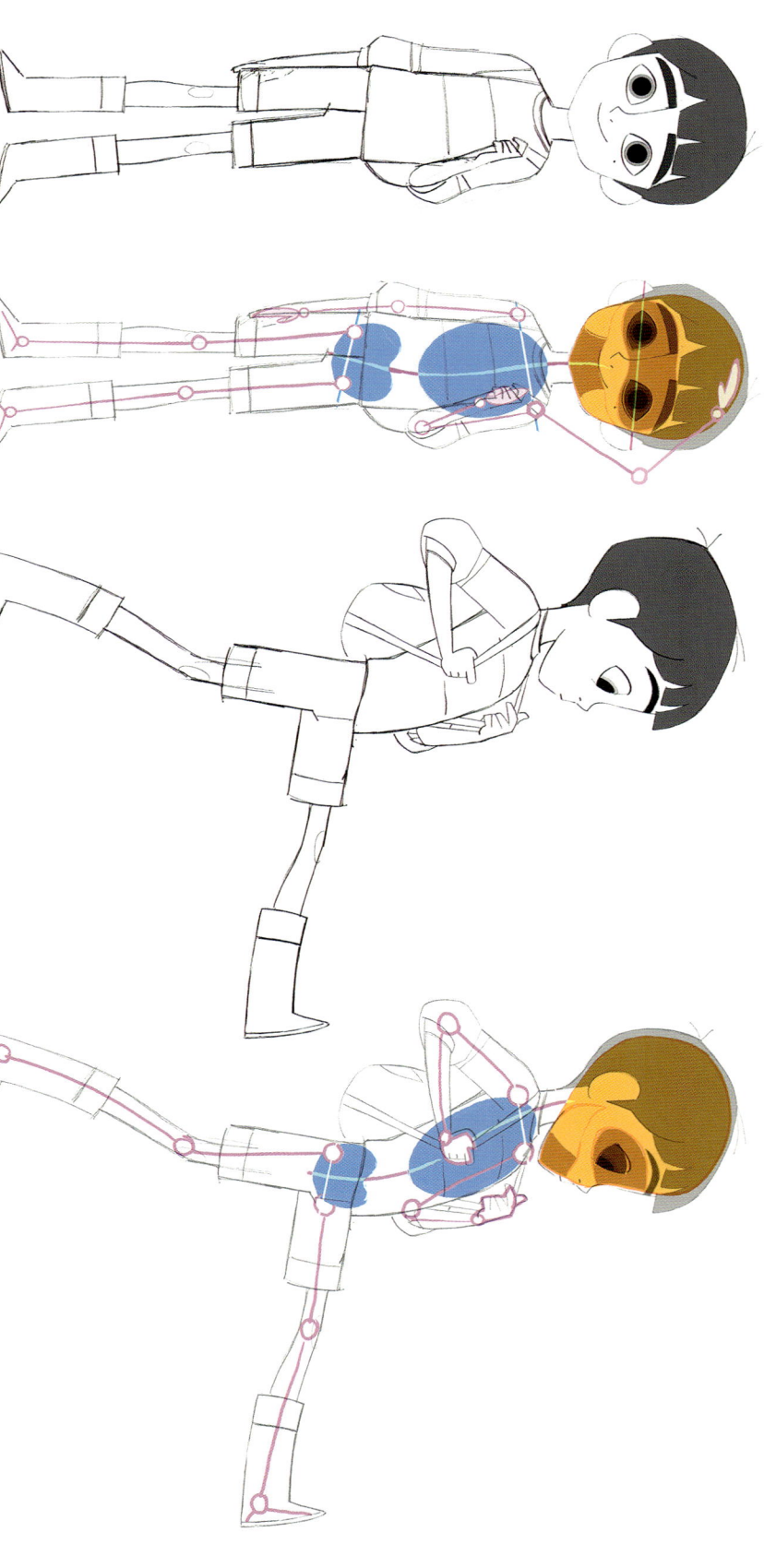

ABOVE Alessandro Toccaceli
OPPOSITE Posing by Esther Morales Sanchez

translated to posing, then further to animation. "Since a lot of the look had already been developed, I had to come up with ways to perhaps push a character or simplify it; for example, I had to decrease the number of stripes on Elmer's shirt from five to three or two," notes Andersen. "Boris was really challenging too. The voice actor [Gaten Matarazzo] gave so much to the character, and he is such a relatable character. But Boris has lots of movements and also a lot of stripes. We had to break the stripe pattern down so it was more understandable and simpler to track and replicate by an entire rough and clean animation team. But I think everyone did a great job, because the number of Boris's stripes remained the same all throughout the movie!"

Andersen personally broke down the storyboards and clarified the scenes for her posing team. "The storyboards we work from are necessarily rough, so there is a lot of interpretation involved. As a supervisor, I break them down for my team and try to visually explain anything vague," she says. "One of the big challenges with this project was the number of four-legged animals we had to deal with. In the previous movies, we had a goat or a horse, but *Wolfwalkers* was the first movie in which we had a lot of four-legged characters—but at least they were all wolves! For this movie, we had animals that were four-legged and two-legged. For Boris, we had to move him smoothly from his four-legged poses to two-legged ones. I'm not sure anyone will notice, but he has different proportions when he stands on his two legs. The same proportions were not appealing for both, so we had to cheat a little bit and move him smoothly from one design to the other. His arms are a bit longer, for example. But it all worked out, because he looks good in the movie!"

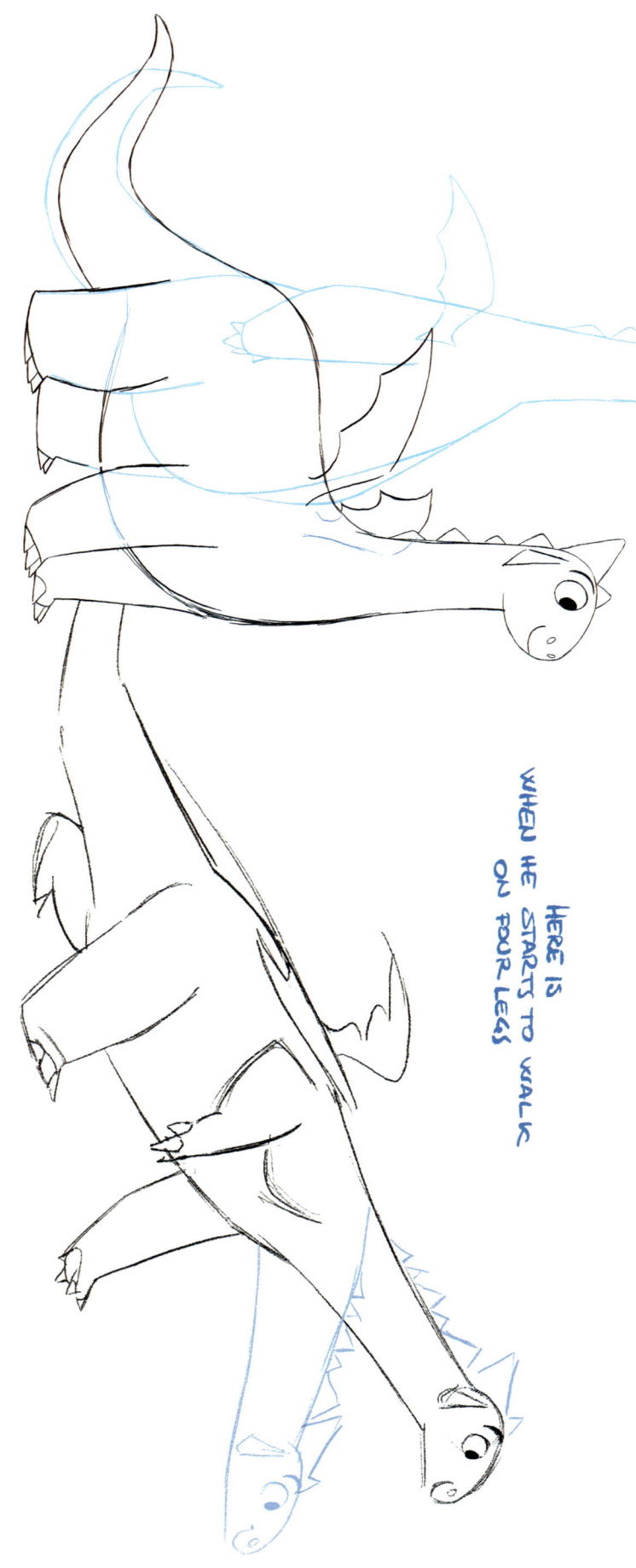

HERE IS WHEN HE STARTS TO WALK ON FOUR LEGS

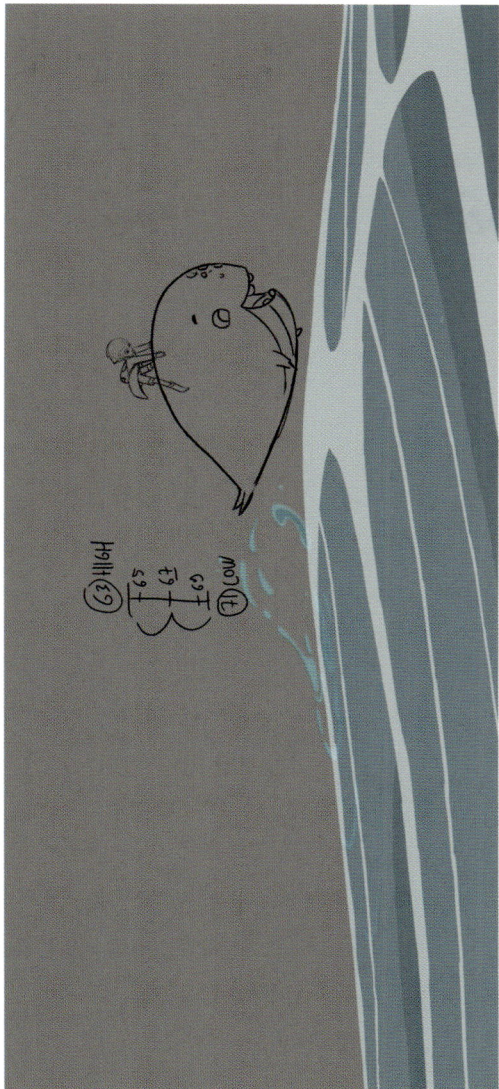
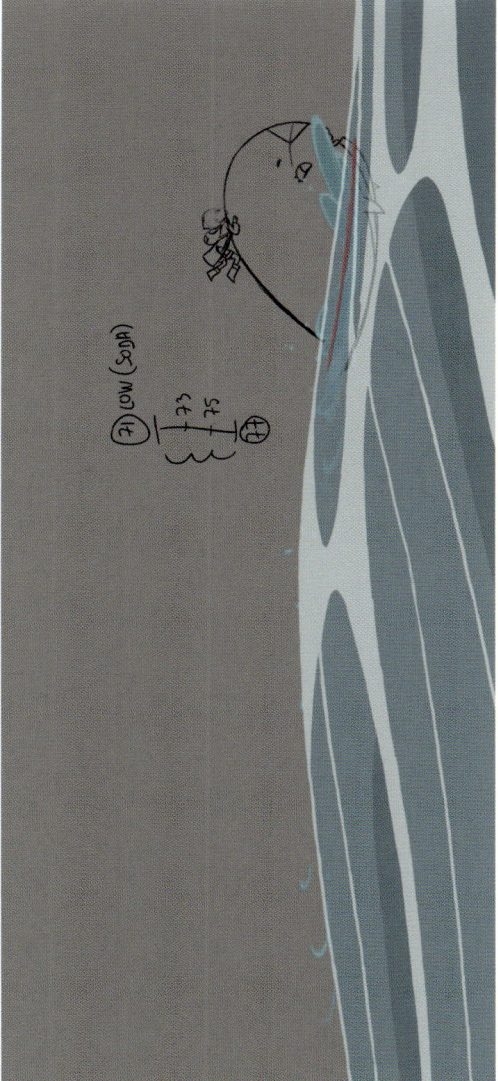

ROUGH ANIMATION

The film has richly emotional performances built into the very core of its narrative. The incredible voice cast gave it everything they had, from Jacob Tremblay and Gaten Matarazzo as Elmer and Boris, to Whoopi Goldberg, Ian McShane, and Rita Moreno. Each actor believed they were in this world of *My Father's Dragon*, battling the elements and expressing their character's essence.

The task of rough animation was split between Cartoon Saloon in Ireland and FOST Studio in Paris. FOST was set up by Didier Brunner, the renowned producer, who was first to put production funds behind *The Secret of Kells*, Cartoon Saloon's first feature, in the late nineties.

My Father's Dragon would benefit from incredible animation talent, old friendships, and new discoveries. Again, pandemic realities dictated the methods of communication between the director, head of department, supervisors, and animation crew. Animators were working from their homes as far away from Kilkenny as Russia and Mexico, so Twomey started by acting out a lot of the central performances timed to the actors' voice recordings in a series of videos as a baseline communication tool for the animators. From there, they were free to interpret the performances while being mindful of the broad, physically personal arc of each character's narrative. For example, Elmer would always have his unique gestures; the way he slips his hand through the backpack strap, the way his pupils flit when he's not saying what he's thinking.

Sequences often had to be split between animators who didn't get to meet each other in person. So often, Giovanna Ferrari (head of animation) roughed out entire sequences so the action would work smoothly across cuts. Veteran animators such as Andrzej Radka and Svend Rothmann Bonde worked with their teams to infuse the lines with their own experiences, to make sure the audience could feel the craft of their expression with every frame.

OPPOSITE Alessandro Toccaceli

RIGHT Rough character animation keys by Esther Lisiki, with water effects by Narissa Schander and Ramon Angelo Jose

CLEAN ANIMATION

The job of the clean animation team is to take the rough animation and pull it back on model, while respecting the fluidity of rough animation. It's one of the most skilled and difficult jobs in 2-D animation. Using key drawings and animation charts from the animator, the clean animation team makes the characters look consistently like themselves, no matter how the rough performance looks.

John Walsh, head of clean animation on *My Father's Dragon*, worked with his team of lead artists to develop the line style and provide feedback and assistance in the creation of the character model sheets. He reviewed all the shots with cleanup supervisor Tatiana Mazzei with final reviews by Twomey, following any retake, review notes, or revisions by Digital Ink and Paint and tech check departments, and working closely with the cleanup leads to support the team. He also worked closely with the team at FOST Studio in France to make sure the whole department worked as one, no matter where crew were based.

The clean animation department had a team of about thirty artists at Cartoon Saloon plus a production manager, Judith Enault, and coordinator, Marick Queven, and a team of around thirty artists at FOST.

Walsh says the biggest challenge for his department was having all team members working remotely. "We had quite a large team, so making sure that communication was as regular and as smooth as possible and that the teams had access to all material was paramount. But thanks to our great production team, it all went very smoothly," he notes. "I loved the enthusiasm and the camaraderie of the team—the bar was set very high, but everyone rose to the challenge. Among the sequences that I'm quite proud of is the sequence in which Elmer meets the cat on the dock, as it was quite challenging to control Elmer's model/clothes, and the cat's overall designs were quite tricky. The sequence right after that where Elmer meets Soda was also quite challenging. We had to do a nice little cheat with Elmer's bag straps as he is riding on Soda's back to Wild Island, but you have to look very closely to catch it. Overall, I had a soft spot for Boris!"

He also points out that whole project felt very inclusive. "As a director, Nora likes to include all the department heads and supervisors in the main sequence kickoffs. We had a director's pass every time a seq was launched. Nora would go through the sequences in depth. All the supes could ask questions, take notes, and get clarification on their particular departments. The supervisors would roughly estimate the level of difficulty for each shot, which was handy for production to track the quotas and follow the progress of the workflow."

The Cartoon Saloon veteran says being able to help guide some of the younger and less experienced artists on the movie has been a very fulfilling experience. "To watch them grow in skill and confidence through such a high-quality production was the biggest reward," he admits.

ABOVE Bryony Evans

1 Gemma Roberts
2 Tatiana Mazzei
3 Basil Malek and Allan Michaut
4 Tatiana Mazzei and Kevin Condron
5 Basil Malek and Allan Michaut
6 Tatiana Mazzei and Kevin Condron
7 Geoff King
8 Tatiana Mazzei

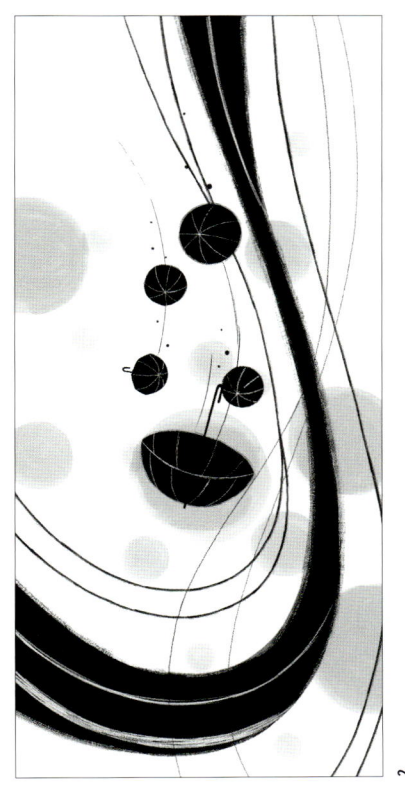

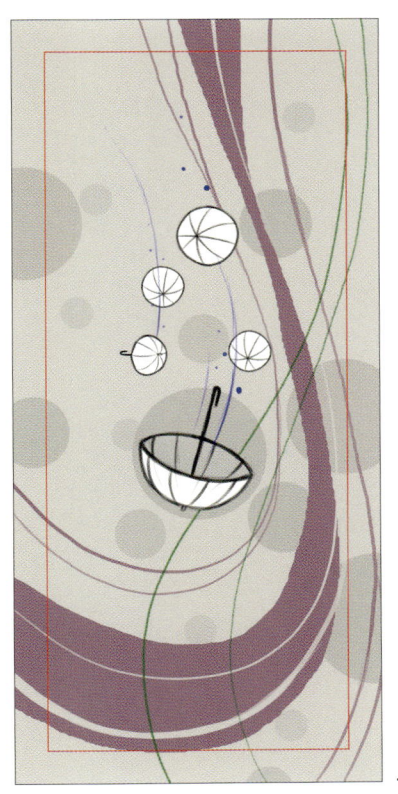
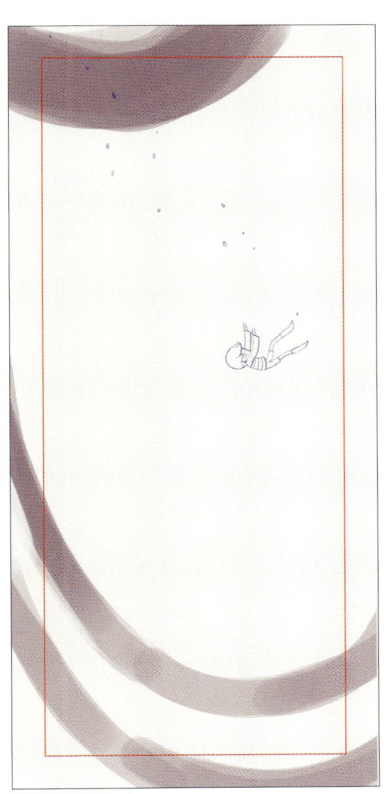

RIGGED ANIMATION

For elements such as the island being pulled out of the water, and the pitcher plants Boris displaces as he makes his grand entrance, Víctor Paredes and his team of rig-based animators took the visual lead. The team used Moho 2-D software to facilitate both the epic elements (roots stretching, riverbanks sinking) and some of the character animation where their models were deemed too detailed for traditional animation and cleanup.

They both imported background-artist-painted Photoshop elements and created their own textured characters in Moho. Crowds of customers, passersby, crocodiles, and pikas were handled in Moho in a way that could blend seamlessly with the TV Paint characters and the background paintings.

Paredes literally lifted and sank Wild Island, and the sense of danger the characters express is earned by the rigged animation team. "We were given a lot of freedom to experiment and problem-solve on *My Father's Dragon*," says Paredes. "As long as we were in line with the graphic style of the film and the physical gravity obeyed the other animation departments (hand-drawn character and effects), we could do what we wanted!"

DIGITAL INK AND PAINT

As both the film's ink and paint supervisor and its technical lead, Helga Kristjana Bjarnadóttir was another integral member of the *My Father's Dragon* team. She had the crucial job of leading a team of up to fifteen. Though the film was hand-animated in TV Paint (and used Moho for rigged animation), they digitally coloured the TV Paint characters using the popular Toon Boom Harmony 2-D software. She says unlike the last

ABOVE Rigged animation by Víctor Paredes

1 Áine Mc Guinness

2–3 Helga Kristjana Bjarnadóttir

LINES
FILLS
eyeline
detail lines
nose line
eyebrow /
sclera
*iris
*pupil
*eye shadow
*ear
*ear inside
nose
nostril
*body
*stripes
*claws
*beans
MOUTH
lines
throat
inside
*tongue
teeth

1

Colour model
Lines
Skin
Nose
Freckles
Eyes
Iris
Undershirt
Jumper
Mouth
Tongue
Hair outer
Hair on face
Hair inner
Eye Shadow
Shadow Nose
Eyebrow over
Eyebrow Under
Beads
Beads String
Star
Star string
Waistband
Tutu detail
Tutu A
Tutu B
Jeans
Shoe R
Shoe L

2

Colour model
Lines
Eye and Pupil
Iris
Eyelid L sep
Eyelid R sep
Eye Patch sep
Ear L and Eye Patch
Ear Detail
Mouth and Teeth
Tongue
Muzzle and Whiskers
Upper Front Legs sep
Inner Ear and Paw Pads
Back Patch Sep
Belly and Chest sep
Head, Belly and Ear R
Paws
Socks sep
Shoulders and Hips
Tail
Tail Hairs
Legs Front, and Back

3

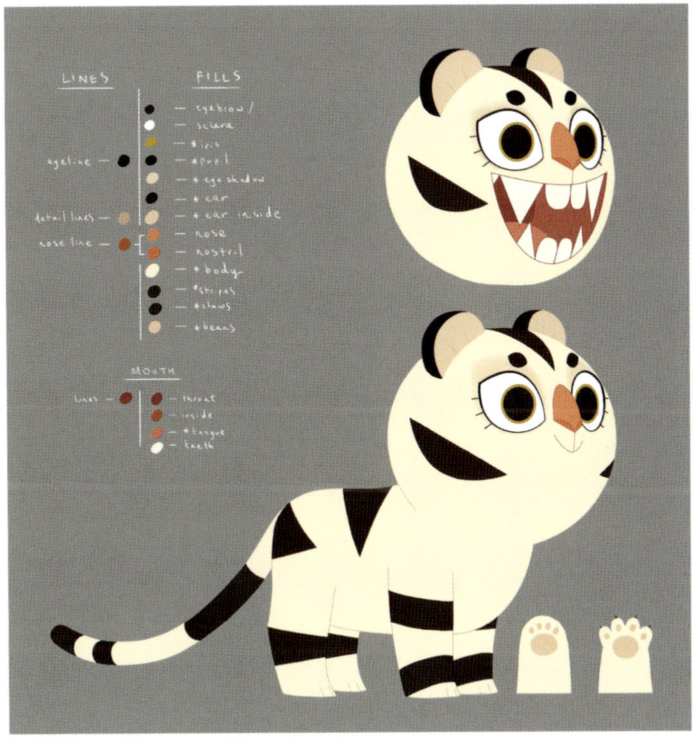

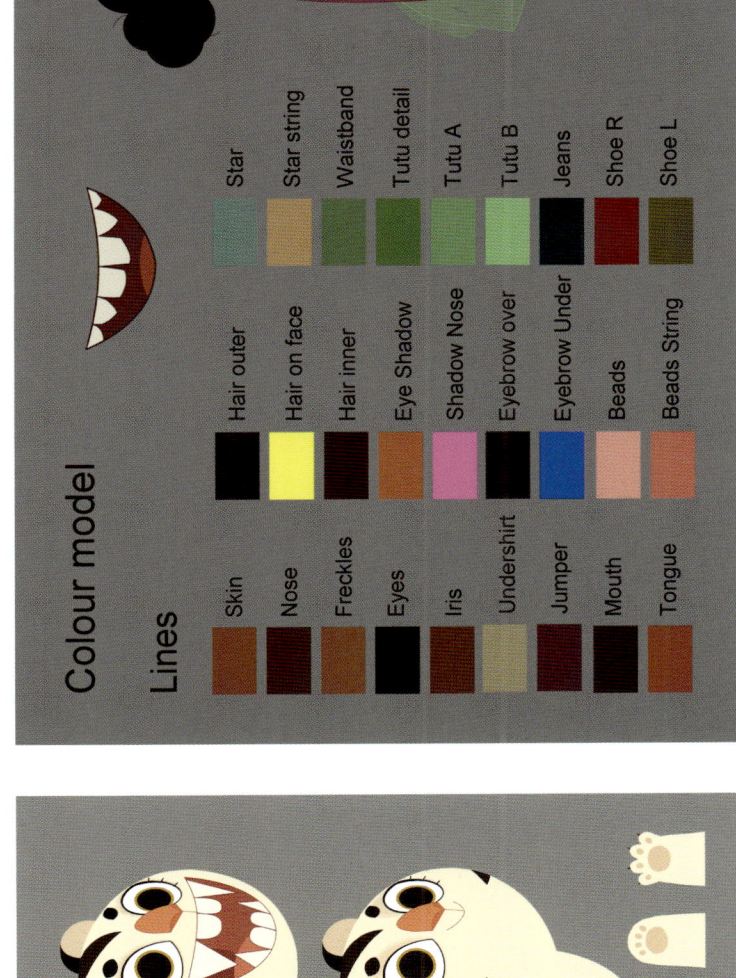

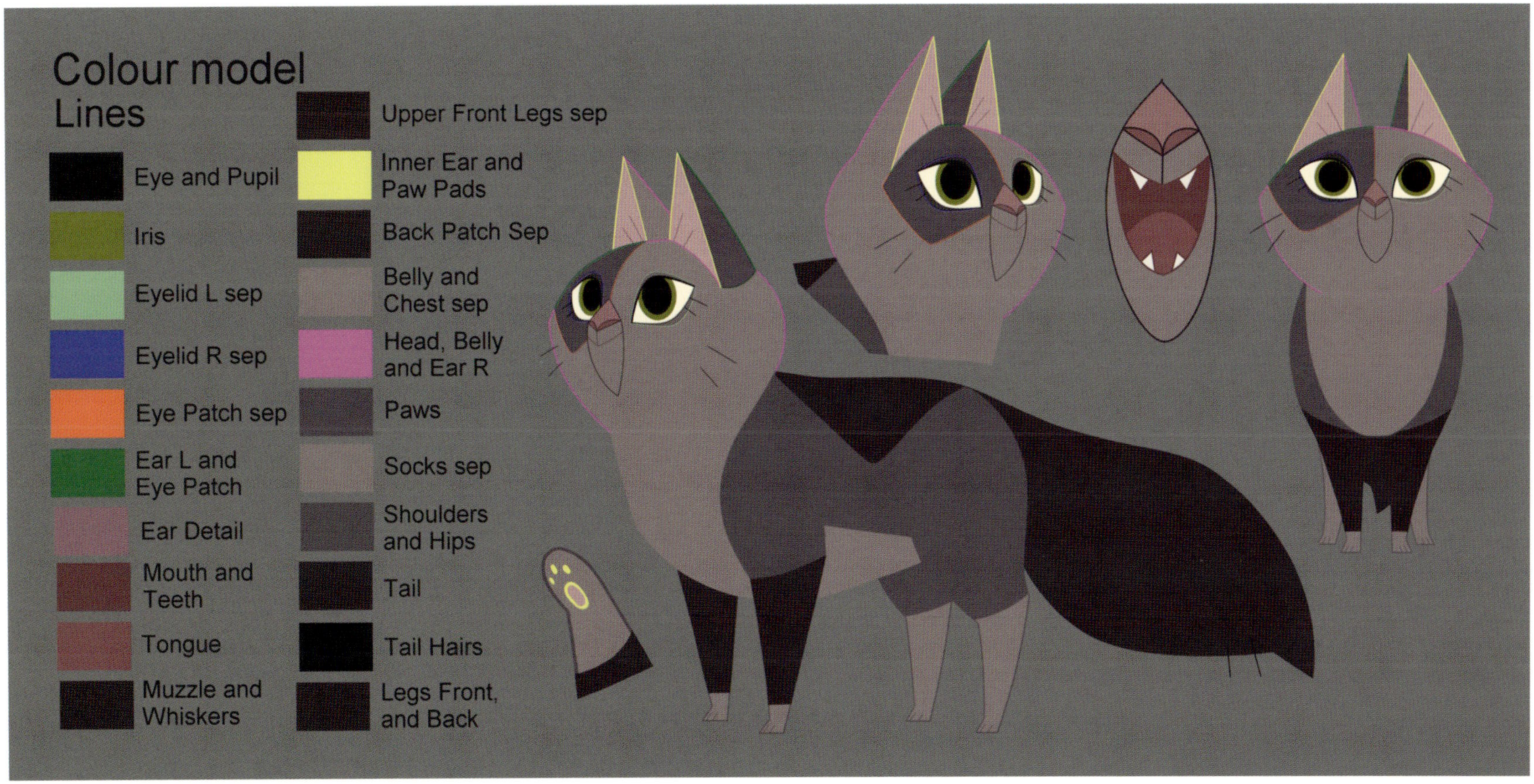

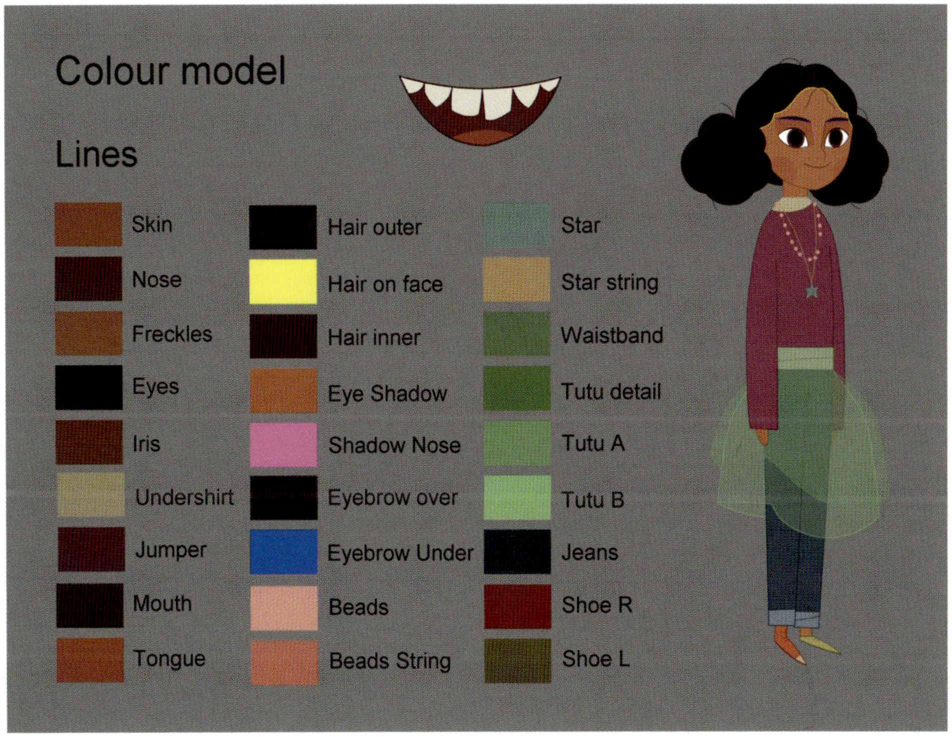

movie she worked on (*WolfWalkers*), which was meant to look as handmade and inconsistent as possible, *My Father's Dragon* required a more controlled and polished approach.

She adds, "We also need to colour all the character outlines, which was a huge amount of work: We didn't have to do this on *WolfWalkers*, for which we only coloured the outlines of the hair and the irises. So we had more work to do and had to build up the colour palettes so that we had the character model's line colour available, and there were lots of important decisions to make."

Bjarnadóttir had to learn how to use Harmony quickly, since she had used TVPaint software on the studio's other projects. "Toon Boom Harmony was the right tool to Ink and Paint this because we needed to do a lot of very precise texturing in the compositing department," she explains. "It also allowed us to change the colours and layers quickly. But it was a bit difficult in the beginning because we had to work out how to construct the palettes. The small animals were also a particular challenge. When the characters are really small, it's more difficult because the software's vectorization process doesn't catch all of the details that we need to take care of, so we had to manually fix all those things!"

The cat (voiced by Whoopi Goldberg) also caused its share of logistical headaches. "That character was complicated because it had double the amount of line colours that you actually see on the screen," she recalls. "We had to use different line colours to delineate. I also did some scripting, which helped us create layers automatically, name them, and put everything in the right place. The studio's software development team was also always ready to build more involved scripts for us, which simplified and organized the process immensely."

VISUAL EFFECTS

Water is a character in *My Father's Dragon*. It expresses Elmer's lack of safety and control, threatening every character and creating a "ticking clock" for the story. Visual effects designer and department supervisor Narissa Schander came on board in January 2020 and had the opportunity to collaborate with the art director to figure out the right look and methodology to make the effects integrated with the film's visual-language motifs. Schander worked with a team of sixteen artists in her Cartoon Saloon project, *WolfWalkers*, which had only six.

"This was the first feature that I worked on that was so effects-heavy," she says. "There were maybe only a handful of sequences that didn't require any—and overall, we did about thirty-two hundred seconds [close to fifty-four minutes] of effects. This included rain, mist, smoke, clouds, all kinds of water splashes, the sinking of the island, tsunamis, as well the magic moments. Every

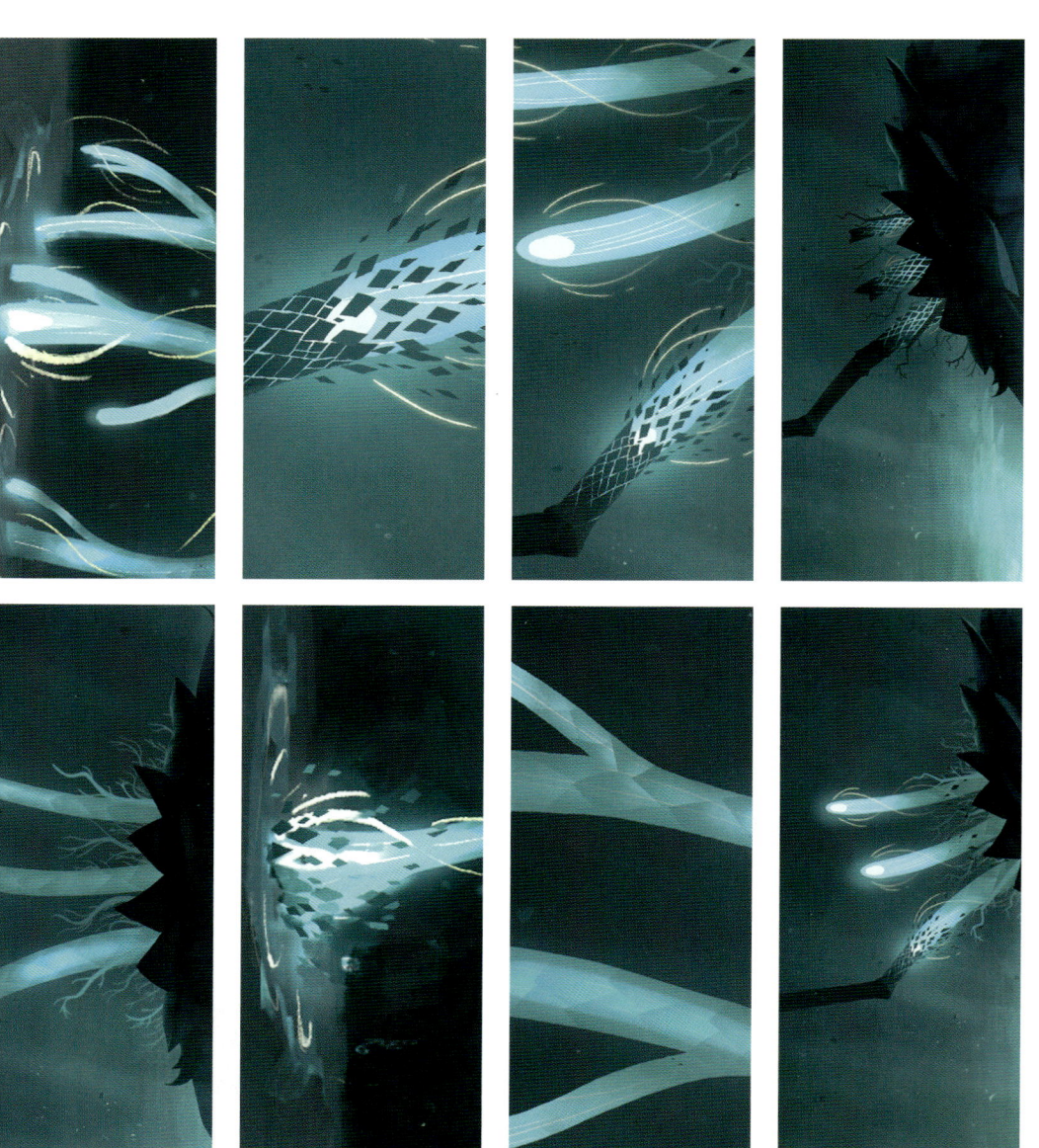

ABOVE Emilie Bach Nielsen

1 Lara Bentassil
2 Narissa Schander
3–4 Emilie Bach Nielsen

CHARTING AN UNPREDICTABLE JOURNEY

OPPOSITE Emilie Bach Nielsen

ABOVE Scene Illustration by Ciarán Duffy and Áine Mc Guinness, based on location design by Julien Regnard and Lara Bentassil. Effects design by Narissa Schander

time the summit is shown in the movie, we had to add more effects to it. Overall, we had to work on five stages of the summit's evolution, and each one had to be more dramatic than the last one, so that we had the big climax in the end."

Among the movie's many effects-heavy shots are the ones involving Elmer and Boris as they pull the island out of the water. "There are all these layers of water flowing off the island, and we had to track all the moving elements," says Schander. "We also had to work on these beautiful smoke dragons on the docks during the first act of the movie, when Elmer runs away from home and meets the cat. He envisions this dragon made up of the mist and smog of the city, which echoes what he'll encounter on the island. It's very illustrative, and we had to make sure it fit in with the rest of the movie, and the textured edges can be a bit challenging to do."

The effects supervisor also discusses the work her team explored to express the way characters interact with the world around them. "We have a character like Soda the Whale, who is very bubbly and fun. So, when we're creating the designs for the effects, they are curvy, elegant, and beautiful. But when we are animating them, we add the character's personality to them as well. In Soda's case, you have bubbles, circles, and splashes around her. For a character like Kwan, we add extra sparks flying off his torch to express his anger and aggression. When Boris flies, we have a pixie dust trail behind him to accentuate how elegant he becomes during his flights. Those are some of the examples of how we used effects to amplify the characters' personalities."

CRAFTING SONIC SIGNATURES

The hidden connection between Elmer's real world and Wild Island is also echoed in the aural elements of the movie. "Nora wanted the sounds of the 'real world' to turn into many of the sonic signatures of Wild Island," says the movie's award-winning supervising sound editor/rerecording mixer, Zach Seivers (*Nomadland*). "The pipes in the apartment become sinking island elements, and some mysterious sounds in Nevergreen City are manipulated animal calls."

Before starting work on any film, the sound team records new sounds specific to the world of the project. This provides them with "fresh ingredients" with which to create a new palette of sounds unique to the movie. "Early on, [supervising sound editor] Justin Davey and one of our designers did an all-day recording session destroying wicker and wooden furniture. We set up ten different microphones, four of them specially designed to hear many times higher than the human hearing range. This was especially important because we took our wicker and wood destruction recordings and pitched them way, way down to create our 'island crunch.' We also used these recordings (not pitched way, way down) as part of the wood creaks for Mom and Elmer's shop at the start of the film, and in the creaky stairs of the apartment building."

This spirit of experimentation is also reflected in how the team designed the unusual sound of the island's pikas. "We tried something not often done in film," recalls Davey, whose previous credits include *Spider-Man: No*

CHARTING AN UNPREDICTABLE JOURNEY 🍋 35

Way Home and *A Quiet Place*. "We combined sound effects and creative loop group to create vocals for these critters. The pikas function as a hive mind in the traditional sense of the definition: many small creatures expressing a single idea. We knew we needed a wide range of sounds to create variation but also needed to communicate a concise idea to the audience."

After designing the pika sound effects, one of the designers made an "instrument" of pikas, so they could perform their vocalizations on a piano keyboard. Then, Seivers worked with the loop group to create another set of sounds with the specificity they could only achieve from directing a group of human beings. "With so much latitude, we were able to shape and control this adorable herd of animals," Seivers notes. "Another of our favorite motifs in the film is the moments when Elmer loses his sense of balance and control. The sound of the world around him shifts into impressionistic textures and tones—the phone booth sequence in Nevergreen is a perfect example of this."

Davey and Seivers point out that unlike in their previous live-action projects, they had more latitude to be experimental, which introduced the challenge of having few restraints. "The film requires sonic textures that feel completely organic," says Davey. "Considering that we were going to be tying sonic themes together and reusing many of the same sounds in dramatically different contexts, we knew we would be doing some heavy and intensive manipulation with the sounds. We went to great lengths to ensure there were no sounds in the film that felt 'digital' or 'processed.'"

SHAPING A MUSICAL SOUNDSCAPE

To compose the music for *My Father's Dragon*, Nora Twomey reached out to the talented team of Jeff and Mychael Danna, who had previously collaborated with her on her 2017 Oscar-nominated film *The Breadwinner*.

"Nora has a great musical sense and allows us to have a free hand to do what we do," says Jeff Danna. "She expertly handles this richly imagined world and doesn't want us to fit in a box. She's always open to try new things and is a great audience as well."

The Danna brothers, who have created the music for a wide range of movies and TV series, including *Onward*, *The Good Dinosaur*, *The Addams Family*, and *Trollhunters*, saw an early cut of the movie in early 2022. "Anytime you work in animation, there are not too many strict rules about the types of music you can come up with, especially when you have a floating island, talking animals, and magical creatures. The gloves are off, and you can be as adventurous and imaginative as you want to be, since you are not hemmed in by reality."

Early on, Twomey discussed the traits and arcs of the characters as well as the role that music plays in each scene with the composers. "Each one of the characters has a special theme or sound," says Jeff. "For example, Boris is often represented by a tuba. He's goofy and doesn't recognize his own strength. At the heart of it, there's something very emotional, vulnerable, and tenderhearted inside. We had a lot of fun with his theme. We also had to come up with a theme for his After-Dragon stage, which is heroic and powerful. Saiwa is scary and low, lots of low brass notes for him, because Elmer sees him as intimidating. Soda had a very unique motif as well, because she was such an unusual Tangerine Island character."

To help evoke the sense of place for the metropolitan backdrop of Nevergreen, the Dannas hinted at the classic sounds often associated with New York City. "We gave it a little bit of a period vibe and played with a traditional New York orchestration. But there is more emphasis on fantasy and otherworldliness. Once we get to the island, we mixed interesting and unusual instruments with core melodic orchestration. You can hear some tribal choral music for the animals, brass and metallic instruments, and a sax choir. We also included a toy piano and lots of bells to create that magical feeling."

The soundtrack was recorded at the iconic Abbey Road Studios in London. Jeff played several guitar instruments, while Mychael was on the piano, accompanied by a sixty-five-member orchestra. "It was a wonderful experience," says Danna. "You couldn't ask for a better collaborator than Nora. Whenever she calls us, we are happy to jump on board."

BUILDING A SOFTWARE-AGNOSTIC PIPELINE

Looking back at his experience as *My Father's Dragon*'s technical director, Fergal Brennan says two things made the movie different from his previous projects: its massive scale and the fact that it was software agnostic, meaning there wasn't one single animation or visual effects software that dominated the process.

"We almost used every mainstream 2-D animation software. Our animation pipeline would have been done with TVPaint, which is the kind of traditional bitmap drawing-friendly program," Brennan explains. "But then, we moved over to Toon Boom Harmony to ink and paint the characters. In addition, we made a lot of use of the vector-based application Moho to rig things, especially when we needed to animate backgrounds."

The team also used Moho for some of the characters that required a lot of texture on their bodies, such as the crocodiles and the pikas, as well as for moving background elements such as the island itself. Mc Guinness wanted their scales and fur to look very flat, as if they were part of their bodies, and they were able to achieve that successfully in Moho.

Brennan points out that Cartoon Saloon has been making movies with Moho since the days of *Song of the Sea*. "The software has evolved along with the studio. One of our directors, Jeremy Purcell [*Puffin Rock and the New Friends*], was a fan of Moho back in the day, and he maintained our connection with the software. We have these specialized people here who understand the type of textured animation we do. It's often the case

OPPOSITE Justin Davey (left) and Zach Seivers (right) mix the score, sound effects, and dialogue for the moment when Elmer first sees Sasha, the huge tiger looming over Boris. Photo by Nora Twomey.

ABOVE Bonnie Mier

CHARTING AN UNPREDICTABLE JOURNEY 37

that we want some sort of rigging solution to help marry the textured elements and maintain a handmade look in the final image. The software allows us to turn things around very quickly with a very high level of quality."

Of course, the film's technical director also faced the challenging task of making sure the team was able to work from home after the studio had to shut its doors due to the COVID-19 pandemic in early 2020. "That was the big story of this movie in terms of the production and technical side of things, because we were just entering this delicate phase of the project when everyone had to go home. Our studio pipeline was created based on the assumption that everyone would be at the studio, so it was scary at first."

He also recalls that slowing down and stopping production was never an option. "We had a lot of new information flying around," Brennan says. "Everyone was trying to learn the process, and we didn't want people to start doing things in the wrong order. It was really important to keep moving and making sure everyone knew how our pipeline was supposed to work. We use the project management software [Autodesk's] Shot-Grid, which is kind of standard in our business. So, we choose what the tasks are and what order they go in, and then deal with the consequences of those choices. The big thing was making sure that everyone had the same understanding of the pipeline and how it all needed to move forward."

Describing the standard order of the studio's departments, Brennan notes that the production began with the creation of the animatic. "Basically, the layout team would figure out the positioning of the camera and which elements needed to be on the screen, which shapes they were, and get a good sense of the background. We'd then have the storyboard's characters placed in approximately the right places, but they're quite crude and not on-model at this point."

Based on the brilliantly imaginative and immersive location designs, the layout department created the monochrome image, which is a schematic for the background to closely follow, which also serves as the stage for the characters in the animation file. Layout began production by analyzing the animatic, and then creating new artwork (the layout) that is the basis of the background and the scene prep. Layout is considered the start of the production pipeline, and it was followed by scene prep. The posing department then drew the on-model characters on top of the layouts.

"Next came rough animation, which created the scenes on the basis of the poses," says Brennan. "They wouldn't be concerned about models at this stage, but they'd pay attention to the things like volumes and just making sure they weren't doing anything that breaks the models at least. The animation was quite loose at this stage."

The cleanup department would then take over the rough animation using TVPaint. "Our incredible cleanup team had this top-of-the-line expertise with this software, so we decided to continue using TVPaint for cleanup," explains Brennan. "We'd then move to Toon Boom Harmony for digital ink and paint. Then it was off to effects and then tonals, which is the last step before the comp stage, where we added shadows and volumes. This would be the standard order, but then we'd have to use Moho for some of the nonstandard shots, if anything in the background was moving or if we needed to do some of the characters in Moho for some niche scenarios [see the "Anatomy of a Scene" chapter on the Crocodile River Crossing]."

Brennan says *My Father's Dragon* has been quite a valuable experience for him and his team. "I think we had some issues by allowing things to become overcomplicated," he admits. "I think I will try to simplify things a bit more on the next project. Sometimes, it's hard to see whether you're making things too complicated or you're simply doing something that's absolutely necessary. After all, you do everything in technical direction in service of creating the best final image."

OPPOSITE Emilie Bach Nielsen

FOLLOWING SPREAD Rosa Ballester Cabo

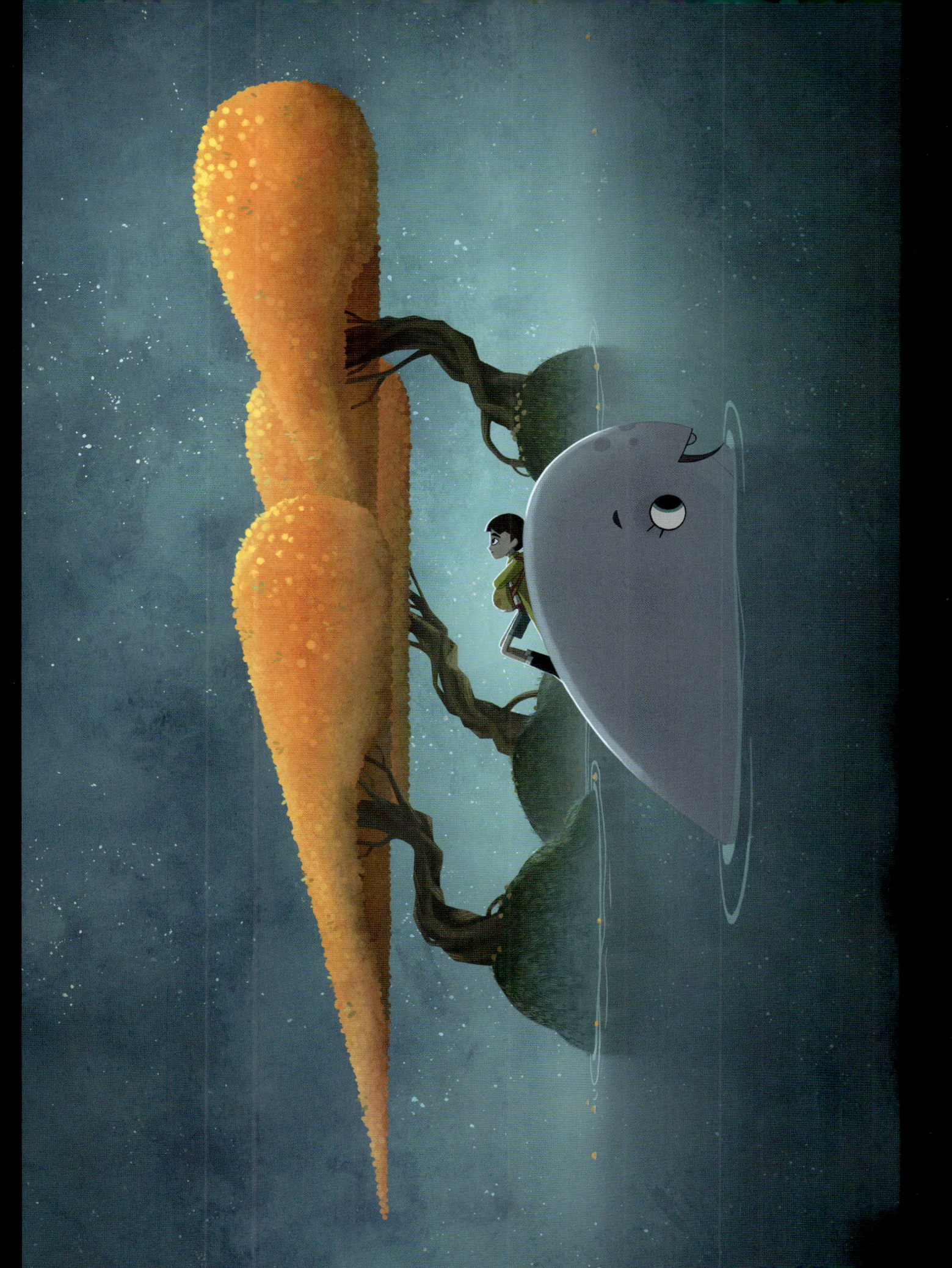

Characters

Elmer

The young hero of the story, Elmer is an adventurous, brave, and empathetic child who has to deal with the changing prospects of his family in the first act of the movie. Voiced perfectly by the young Canadian actor Jacob Tremblay (*Room*, *Wonder*, *Luca*), Elmer is a timeless character, anchoring the characters from both realms: those from his life back home and the ones he meets on Wild Island.

"I love the way he's set up from the beginning as a doer; he's not precious," says Twomey. "Jacob handled that brilliantly and gave us such inspiration. When Elmer feels secure, he can answer someone's question even before they ask it; he thinks he can predict life's course. But then the rug gets pulled out from under him, and everything he knows is gone. Even his mother seems to have changed. We really wanted to put a real-life challenge on the screen and handle it imaginatively and sensitively."

Elmer was the first character that the film's characacter and production designer, Rosa Ballester Cabo, worked on. "It was a big deal because his design was going to set the aesthetic for the rest of the characters," she explains. "At this early stage of design I like to do as many versions of the characters as possible. I wanted to give Nora many options to choose from and see what her preferences were, which designs would feel like Elmer to her. At this stage it's not only the style, proportions, and shapes that sell the character; it's also the poses and expressions you give them. So little by little we started narrowing down Elmer's design until we got it. This journey took many exciting months. You'd be amazed if you saw how many of the different Elmers we worked on *almost* made it, but I love the final version of Elmer!"

Ballester Cabo mentions that while the general graphic style for the young boy looks cool, it did provide a certain set of challenges for angles, poses, and expressions to work. "Every single element of Elmer was tested out to see if it worked both in a practical way and in an aesthetic way," she recalls. "Every little detail is checked thoroughly. Even the small freckle on his face was a big decision. I actually based that one on my own son's freckle."

Another crucial detail was to connect the movie's version of Elmer to Ruth Chrisman Gannett's illustrations from the original book. "We had to give him as many elements as possible to link our Elmer to the book. His outfits [the red-and-white striped shirt, the boots, the blue hat, the raincoat, etc.] and the way they're coloured come straight from the book illustrations."

The big difference can be seen in the design of his head. "We gave him hair and we didn't keep his dotted eyes," she points out. "Instead, we gave him big eyes with irises and pupils so he could show more expressions."

LEFT Scene illustration location by Ciarán Duffy and Lily Bernard. Characters by Rosa Ballester Cabo

RIGHT Rosa Ballester Cabo

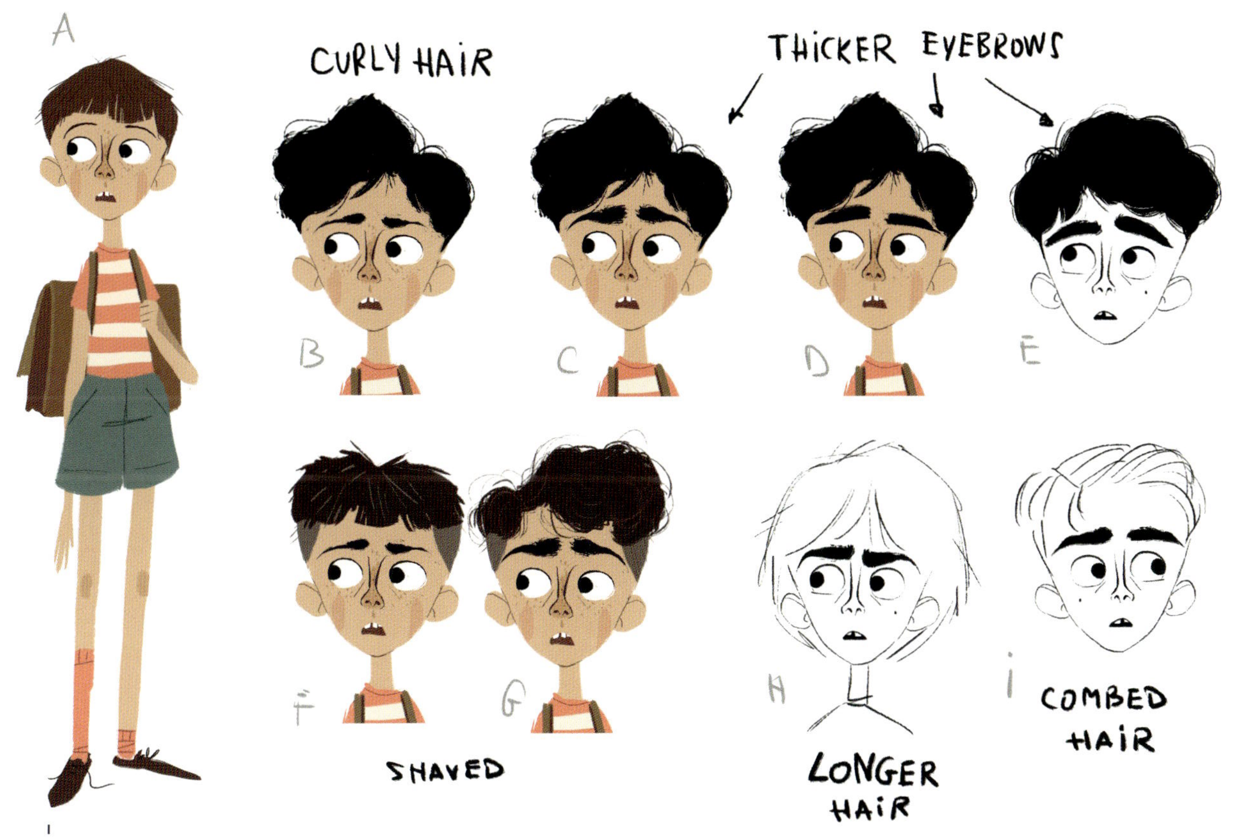
A
CURLY HAIR
THICKER EYEBROWS
B
C
D
E
F
G
H
I
SHAVED
LONGER HAIR
COMBED HAIR

1

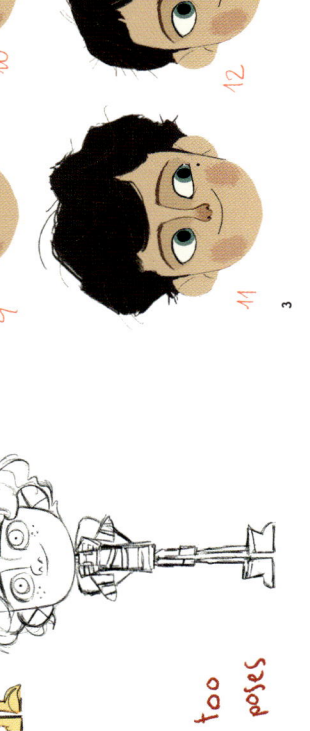

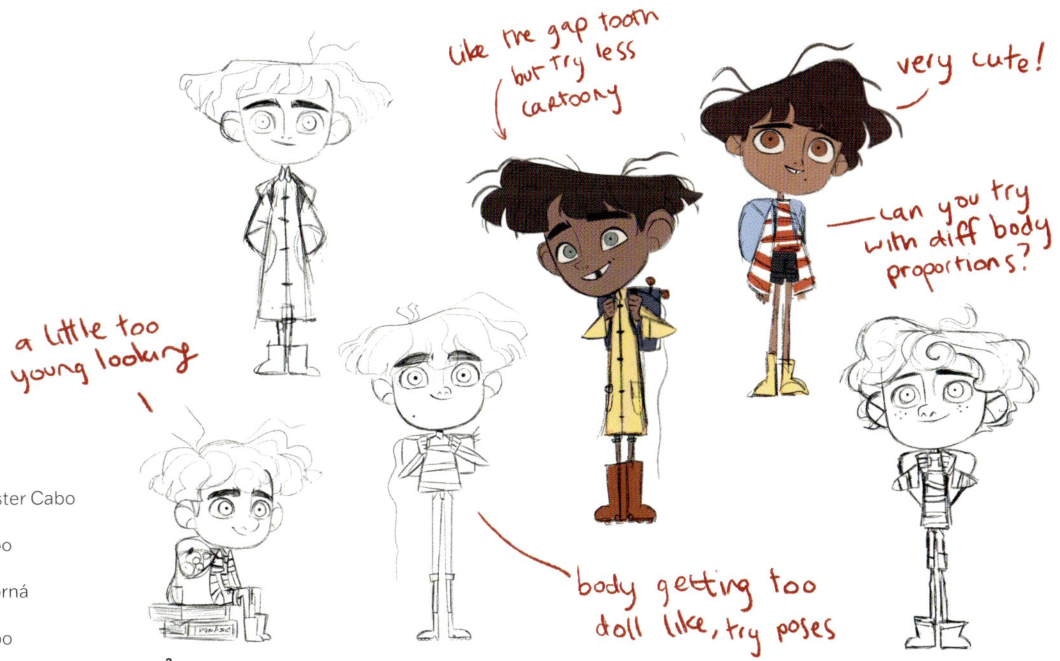
like the gap tooth but try less cartoony
very cute!
can you try with diff body proportions?
a little too young looking
body getting too doll like, try poses

2

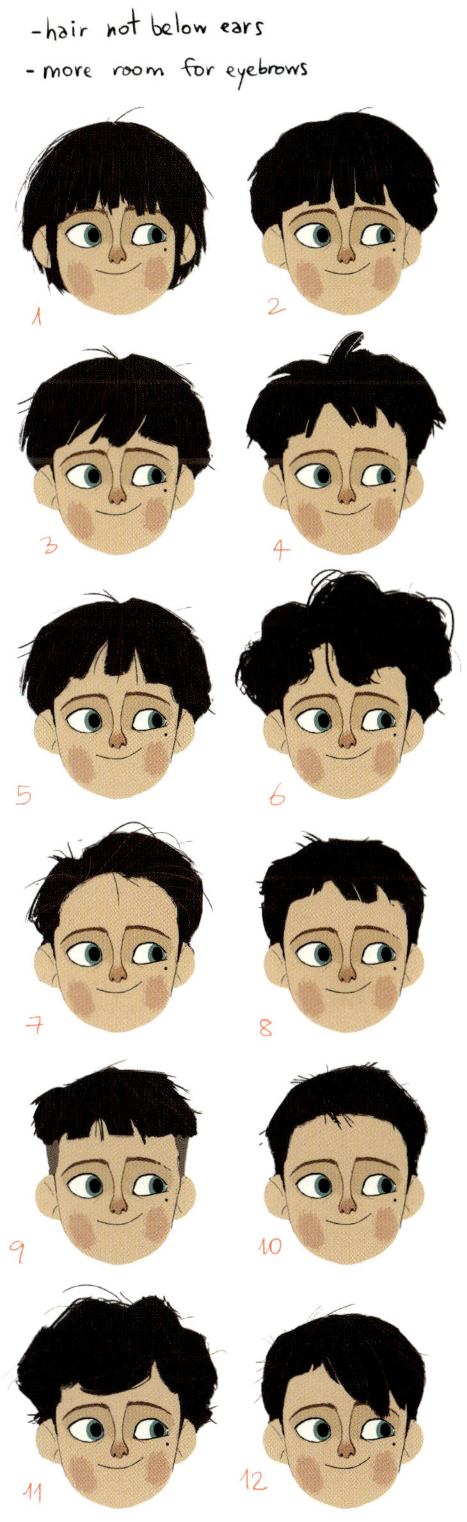
-hair not below ears
-more room for eyebrows
1
2
3
4
5
6
7
8
9
10
11
12

3

OPPOSITE Rosa Ballester Cabo

1 Rosa Ballester Cabo

2 Maria Madelaire Forná

3 Rosa Ballester Cabo

CHARACTERS

1 Sandra Norup Andersen
2 Rosa Ballester Cabo
3 Kayvon Darabi-Fard
4 Rosa Ballester Cabo
OPPOSITE Rosa Ballester Cabo

— slightly too old!
— love how the body feels real, carries weight.

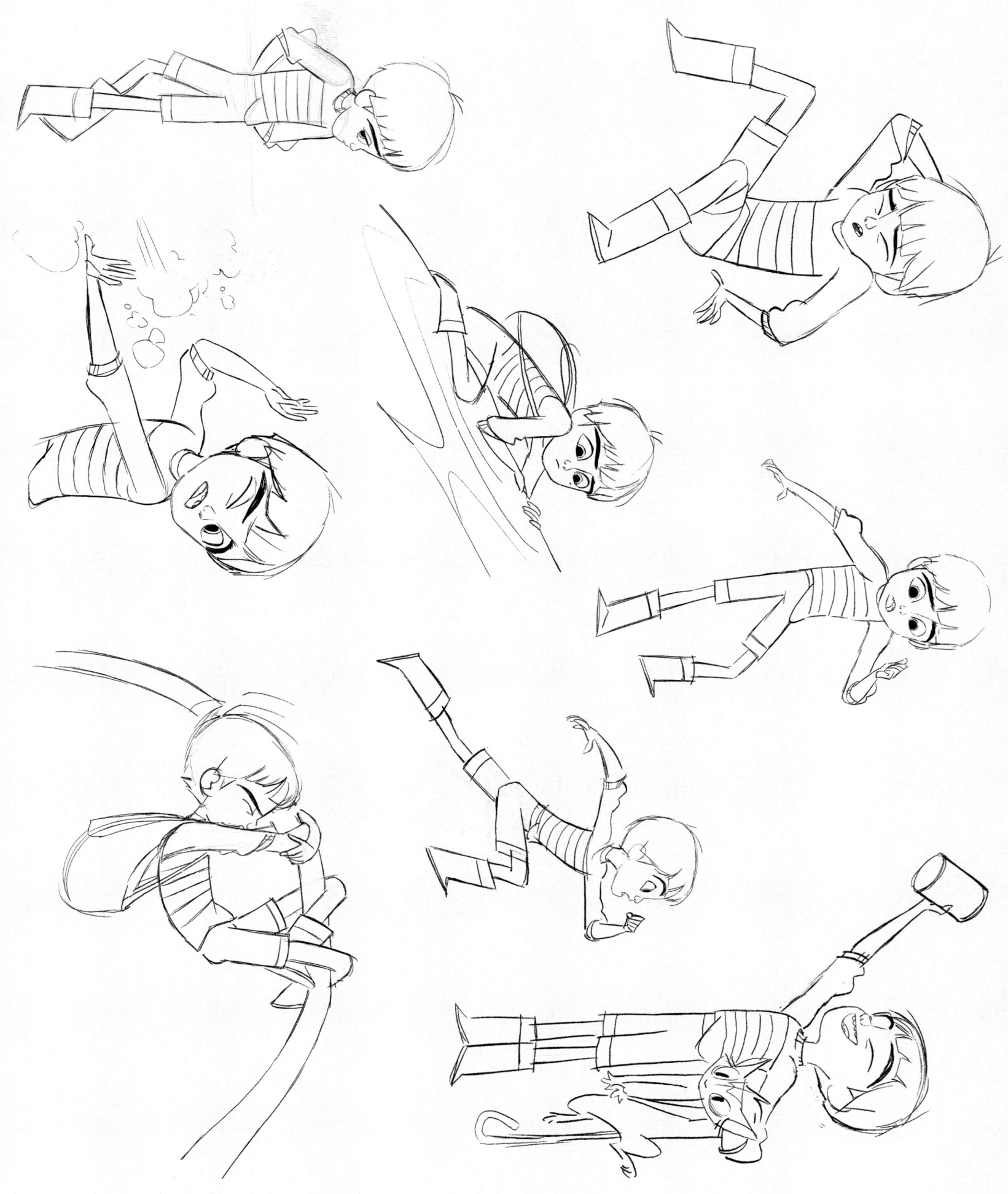

OPPOSITE Alessandro Toccaceli

1–2 Maria Blowers
3 Alessandro Toccaceli
4 Vir Prieto Calvo

Mom

Elmer's mother plays a pivotal role in the first act of the movie, as she attempts to move the center of their family's life without really explaining anything to Elmer. She's scared and doesn't want him to see it. She begins to shut him out.

"She does what she can," says Twomey, "but she makes mistakes. Early on when we were discussing the catalysts that had to propel Elmer to the journey and to Wild Island, we were trying to figure out: What could that be? Our writer Meg LeFauve pointed out that it's unusual to see a mom who is flawed in family films. It's often expected that the mother is great at everything. She's really strong and a superwoman. That's not Elmer's mum; she's real! Golshifteh Farahani had both a warmth and a fierceness to her performance that made her humanity shine through emotionally tough scenes."

Ballester Cabo pointed out that it was important to make sure Mom looked a bit tired, since she is always working hard to shield Elmer, while keeping a sense of security. The designer also mentions that she had originally drawn the character as one of the background people seen on the streets of Nevergreen. "Nora liked one of the faces on those crowd scenes and decided that she would be great as the mom, so we started developing her further," Ballester Cabo remembers. "I also had a lot of fun looking at pictures of women from the 1930s and '40s to come up with ideas for her outfits. What you see her wearing in the early scenes in Dust Town is actually directly inspired by a photo of a woman in the countryside that really grabbed my attention."

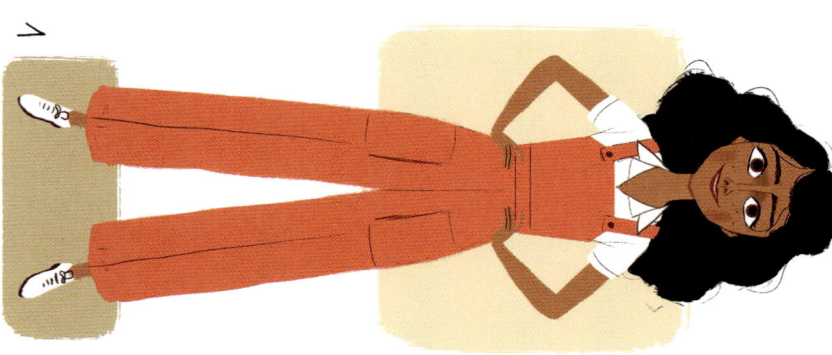

1

2

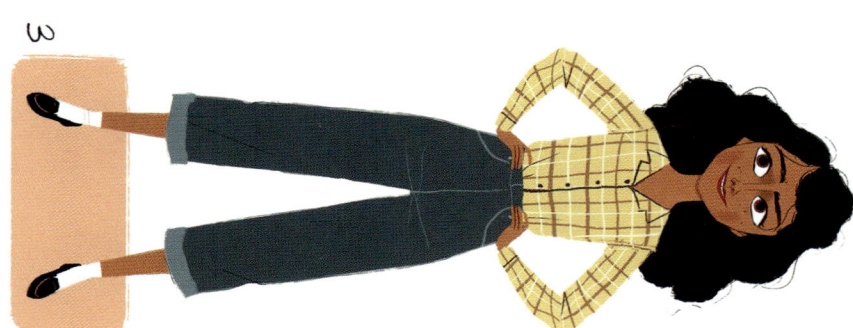

3

THIS SPREAD Rosa Ballester Cabo

1

Mom
wild
island flowers

2

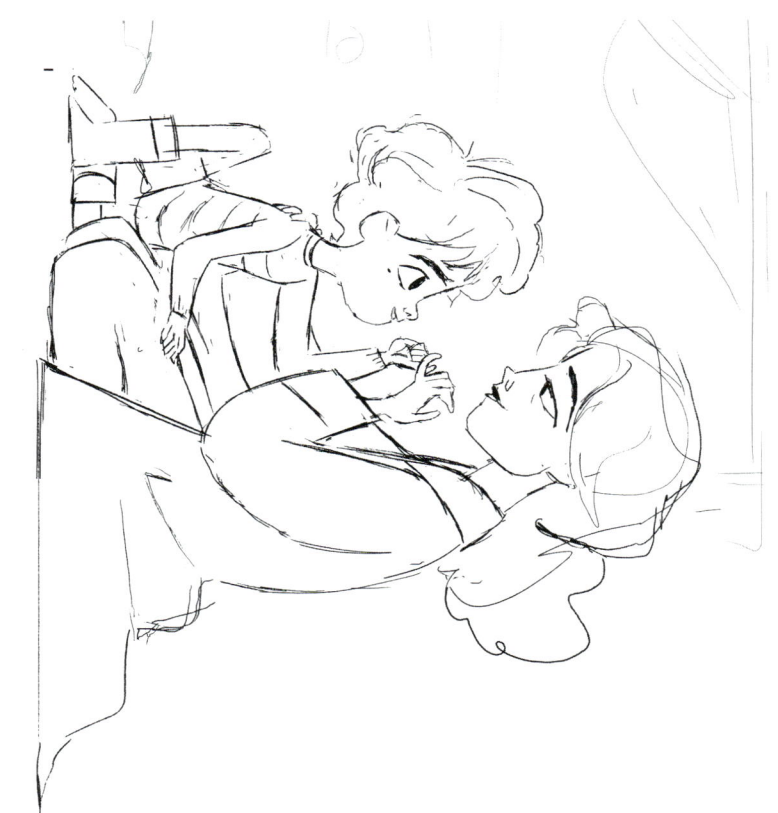

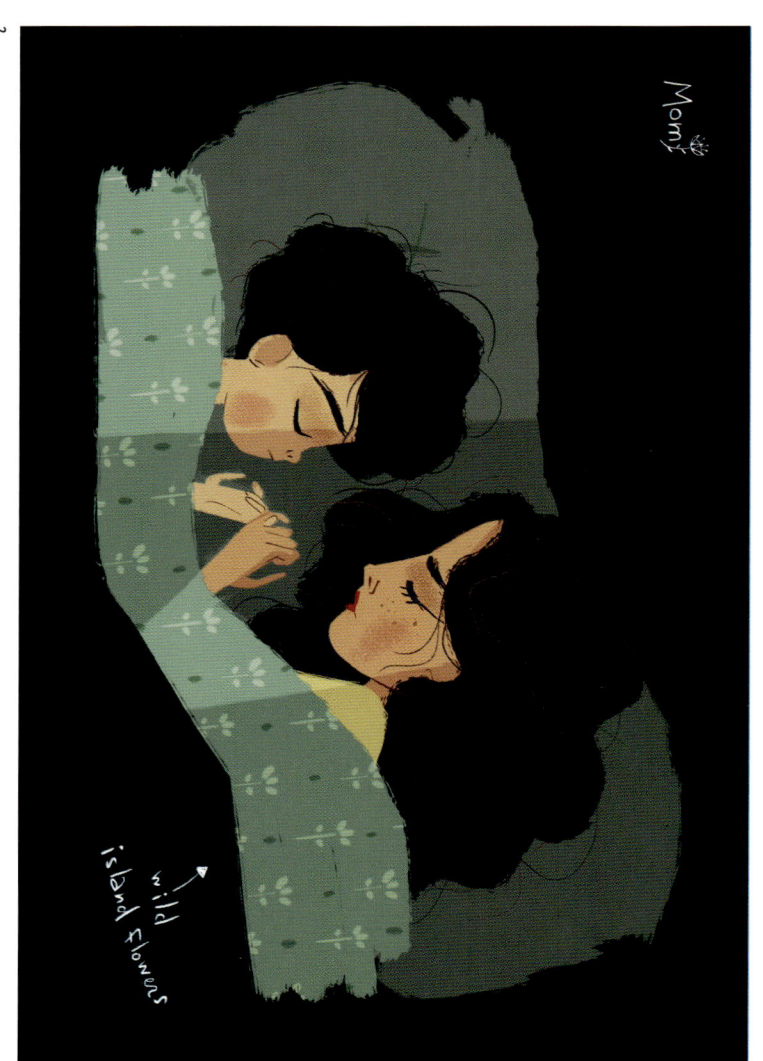

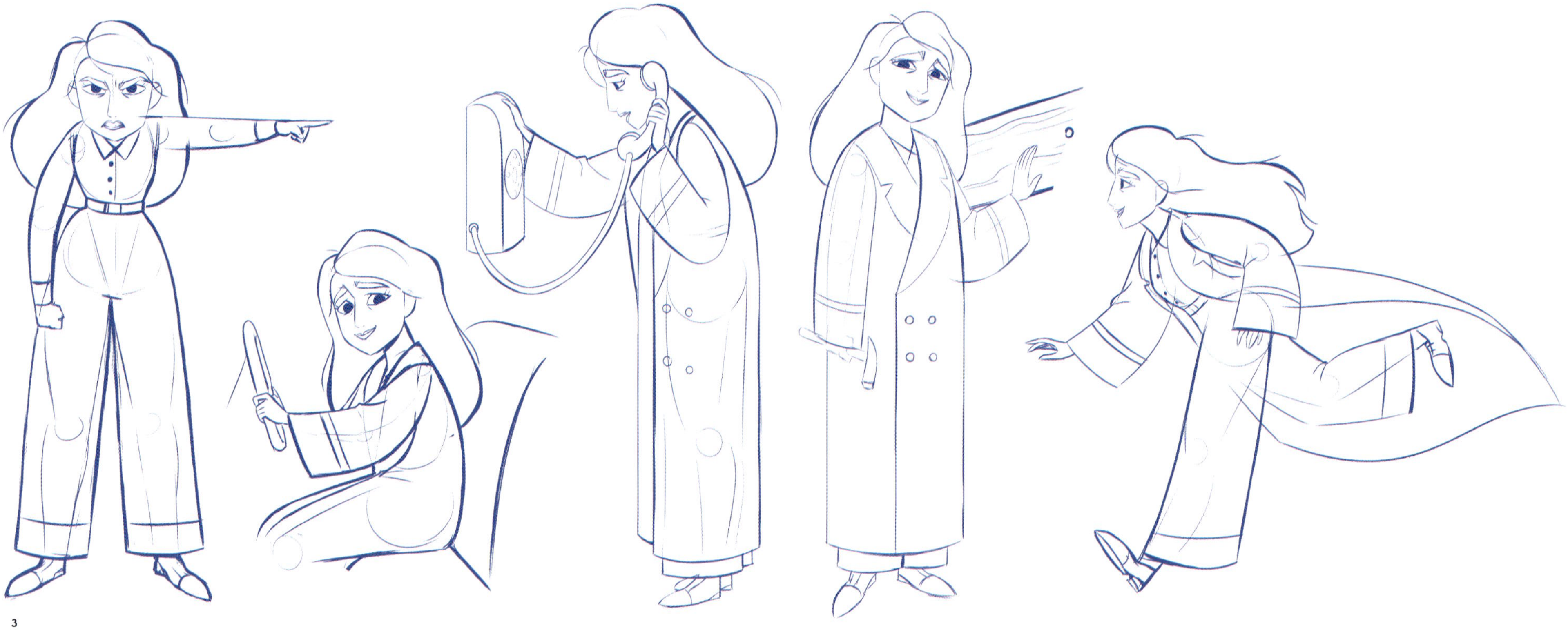

3

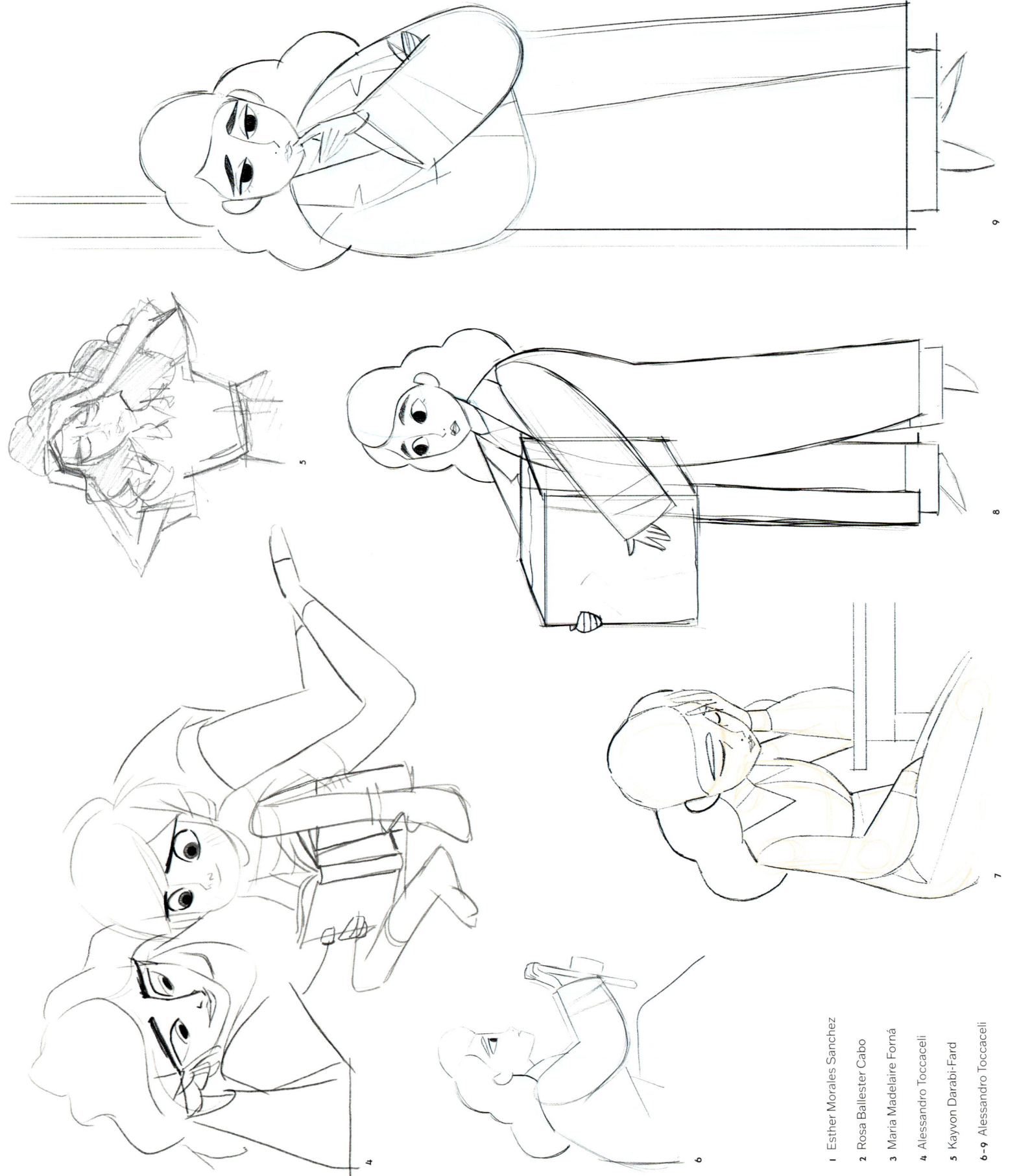

1 Esther Morales Sanchez
2 Rosa Ballester Cabo
3 Maria Madelaire Forná
4 Alessandro Toccaceli
5 Kayvon Darabi-Fard
6–9 Alessandro Toccaceli

The Cat

She watches Elmer's attempts to acclimatize to Nevergreen City. She accepts Elmer's generosity, a saucer of milk. It's a key moment from the book, and a wonderful device to show Elmer's intrinsic kindness—a kindness that should be rewarded. The cat is voiced by Whoopi Goldberg with playful ease; Whoopi showed Twomey pictures of her own cats and her grandchildren before exploring the gruff, mischievous character through her performance. "In some of the earlier drafts of the movie, the cat was a mother to a litter of kittens, says Ballester Cabo. "We wanted to make her look a little bit disheveled and unkempt because she was found on the street," says the production designer. "In one of the early versions, a piece of her ear was missing because of a street fight."

Ballester Cabo says the designs of the cat became finalized after the team was done with the tigers. "Once we decided that she was going to resemble the tigers, our direction was clearer. They come from the same family. We based her design on the tigers. You can see the similarity in the eyes, the nose, and the general flow of the body lines."

ABOVE
1 Lily Bernard
2–4 Rosa Ballester Cabo

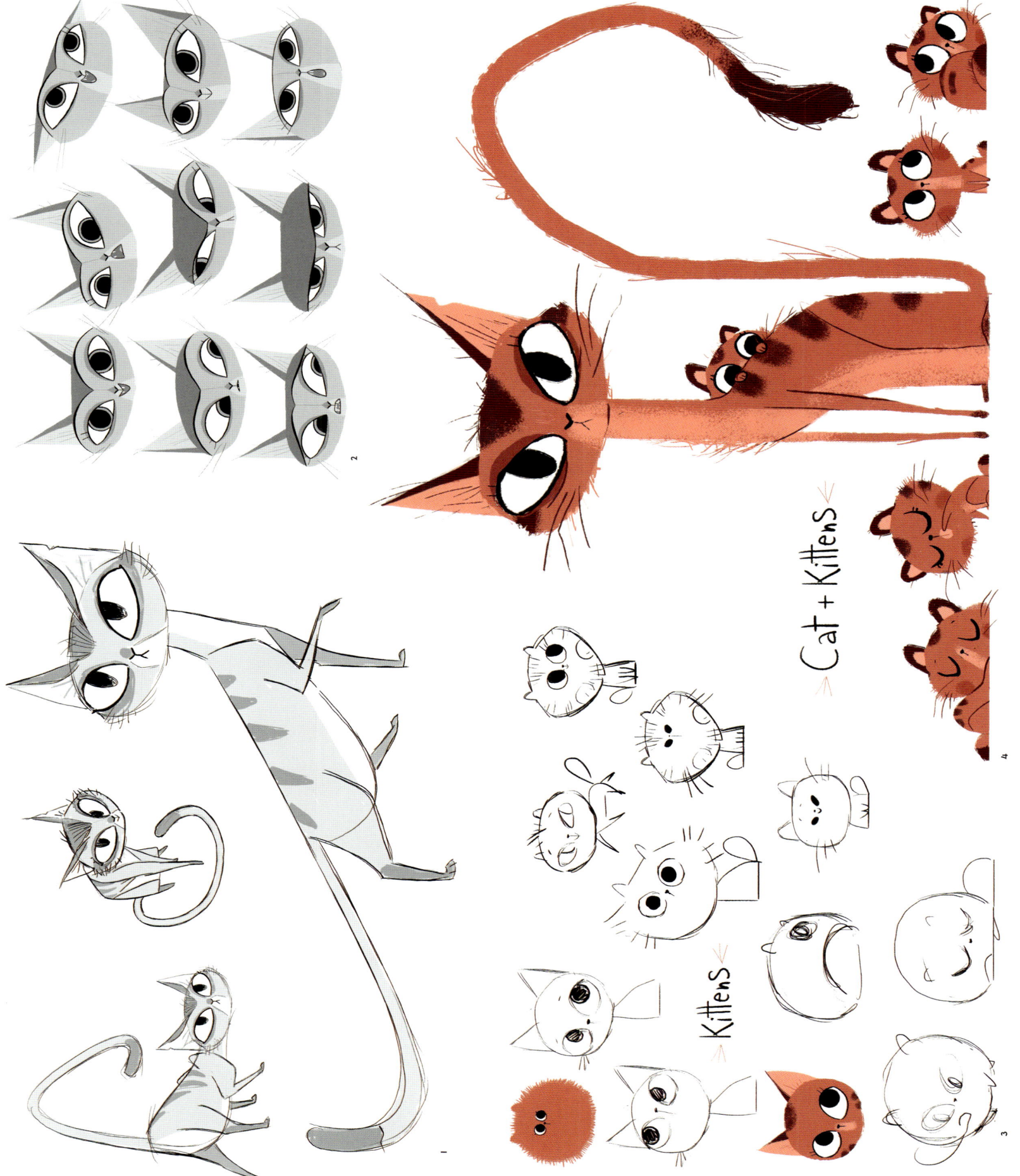

CHARACTERS

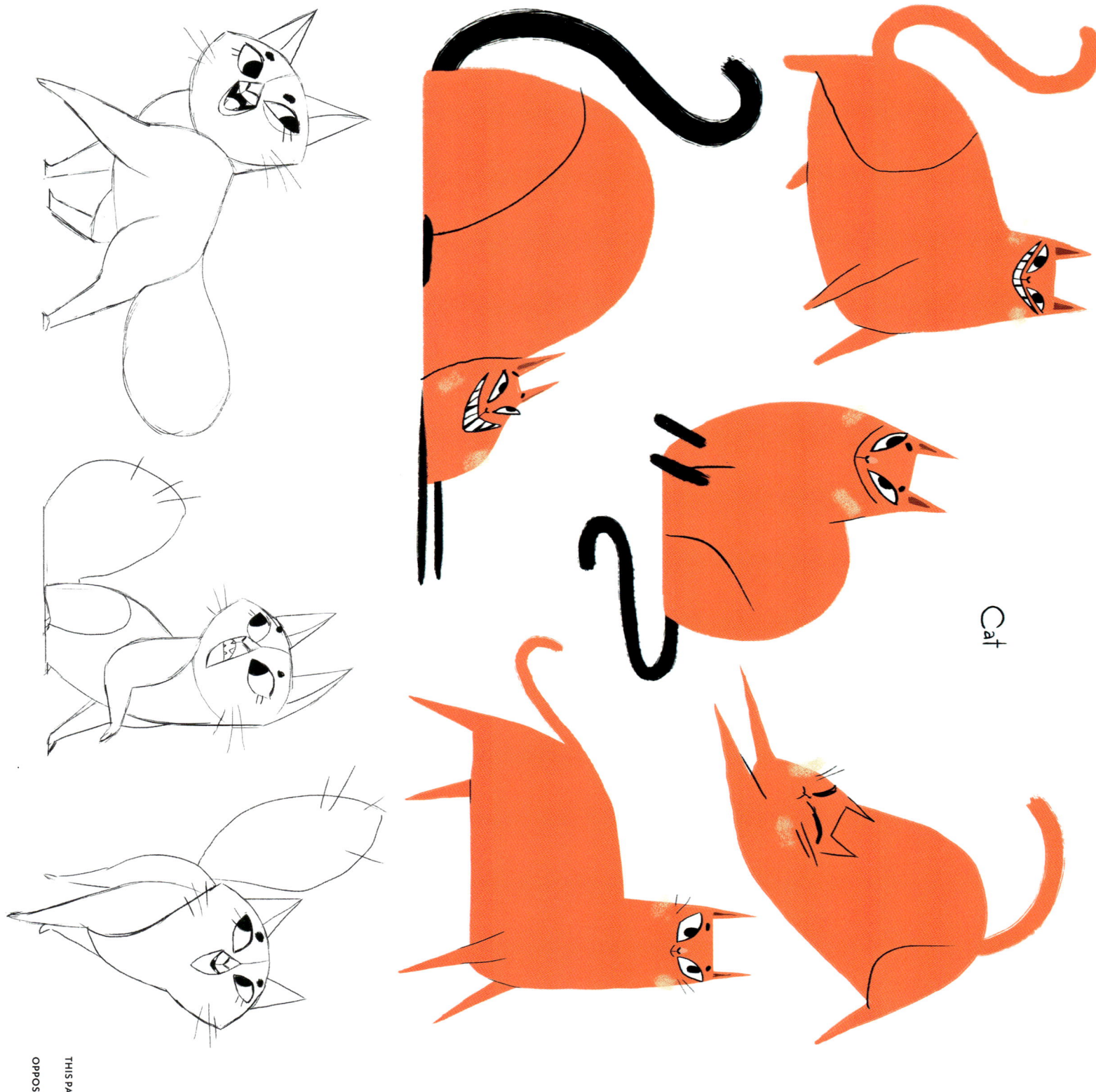

Cat

THIS PAGE Rosa Ballester Cabo
OPPOSITE Esther Morales Sanchez

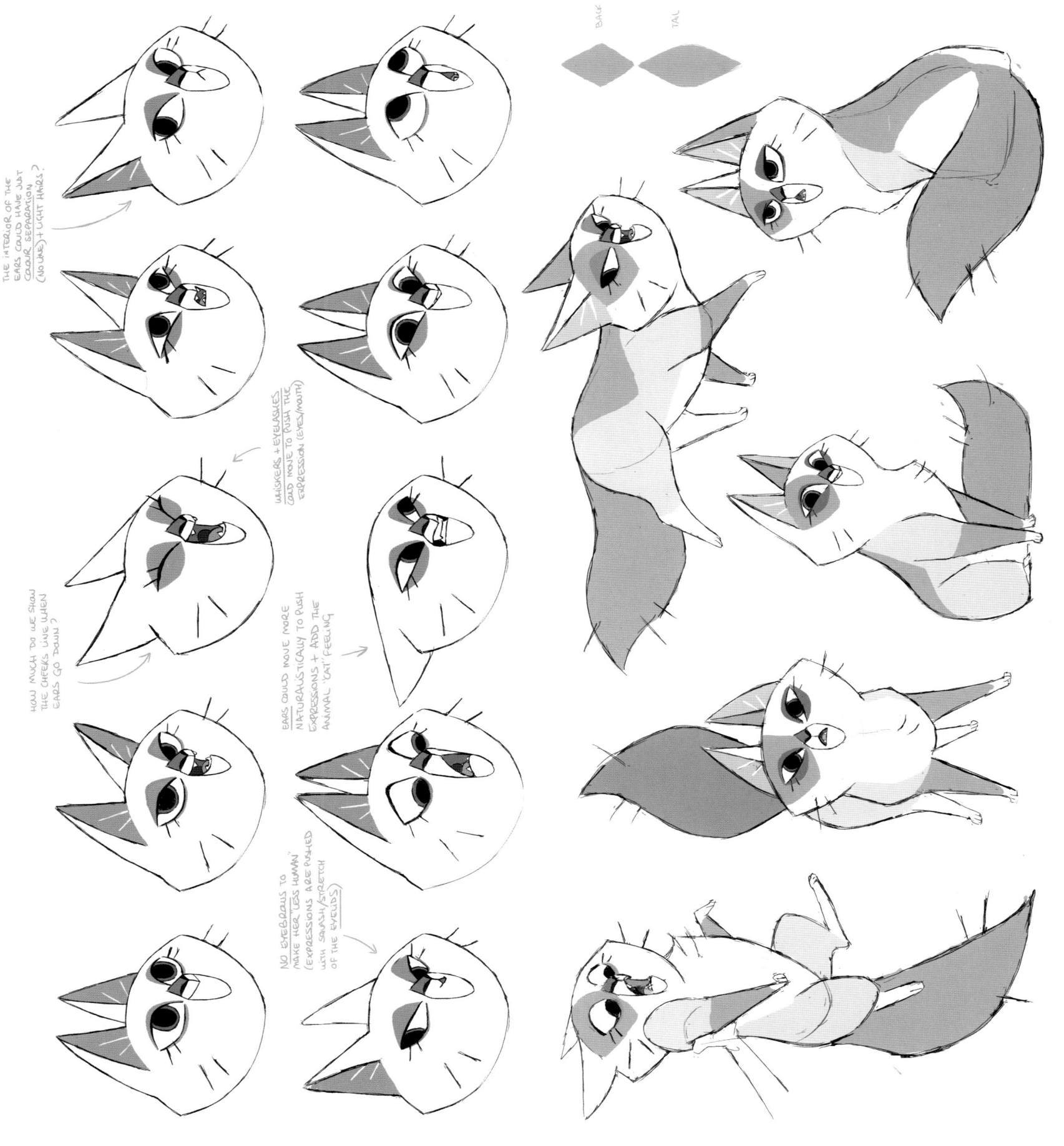

Mrs. McClaren

When Elmer and his mother arrive in Nevergreen, they meet Mrs. McClaren, the no-nonsense landlady of their new apartment in the big city who doesn't have time for tenants who can't pay their rent on time. In the original script, she is described as having a face "set with a permanent sour expression," and the designers definitely took their cue from those few words. They tried a variety of different visuals for the older woman and finally settled on the visuals that we see in the final movie.

"We had a lot of fun coming up with all the different variations," notes Ballester Cabo. "We tried all kinds of body types and expressions. We knew that she was a grumpy landlord who lives by herself and looks a bit mean, but we find out that she is actually a nice woman by the end of the picture. We tried an overweight version, one that was a bit dirty and unkempt, a version that dresses way too young for her age and reveals a bit too much cleavage, and finally settled on the version that Nora picked and appears in the movie."

Twomey adds that "Rita Moreno gave Mrs. McClaren such a fantastically comedic voice. Her timing is impeccable, and she uses every little lilt and pause to best effect. I've seldom witnessed someone who enjoys what they do as much as Rita; she's incredibly generous as a collaborator."

ABOVE Rosa Ballester Cabo
1–2 Rosa Ballester Cabo
3 Lamberto Anderloni

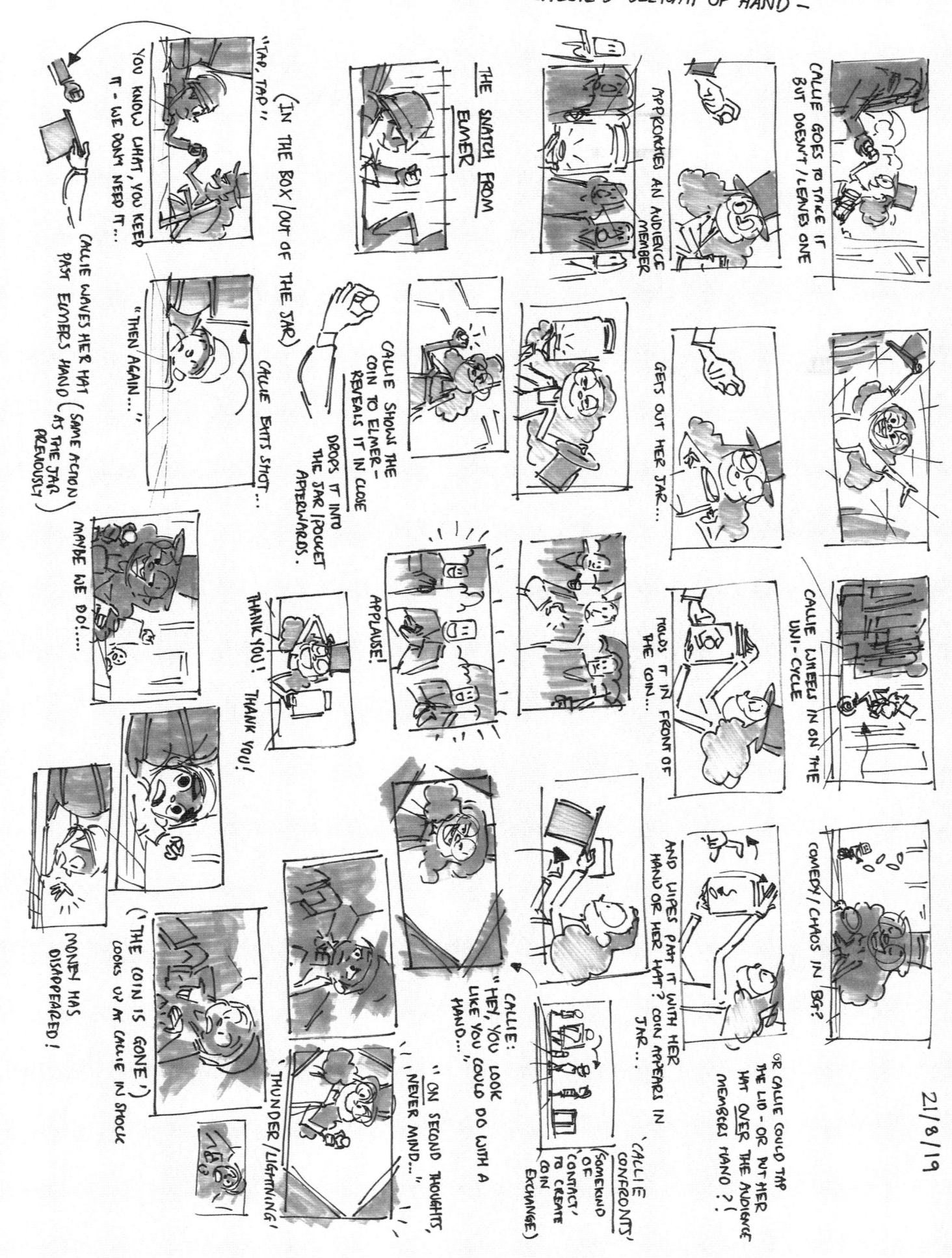

Callie, Gertie, and Eugene

The three neighborhood kids who shun Elmer when he first arrives on the scene went through a variety of design changes as well. As Ballester Cabo points out, "Nora wanted them to wear outfits that they could have picked up in a thrift store. Voiced playfully by Yara Shahidi, Callie is a little bit confrontational. We gave each one of them different physical characteristics to make them stand out. Eugene's cardboard bee costume on one of them was challenging to prep for the posing department. Little Gertie is wearing a cape to illustrate her dramatic qualities."

OPPOSITE Kayvon Darabi-Fard

1–2 Nora Twomey

3 Colour script by Ciarán Duffy, Martí Furgber Morales, Alice Dieudonné, and Emilie Bach Nielsen

CHARACTERS

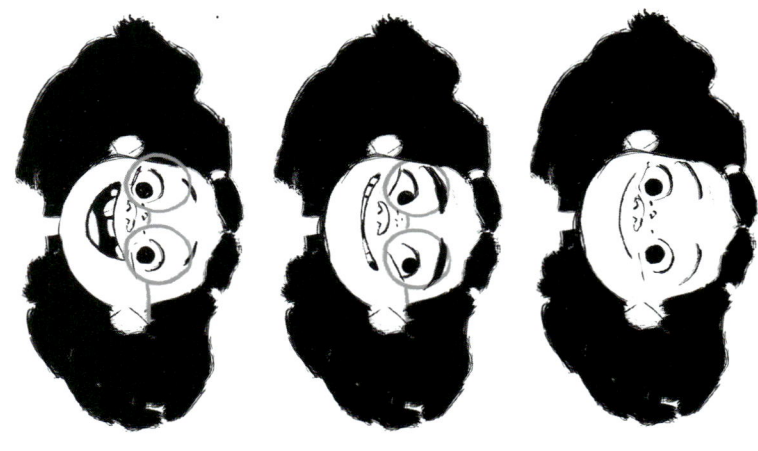

MAYBE THEY REPAINT THE HEAD TO MAKE IT MORE BORISH? (maybe they add the stripes as well?)

1-2 Rosa Ballester Cabo
3 Louise Bagnall
4 Rosa Ballester Cabo
5 Naomi Calvo Morales
6 Elle Power

FOLLOWING SPREAD
Rough animation
by Laurent Kircher

Background Characters

The movie's artists and designers studied archival photos and classic movies from the 1930s and '40s to find inspiration for the background characters we see in both the Dust Town and Nevergreen sections of Elmer's life. The people who interact with Elmer and his mom in the small town are seen as colourful and happy, corresponding with the orange- and yellow-hued backdrops of the first sequences of the movie. In contrast, the harried and stressed-out characters seen on the rainy streets of Nevergreen needed to look dour and angry. "We played with a lot of lights and shadows," says Ballester Cabo. "When Elmer steps out of the car, we had a parade of umbrellas, making him feel small and disoriented. I sketched a lot of background characters for the city scenes, and I had a lot of fun imagining all these different characters, wearing these wonderful outfits from that era. I would show them all to Nora, and she would decide which ones she liked and would fit in with those scenes."

RIGHT Rosa Ballester Cabo

CHARACTERS

long coats! umbrellas! hats!

angry faces under big hats

1 Almu Redondo
2–4 Rosa Ballester Cabo
OPPOSITE Rosa Ballester Cabo

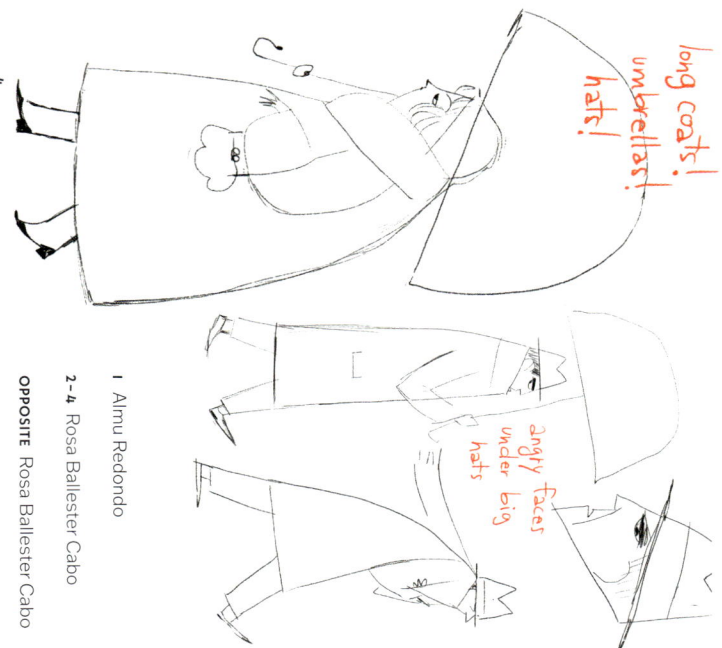

Soda

Judy Greer walked into the recording booth and jammed on the accelerator from the moment she started recording. Soda was to be an unbalancing force in Elmer's life, just as the rug had been pulled out from under Elmer when he moved to Nevergreen. Soda won't let him feel secure for an instant of their journey to Wild Island.

One of the main challenges the designers faced was how to quickly impart the visual cues about her young age. "We needed to show that she was the equivalent of a six-year-old human girl," says Ballester Cabo. "In the initial concepts, she looked older because her body was too long. So, I decided to simplify her shape as much as possible: I gave her a perfectly round body shape where the tail and fins were the only elements breaking the form. But that design was too pushed and graphic. In the end, we went for something in between—a round head with a longer body. We made her tail and fins really small compared to the body, gave her huge round eyes and a big mouth with a set of teeth [suitable for a six-year-old] The final touch was some freckles, which, as a rule, always bring some extra playfulness to a face."

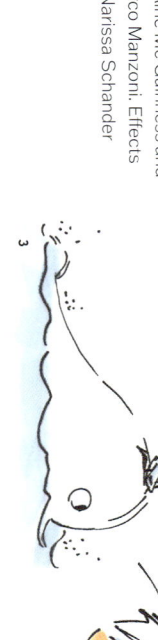
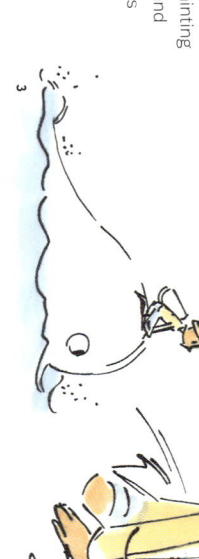

1 JB Vendamme
2 Rosa Ballester Cabo
3 Kayvon Darabi-Fard
4 Rosa Ballester Cabo
5 Scene Illustration painting by Áine Mc Guinness and Marco Manzoni, Effects by Narissa Schander

CHARACTERS

Boris

Elmer doesn't come face-to-face with Boris, the lovable and clumsy dragon of Wild Island, until the tenth and final chapter of the original book. Since the movie's central story depends on the bond between the two characters, the creative team had to introduce him much earlier and open up the relationship between the boy and the magical creature.

"He actually reminds me of some classmates I knew as a child; a 'type'—someone who laughs at themselves before someone else gets there first. He is an adolescent dragon, which makes him more awkward. Gaten Matarazzo brought a depth of feeling as well as brilliant comic timing to Boris. He's an incredible actor, and he understands story brilliantly. The comradery between Jacob and Gaten was instant. The recording stage was electric with their energy," comments Twomey.

Assistant director Louise Bagnall adds, "There is no shortage of dragons in films and in animation, so we wanted to create a character that hadn't quite been depicted the same way before. This was not going to be the most impressive dragon, not something that would make your friends think that you're the coolest thing ever. We opted for the least conventional dragon: He's different, awkward, and fumbling, but he is still the best friend you could possibly hope for in life."

Ballester Cabo mentions that it took the team the longest to finalize the visuals for Boris: "We started with the original illustrations in the book, but our Boris needed to look clumsy, with a soft belly and small wings," she says. "We were constantly discussing every physical detail: How many spikes would look good on his head? How many stripes, freckles, and teeth would look best on him? Is the tail yellow or blue? We kept tweaking the designs until we ended up with the best version possible."

1. Rosa Ballester Cabo
2. Rozenn Grosjean
3. Maxime Mary and Tomm Moore
4. Rosa Ballester Cabo
5. Maxime Mary

CHARACTERS 73

CHARACTERS

1 Eva Roycroft
2 Tito Ballester Cabo
3 Aislin Konings Ferrari
4 Oliver McGrath

OPPOSITE Rosa Ballester Cabo

"We asked the children in our lives to draw from the book in order to loosen up our imaginations and imagine the film's characters through a child's mind."

NORA TWOMEY

CHARACTERS

1 Rozenn Grosjean
2 Rosa Ballester Cabo
3 Maria Madelaire Forná
4–5 Esther Morales Sanchez

OPPOSITE Rosa Ballester Cabo
THIS PAGE Kayvon Darabi-Fard

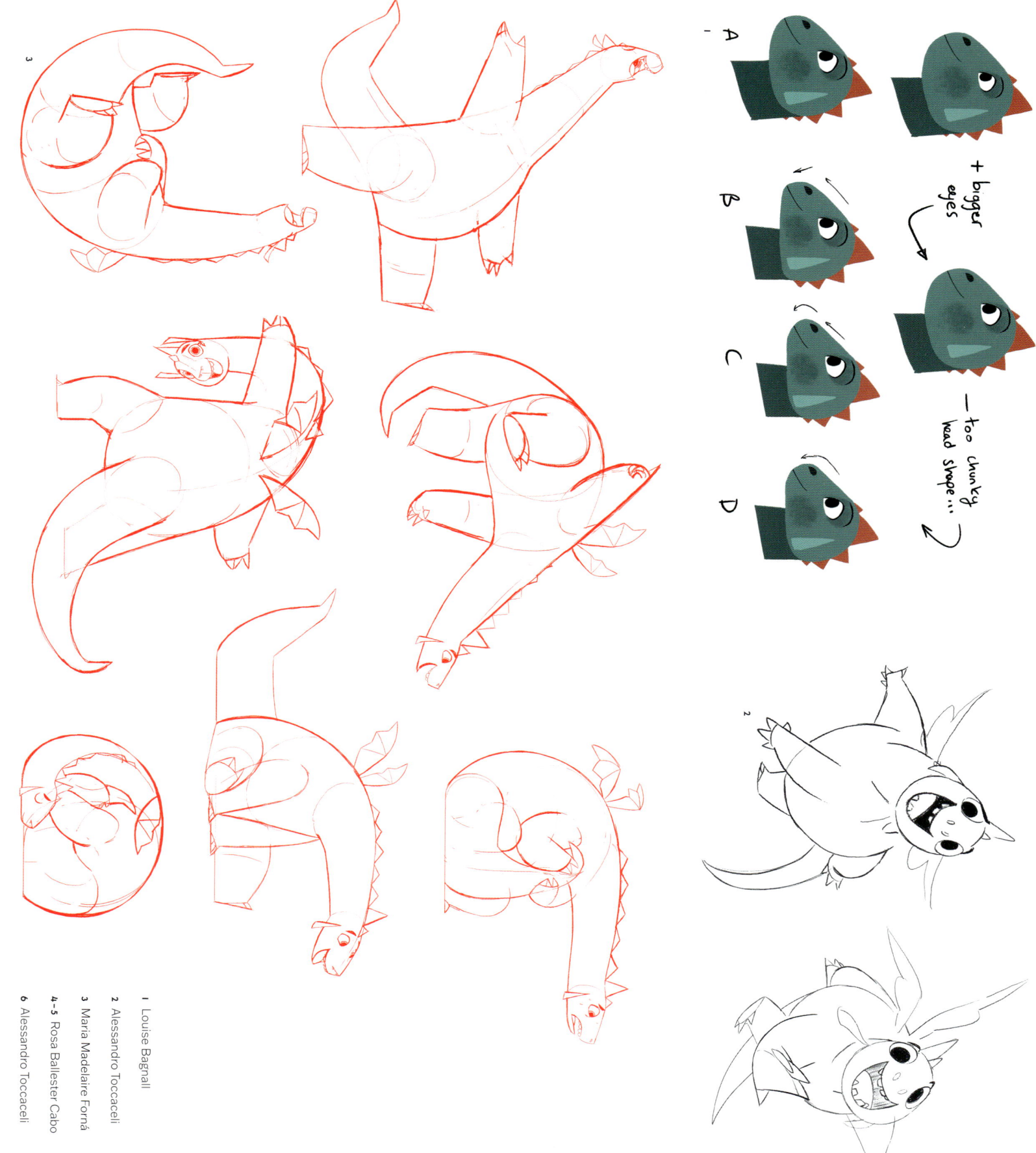

1 Louise Bagnall
2 Alessandro Toccaceli
3 Maria Madelaire Forná
4–5 Rosa Ballester Cabo
6 Alessandro Toccaceli

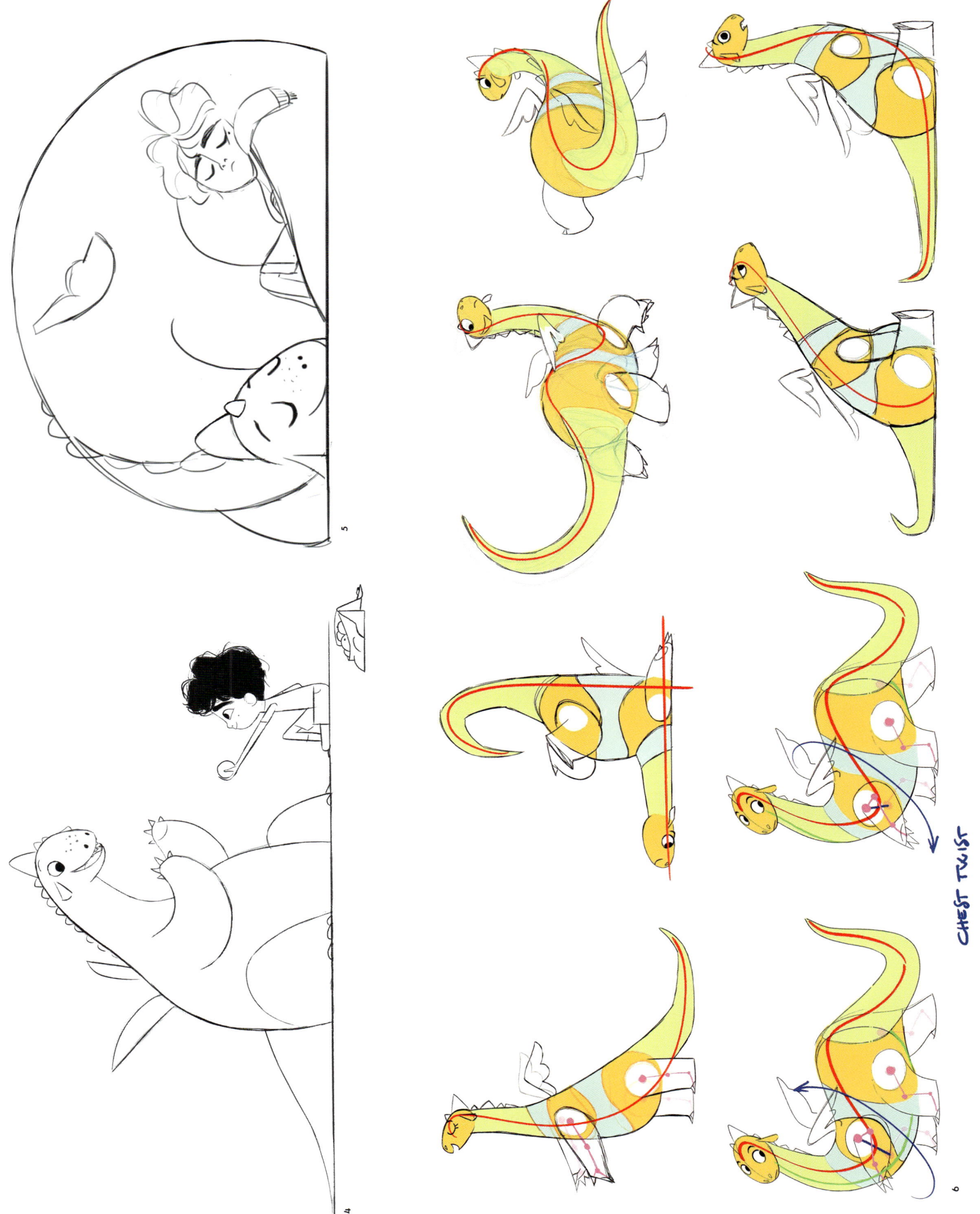

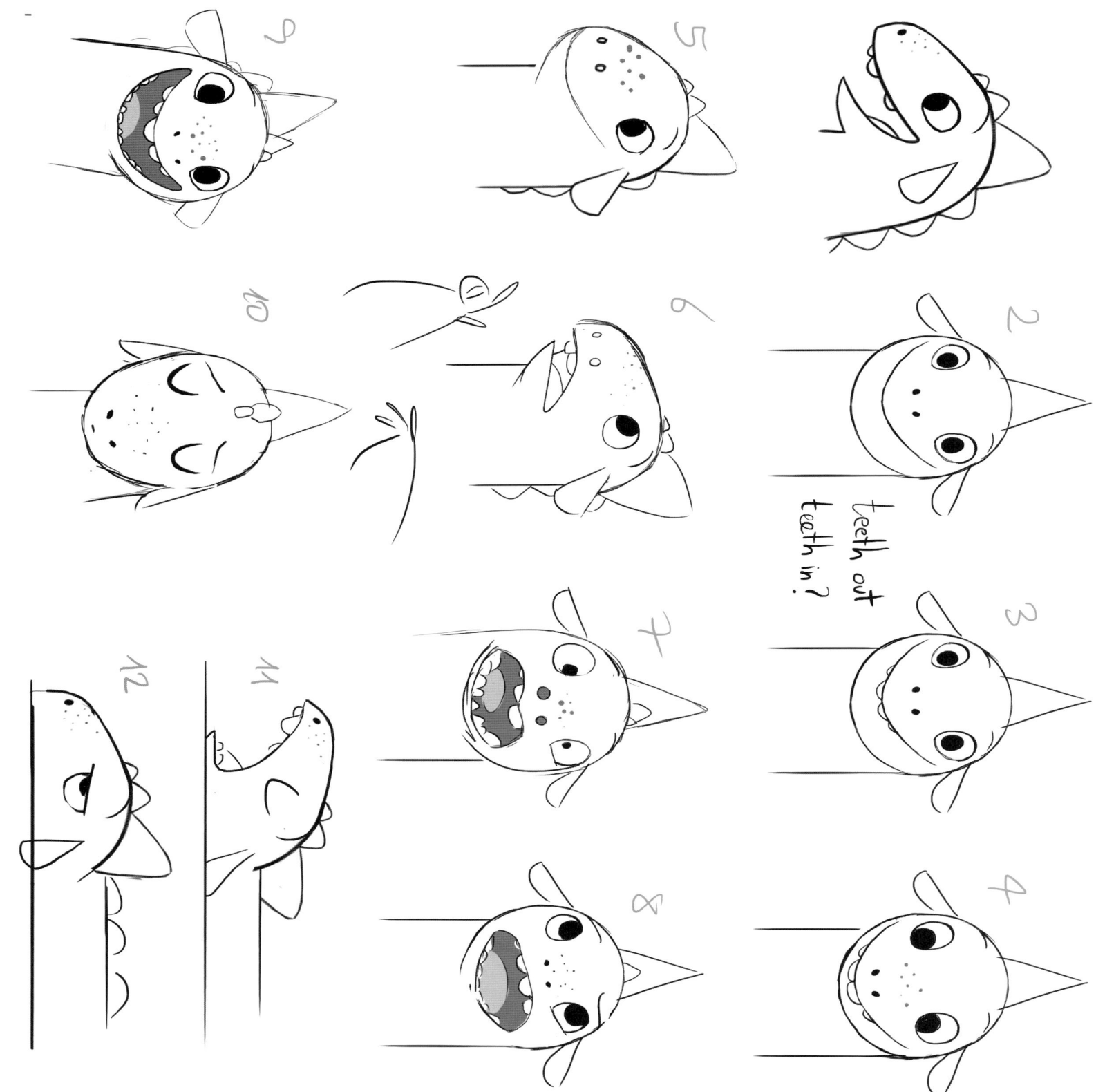

1 Rosa Ballester Cabo
2 Sandra Norup Andersen
3 Rosa Ballester Cabo

Kwan

We get our first glimpse of Kwan (voiced by Chris O'Dowd), a lean and lanky reddish-brown Sulawesi monkey, as he tries to quiet down the group of anxious animals who are worried about the fate of their island.

"Kwan is a character who feels utterly betrayed," says director Nora Twomey. "He knows that what they're doing to the dragon is not the answer to saving the island, but he doesn't know what the right answer is. To me, he's someone that I think of as having a kind of young man's energy. He's very direct. He seeks out what he believes is the right way forward. Both Saiwa and Kwan are versions of what Elmer could become if he kept going down the path that he is going. I understand Kwan's perspective; Chris got him straightaway—there's a desperation in his voice at all times, no matter what he's saying. When we're writing or directing characters, I need to know where they're coming from. They can't just act the way they act because that's their function in the story—they have to be real; real people with realm problems."

"He has a rhombus-like, triangular head, says Ballester Cabo. "His body is lanky with muscular legs. We needed to show that he's still in his developmental stage.

THIS SPREAD JB Vendamme

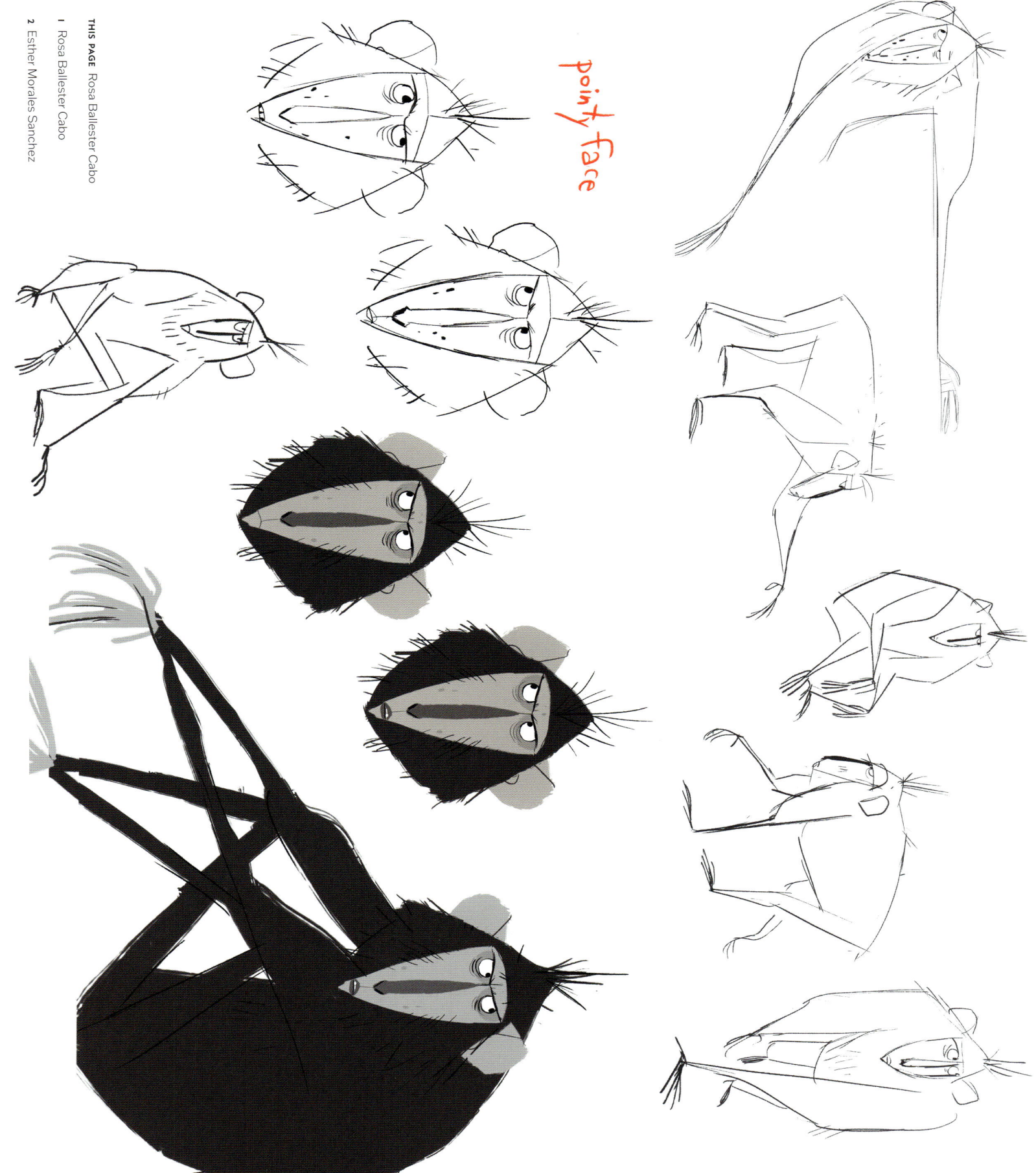

THIS PAGE Rosa Ballester Cabo
1 Rosa Ballester Cabo
2 Esther Morales Sanchez

pointy face

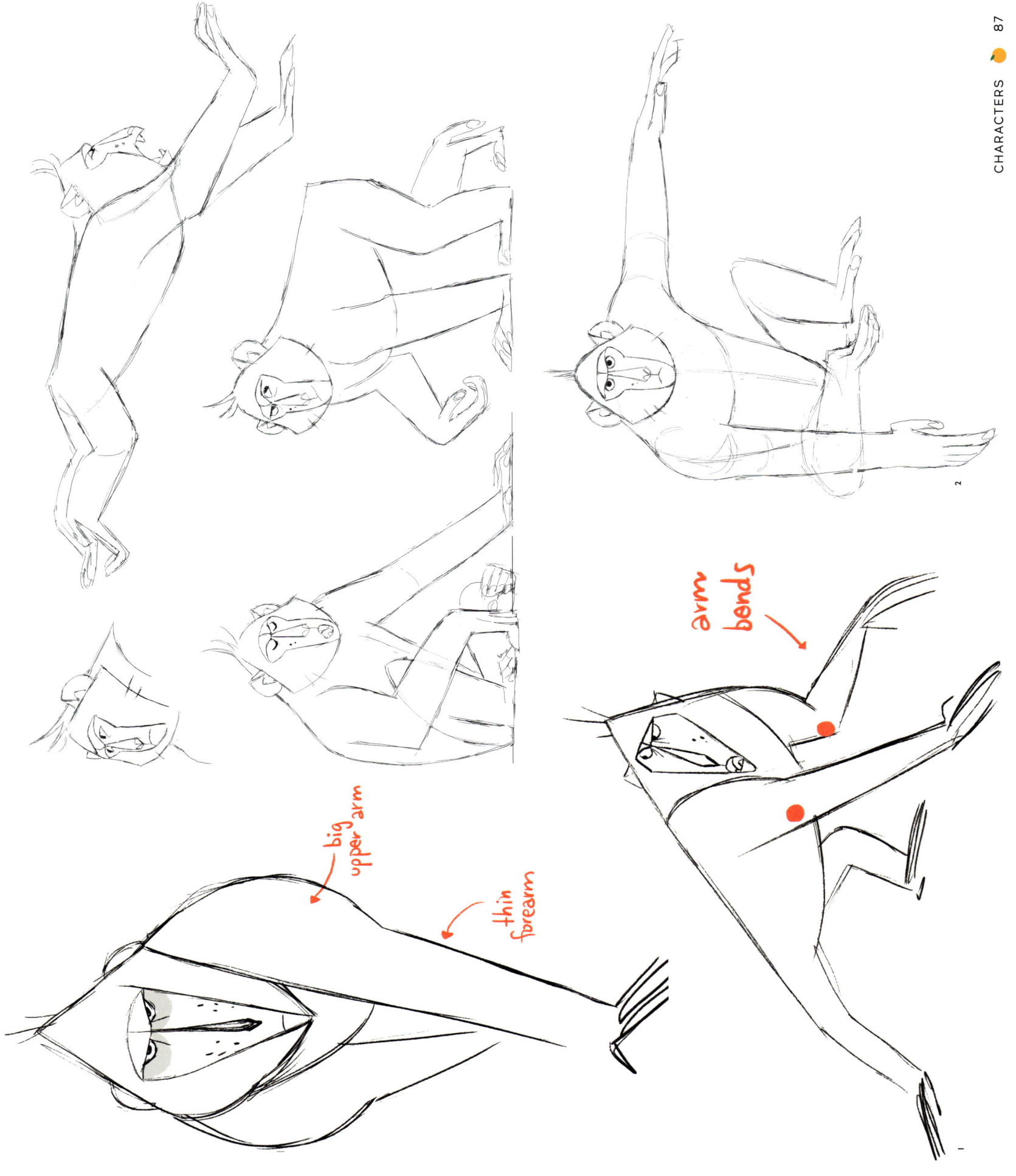

Saiwa

"The most important thing is that we all keep calm," says Saiwa, the tired grey gorilla who acts as the leader of the animals on Wild Island, voiced beautifully by an authoritative Ian McShane.

Twomey points out that it was really important for her that the audience believes the motivations behind this character's actions. "We really wanted to make sure that he was not a carbon-copy bad guy and that there was a real depth to him," she says. "He is perhaps doing the wrong thing for the right reason. He feels the weight of Wild Island on his shoulders. He's just doing the best he can. He is somebody who perhaps doesn't have the most amount of energy in the world, but he knows that he's holding on to things. I love it when Saiwa tells Elmer that he is sure that 'fear would have drowned [the animals] long before the sea did.' His sense of responsibility is connected to both Elmer's and his mom's similar feelings. I love the final interaction between Saiwa and Boris, because Boris doesn't simply forgive him. He tells him what he can do so that it will never happen again. We worked very hard in the story department to get that right."

The design for the character also evolved as the story evolved. "In the beginning, he was mostly long-limbed, skinny, and saggy, with lots of angles. Eventually, we had to make him stronger, with wide shoulders, a solid shape and posture. His design language changed, and his face also became round and bulky. We had to reveal his strong character with an economy of lines on his face. Every line needs to reveal a lot of information about his nature, and the dignity and truth of Ian McShane's performance."

THIS SPREAD JB Vendamme

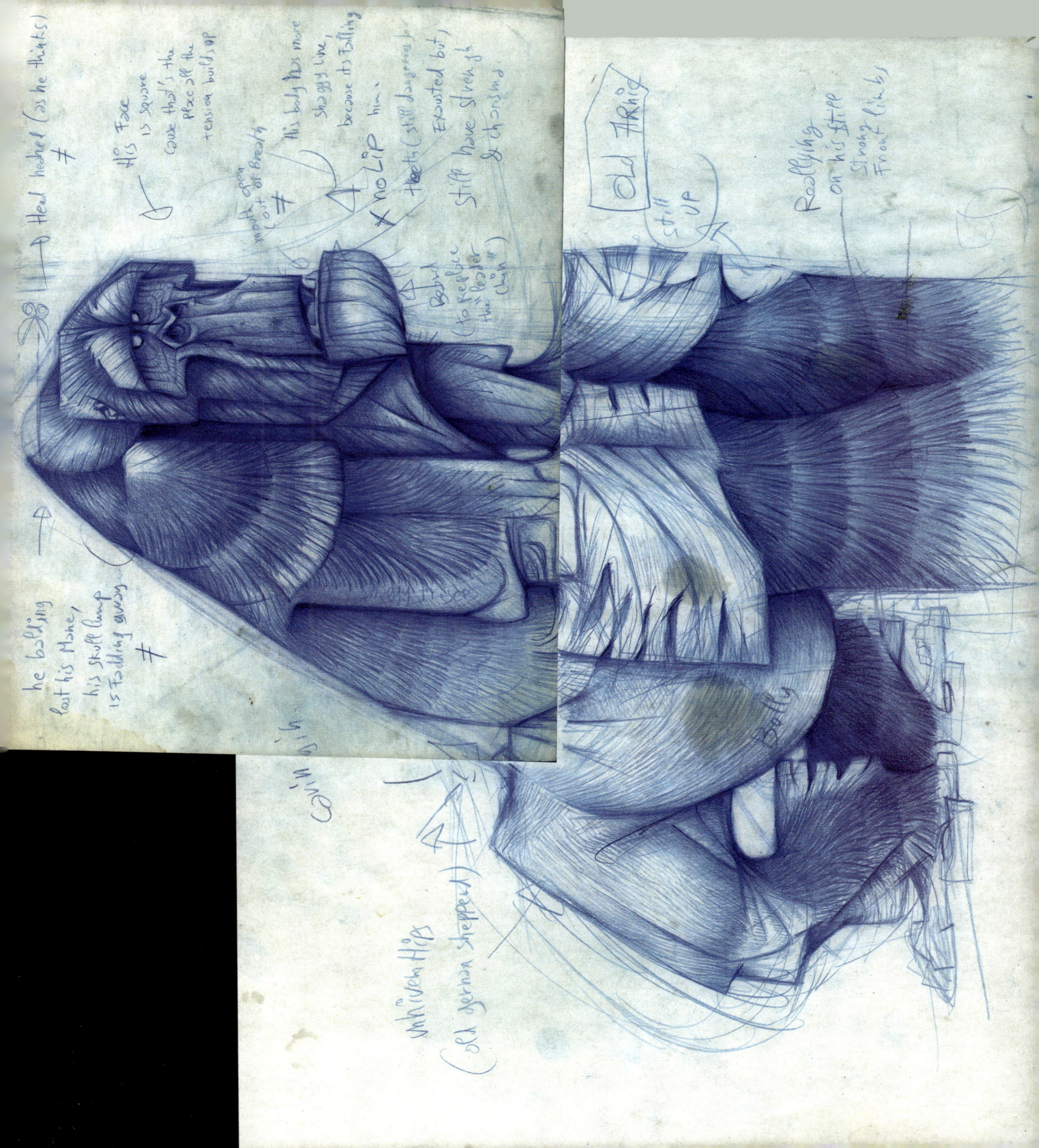

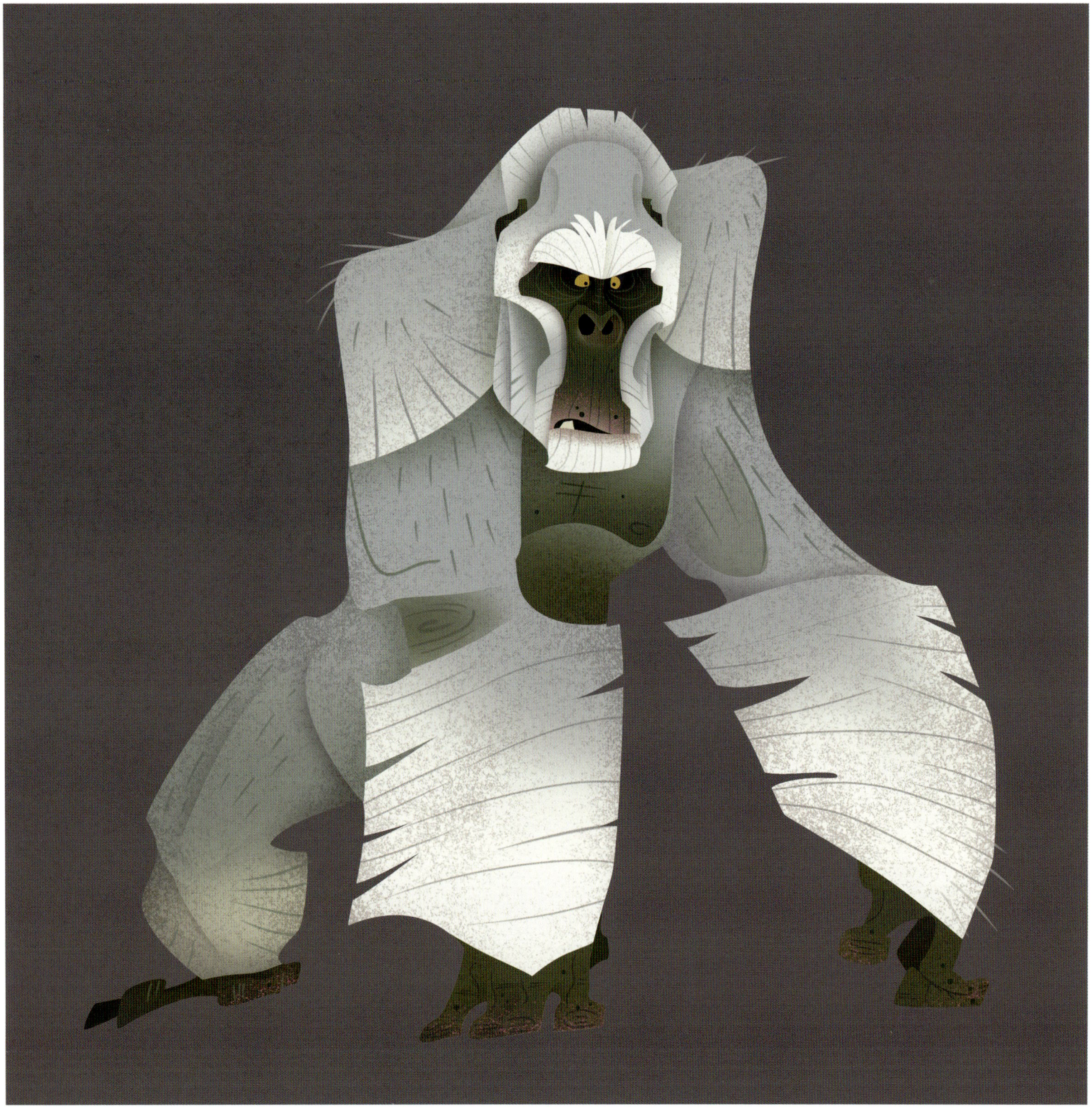

1

1–2 JB Vendamme

3–4 Rosa Ballester Cabo

Tamir

If you were to come up with one adjective to describe Tamir, the wide-eyed little tarsier who likes to sit on Saiwa's shoulders, it would be "anxious." "He is always very, very, very afraid," says Ballester Cabo. "His head is bean shaped, and he often has the same scared expression. His design remained constant throughout. We were able to nail down his nervous face early on."

Twomey adds, "Jackie Earle Haley voiced Tamir as though he had no control over what came out of his tiny mouth. Tamir tells the truth, to everyone's alarm."

1 Rosa Ballester Cabo
2 JB Vandamme
3 Rosa Ballester Cabo
4 Louise Bagnall
5 Esther Morales Sanchez
6 Rosa Ballester Cabo

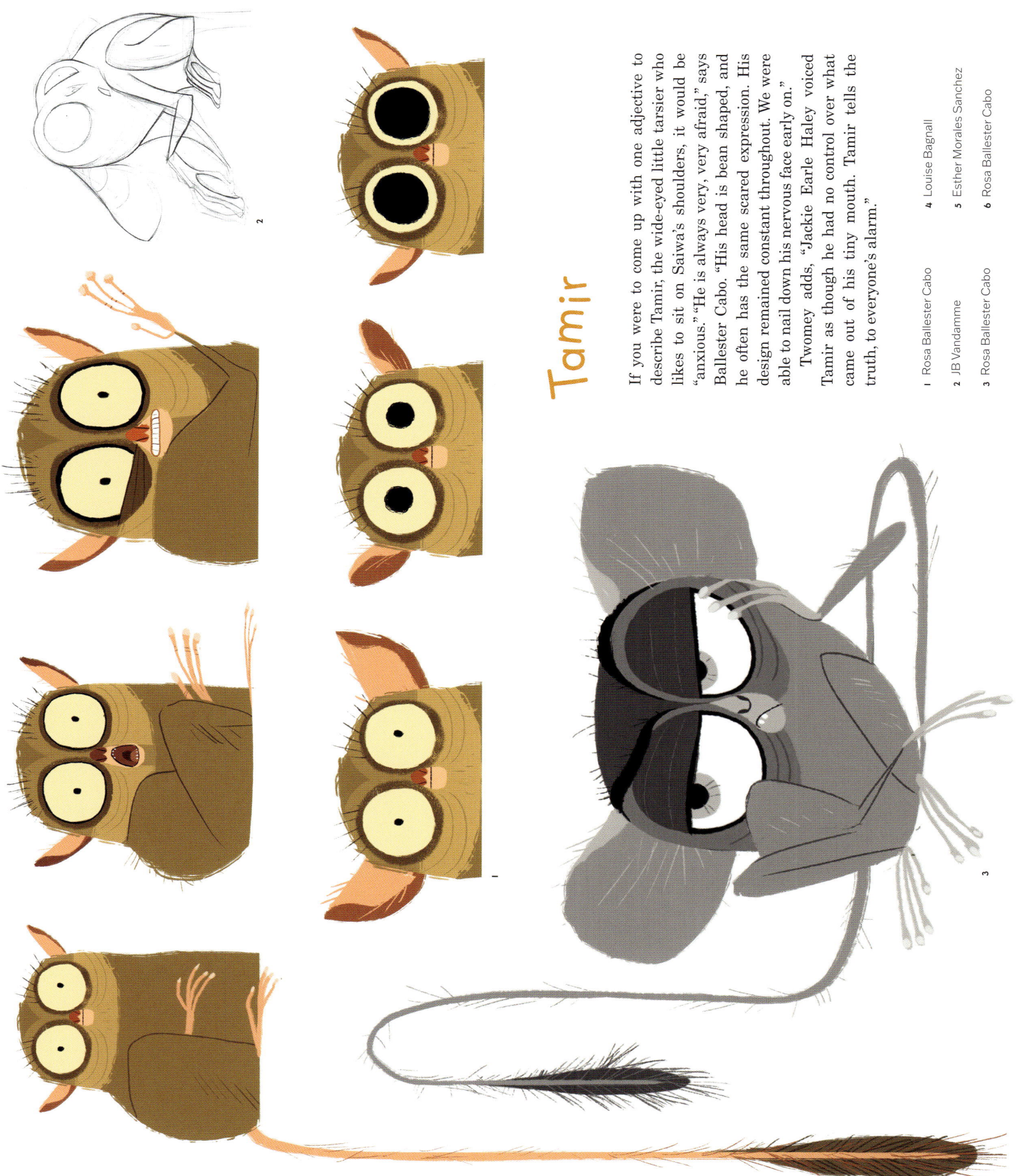

CHARACTERS

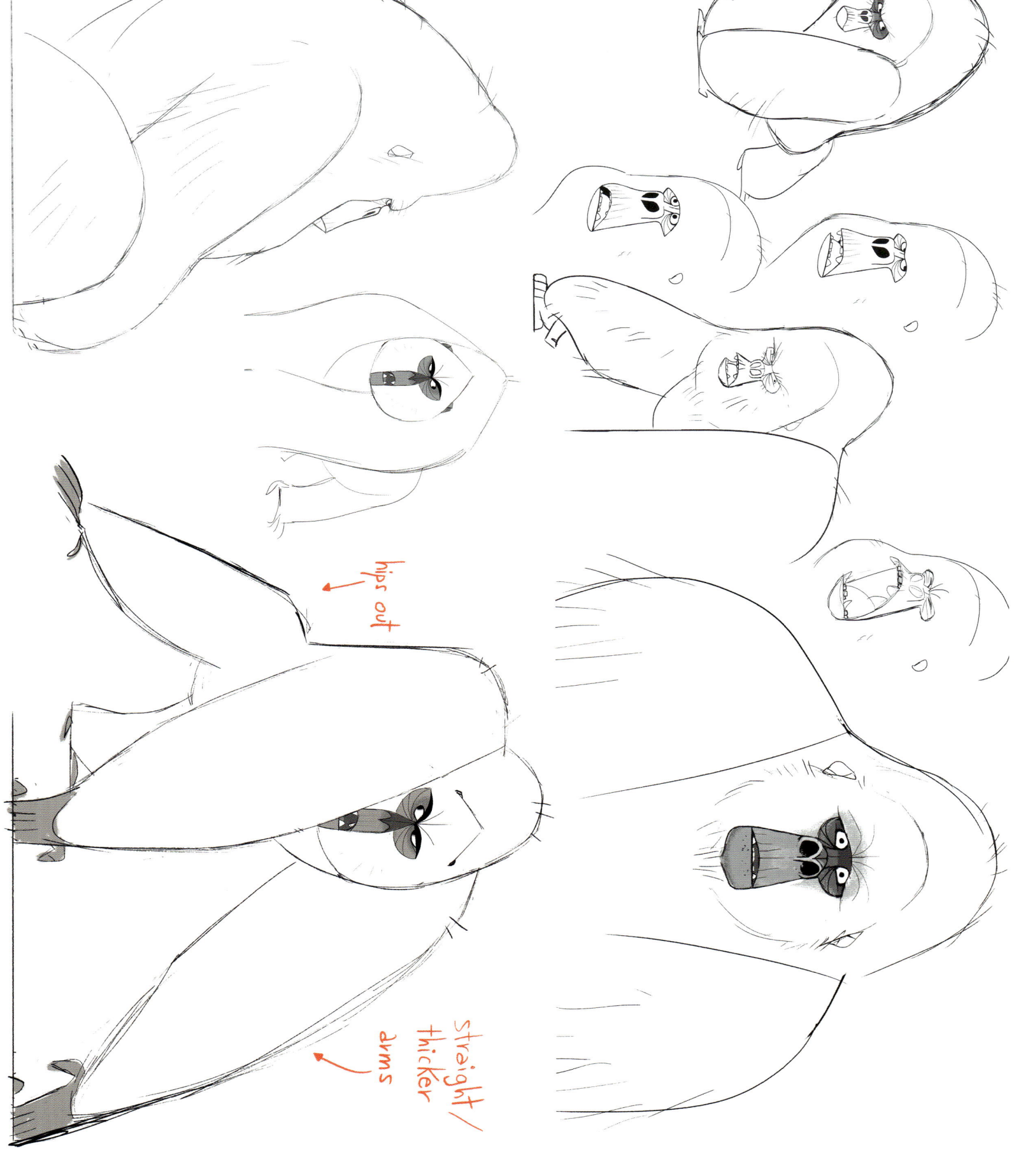

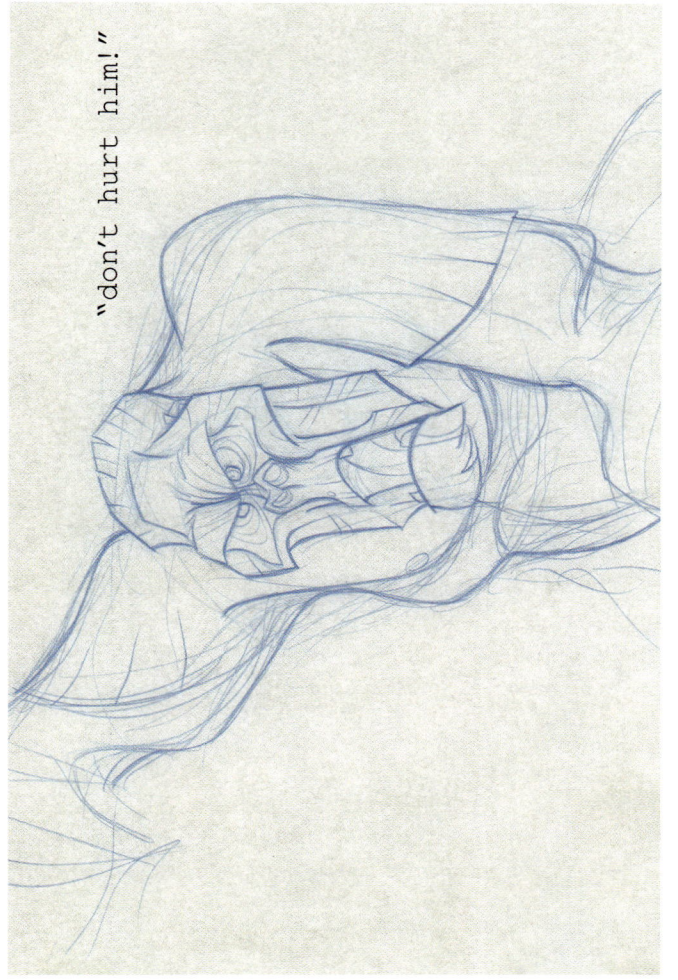
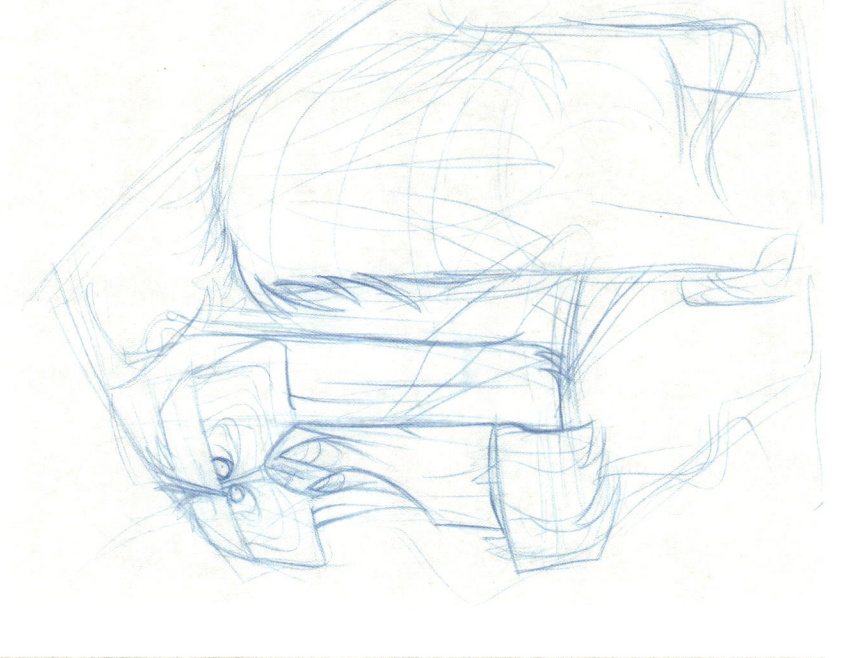
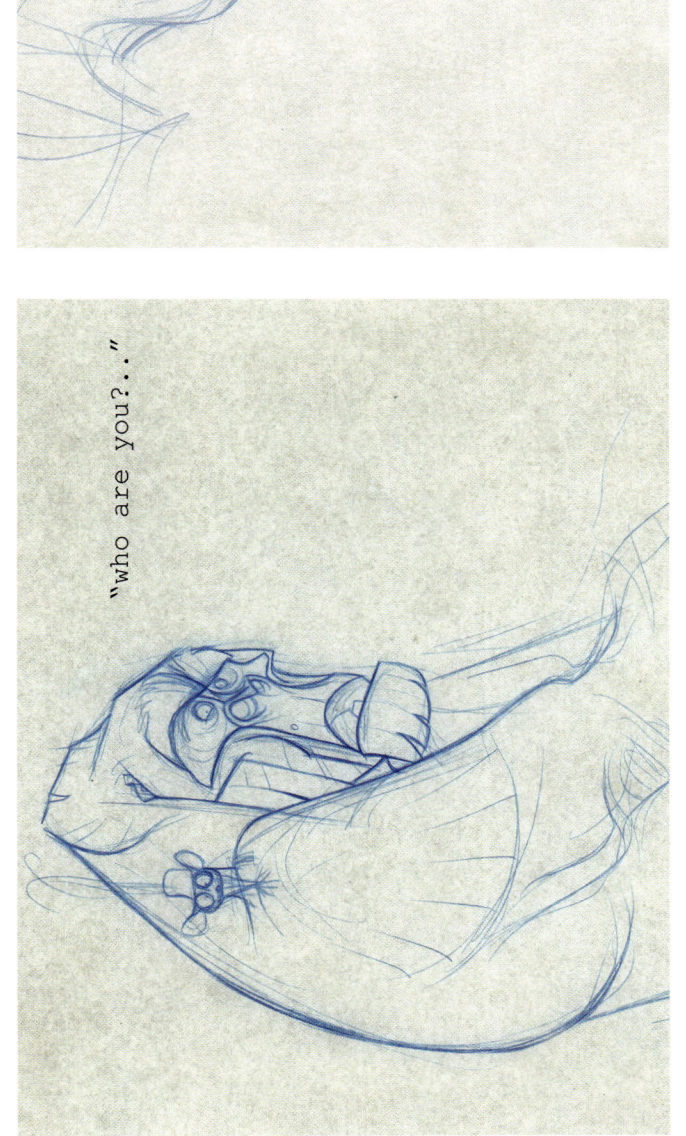

THIS PAGE
JB Vendamme

OPPOSITE
Rosa Ballester Cabo

CHARACTERS 91

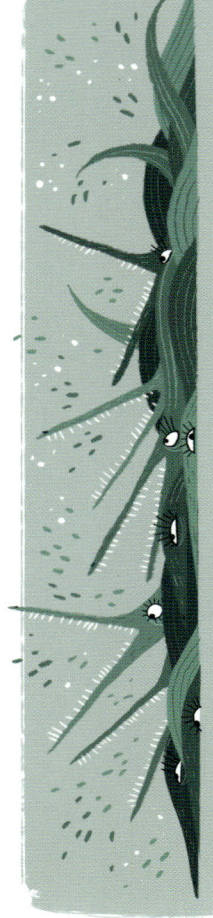

Cornelius Crocodile and the Baby Crocs

One of the memorable and eccentric characters of Wild Island, Cornelius Crocodile is constantly protective of and at the same time irritated by his little army of mischievous baby crocs. The designs of the crocodiles was also something of a bold adventure for Ballester Cabo and the team. "We wanted to step away a little bit from what we usually picture in our heads when we think about a crocodile, so I made them extremely long and skinny," she recalls. "Cornelius is almost snakelike, but he has the physical characteristics of a crocodile. Since the early brief I got about the characters told me that the crocodiles had to look like water moving, I added this wavelike quality to their back as well. That early brief also told me that the crocodiles were old ladies that desperately wanted to go near Elmer and probably eat him. A fun fact about this design is it was really difficult to make their 'hinge' heads look good in the straight-up frontal views, so we decided to always show the crocs in profile. The baby crocs are basically a tiny version of the adults: small hinges with huge eyes!"

Alan Cumming's performance, along with an entire "loop-group" of actors who make up the baby crocodile babble, brings an entertainingly odd dimension to Elmer and Boris's first encounter with Wild Island animals who try to stop their journey to Aratuah. During pandemic lockdowns, Alan performed Cornelius with a mobile recording kit in a room in his house chosen for its lack of reverberance. If voice actors need a lot of imagination for animated parts, it's doubly so for an actor who has to perform while connecting with the sound recordist and director over a video call, while holding a pencil in his mouth to mimic what it's like to have six baby crocodiles hidden in there!

OPPOSITE JB Vandamme

THIS PAGE Rosa Ballester Cabo

water level raises up and camera follows it

BODY SHAPE

4 Federico Chericoni
5-6 Rosa Ballester Cabo

CHARACTERS

Tigers

Sasha and George lead a group of adolescent tigers. Their playful designs were based on children's drawings. Leighton Meester and Spence Moore II had such fun making these lethal kittens own their scenes.

"They had to generally look harmless, but seem menacing when the story required it, so when their small mouths open, they become huge, showing off their long, pointy teeth to look scarier," explains Ballester Cabo. "This extreme change of size for the mouth [from closed to open] was a challenge, since the same set of teeth had to work for both mouth sizes. These characters had to camouflage in a birch forest, so I coloured them white like the birch trunks so that they would blend well with the background."

1 Rosa Ballester Cabo
2 Nora Twomey
3–4 Rosa Ballester Cabo

no gums

CHARACTERS

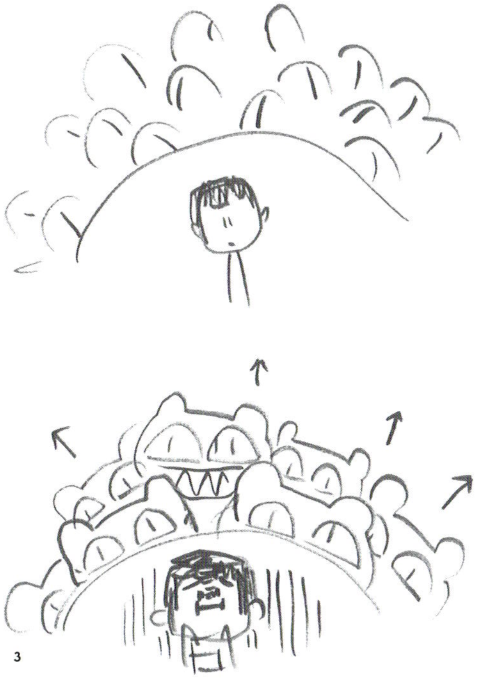

3

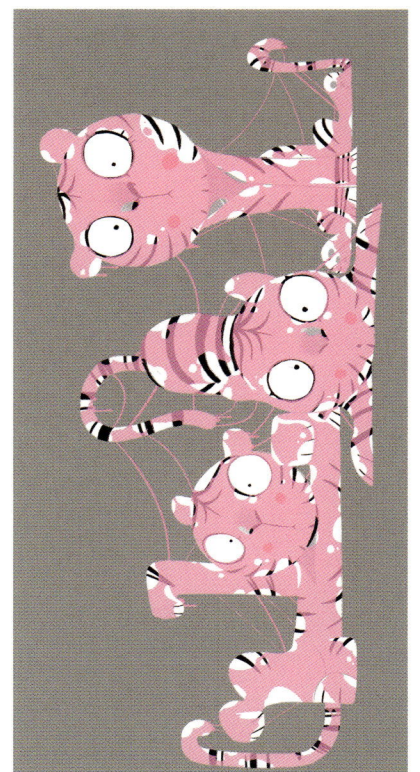

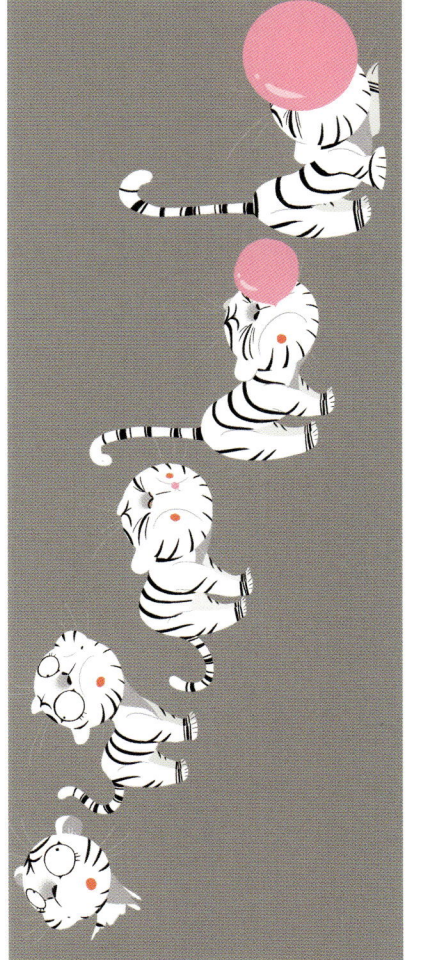

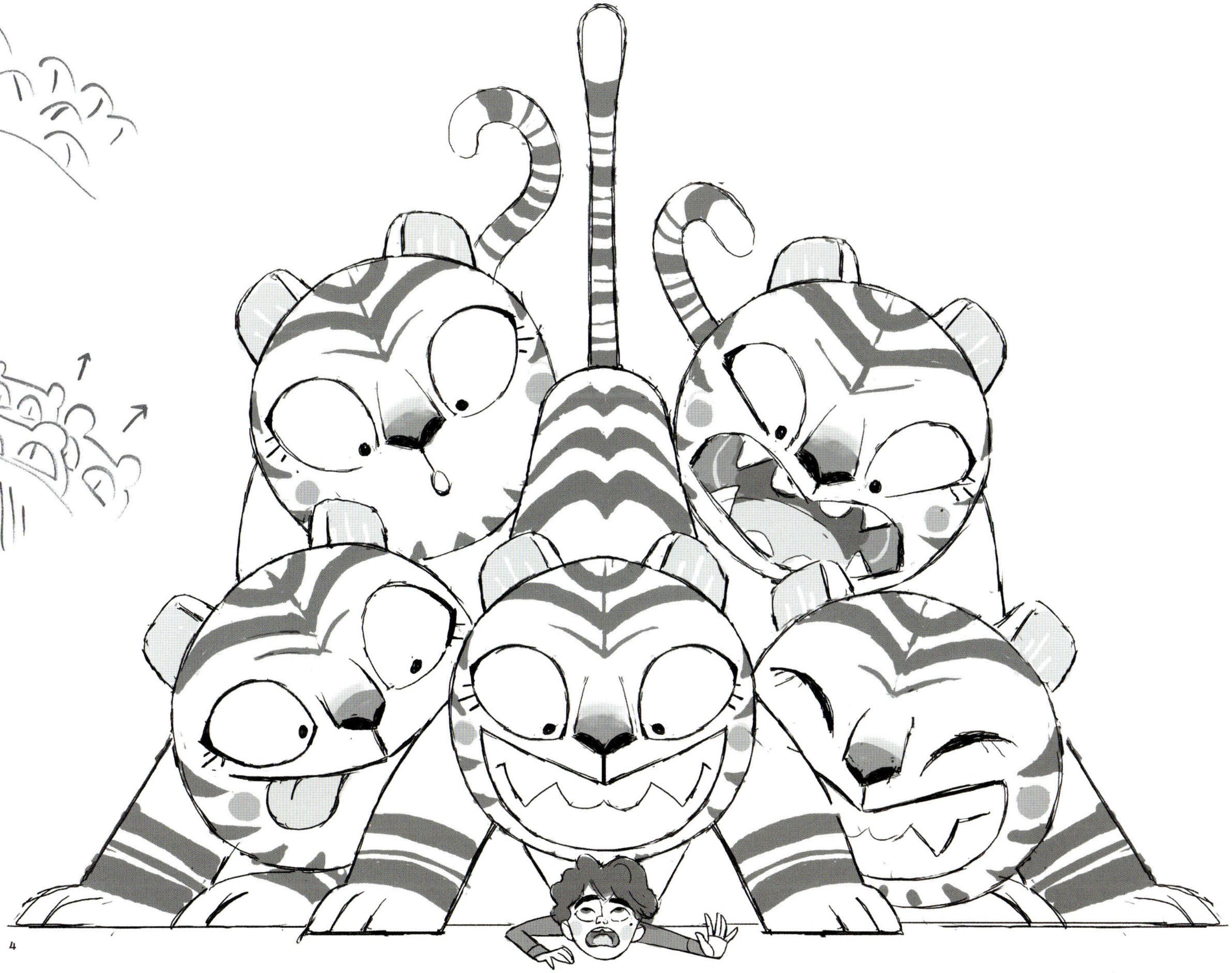

4

5

1 Alessandro Toccaceli

2 JB Vendamme

3 Story team

4 Esther Morales Sanchez

5 JB Vendamme

Pikas

"The shape of the pikas is entirely connected to the round bubble-head of the tigers, and also to the round shape of the cat's kittens that never made it to the final stage of the film," says Ballester Cabo. "They weren't going to speak, so I drew them with tiny mouths, but I had to express their emotions with their big, round eyes. Oh, and their eyes also echoed the features of the island's rabbits—but they also ended up on the cutting-room floor!"

1 Naomi Calvo Morales
2 Rosa Ballester Cabo
3 Naomi Calvo Morales
4–5 Rosa Ballester Cabo

Iris Rhino and Baby

The story and the personality of Iris were another of the movie's evolving aspects.

Originally, the island's rhino character was always sad and was often seen crying, as she is in the book. But it was very miserable as a cinematic sequence. Initially she had a droopy body shape and a mournful expression, but that changed as the character was rewritten. Dianne Wiest somehow gave Iris a comedic side, while also hanging on to the fierce desperation her character feels when Elmer first meets her—a desperation that deepens Elmer's understanding of Wild Island and his empathy for its inhabitants.

"A real rhino has a lot of armor-like segments on its body," says Ballester Cabo. "We wanted to make sure those pieces were visible in the design, but also we didn't want them to be too complicated. We needed to give Baby a graphic look, so we started simplifying the design into big pieces with details inside. Before approving a design, we need to see if it works in all possible angles and in movement. The wonderful Sandra Andersen would test the characters by doing poses and expressions of them, and after that some more tweaks on the design were made."

1 Rosa Ballester Cabo
2 Maria Madelaire Forná
3 Kayvon Darabi-Fard
4 JB Vendamme
5 Naomi Calvo Morales
6 Rosa Ballester Cabo

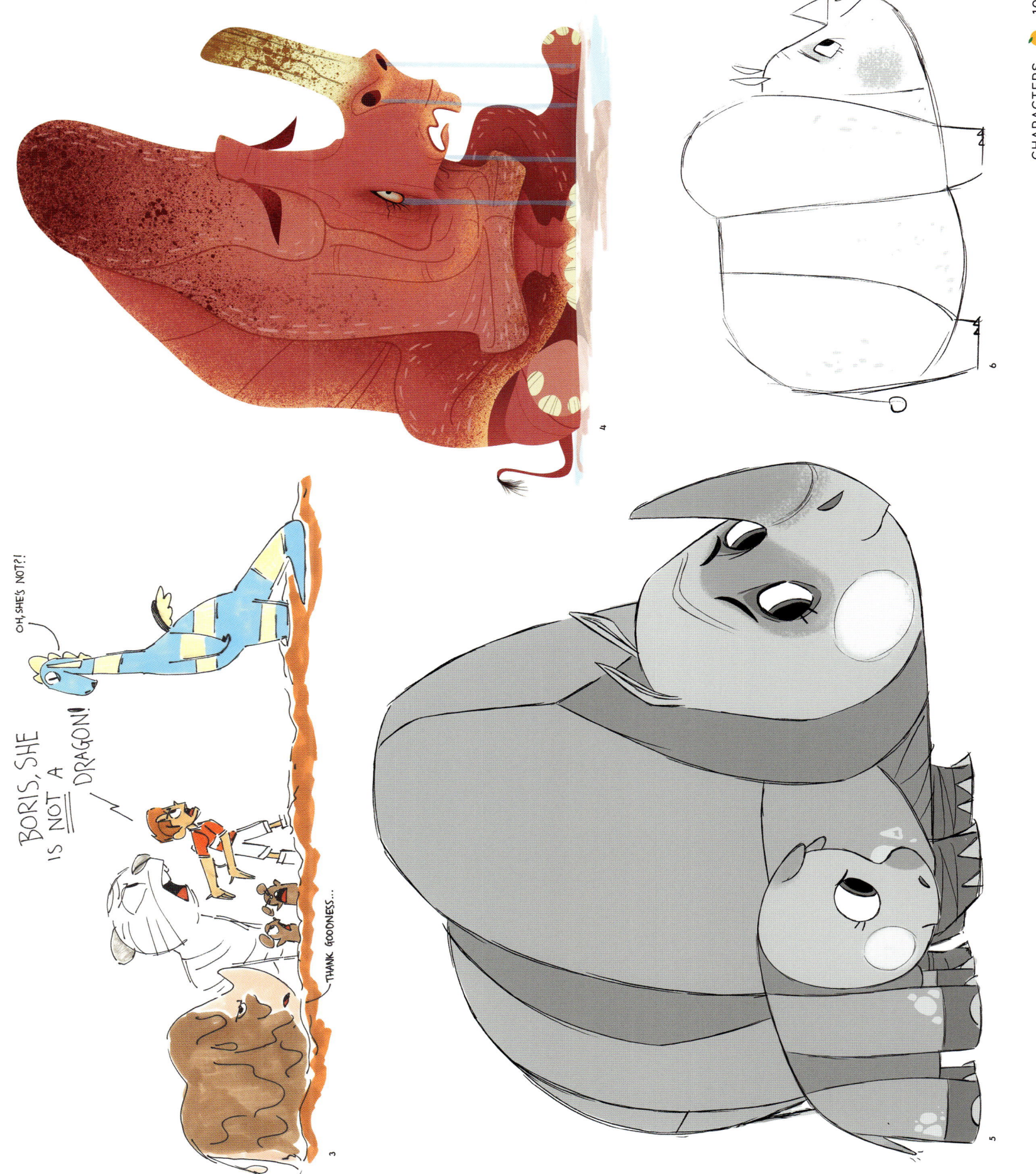

Howler Monkeys

The hooting howler monkeys of the movie went through their share of visual evolutions as well. These noisy simians were initially just called "monkey guards," so the character designers created various different monkey designs. Then, when it was decided that they would all be howler monkeys, Ballester Cabo came up with a group of the stout, bearded species. "What I liked about the real monkeys is that they're always together and constantly howling next to each other, so I wanted to portray them as clone-like versions. Another aspect that I found appealing was that are able to fold themselves into these round shapes when they're still, and then they stretch out and show their limbs and tails all going wild when they move. This idea of changing shapes would translate in a very playful way when we see them animated on the screen."

1–2 Rosa Ballester Cabo

3–4 JB Vendamme

5–8 Rosa Ballester Cabo

Background Animals

Aratuah wasn't the only inhabitant of Wild Island that ended up on the cutting room floor. As director Nora Twomey reveals, Elmer and Boris encountered various other creatures in the earlier drafts of the movie. "When we first began exploring the inhabitants of Wild Island, our minds lit up with dozens of fabulous species," she recalls. "But everything had to serve Elmer's narrative needs; anything that took attention away from his arc at key moments had to go. For example, we had written, designed, recorded, and boarded three rabbits: Daisy, Nibbles, and Buttercup. They functioned as characters Elmer didn't know whether he could trust or not. But as the animatic's themes of fear and control deepened, the rabbits ceased to push the story forward, and they were cut from the film. Everything has to serve story!"

Underwater life

1 Colour script by Ciarán Duffy, Martí Furgber Morales, Alice Dieudonné, and Emilie Bach Nielsen

2–6 Rosa Ballester Cabo

7 Alice Dieudonné

CHARACTERS

CHARACTERS

1–2 Rosa Ballester Cabo
3 JB Vendamme
4–6 Rosa Ballester Cabo
7 JB Vendamme
8 Rosa Ballester Cabo
FOLLOWING SPREAD
Nora Twomey

Dust Town

The film opens in the charming bucolic world of Dust Town, where Elmer and his mother enjoy a happy life before they are forced to close their store and move away to the big city to survive. The name of the town itself echoes the Dust Bowl, the name given to the drought-stricken southern plains of the United States, which experienced brutal dust storms during the 1930s.

Since the movie is set sometime in the late 1930s or early '40s, the background designers were inspired by photos and films from that era. Another influence was the book author Ruth Stiles Gannett's own bright-yellow-coloured home in upstate New York. The artists took a page from her home and referred to the colour yellow whenever Elmer is feeling happy. "We used the colour gold as a symbol of home and the center of warmth and safety throughout the movie," says Twomey, as a reminder of the golden, sunny day spent in Ruth's family home.

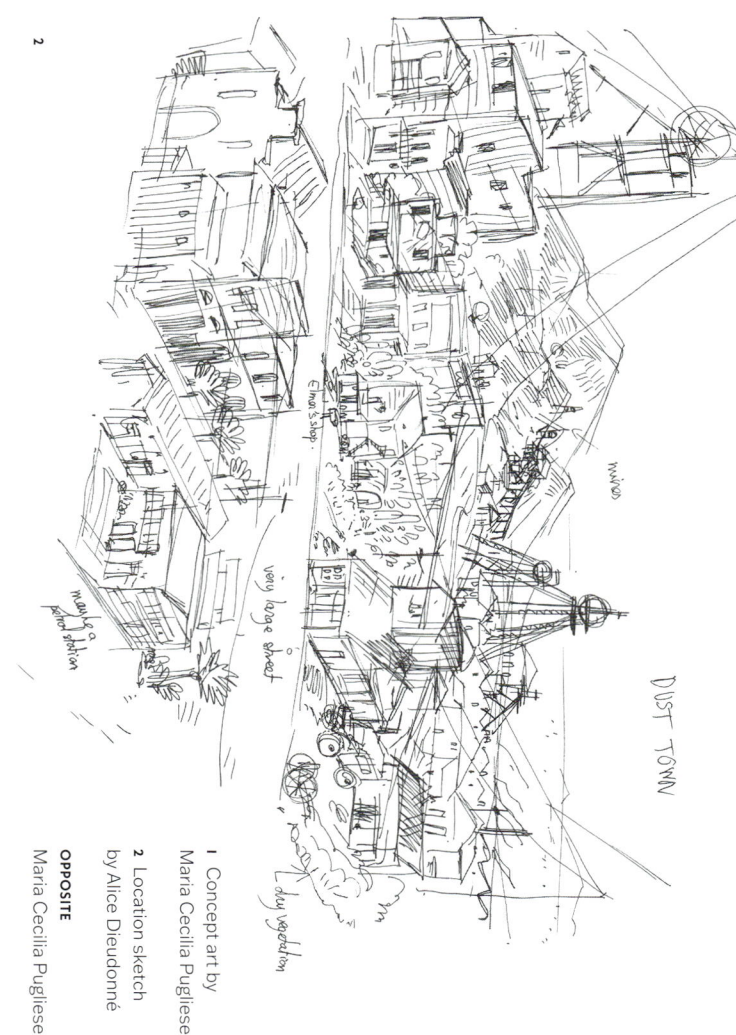

1 Concept art by Maria Cecilia Pugliese

2 Location sketch by Alice Dieudonné

OPPOSITE
Maria Cecilia Pugliese

The Store

Elmer's mother's store was designed to look very modest, straightforward, and not uncommon to find in a small town in the United States during the 1940s. The film's art director, Áine Mc Guinness, mentions that the goal was to make it simple, yet inviting and colourful. You can find a lot of wooden shelves packed with fresh goods for the town's residents, which become alarmingly empty after the community is hit by hard times. Like the rest of the town, the store is filled with hues of yellow and gold, signifying the earlier, prosperous days of the mother and son.

1–3 Alice Dieudonné
4 Kayvon Darabi-Fard
5 Alice Dieudonné
6 Ciarán Duffy

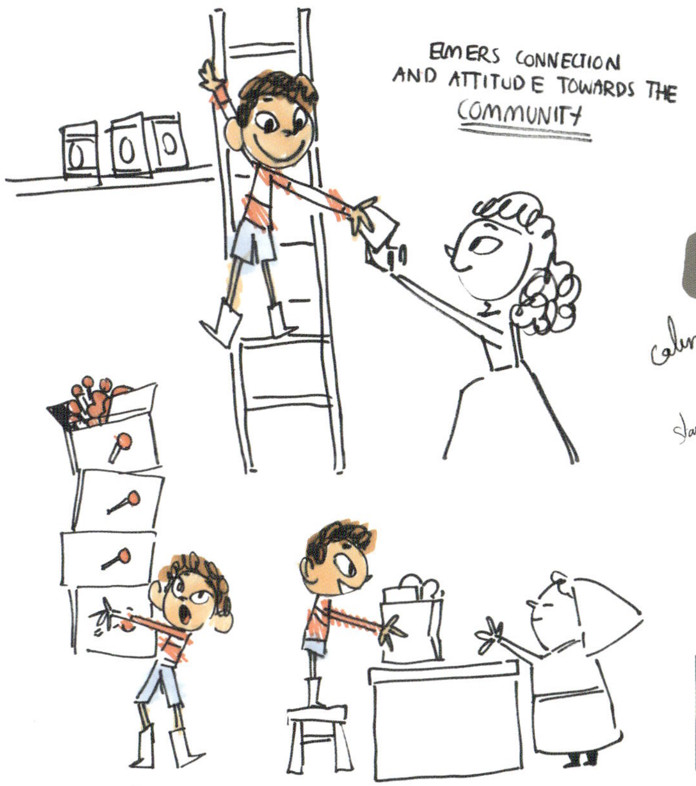
EMERS CONNECTION
AND ATTITUDE TOWARDS THE
COMMUNITY

4

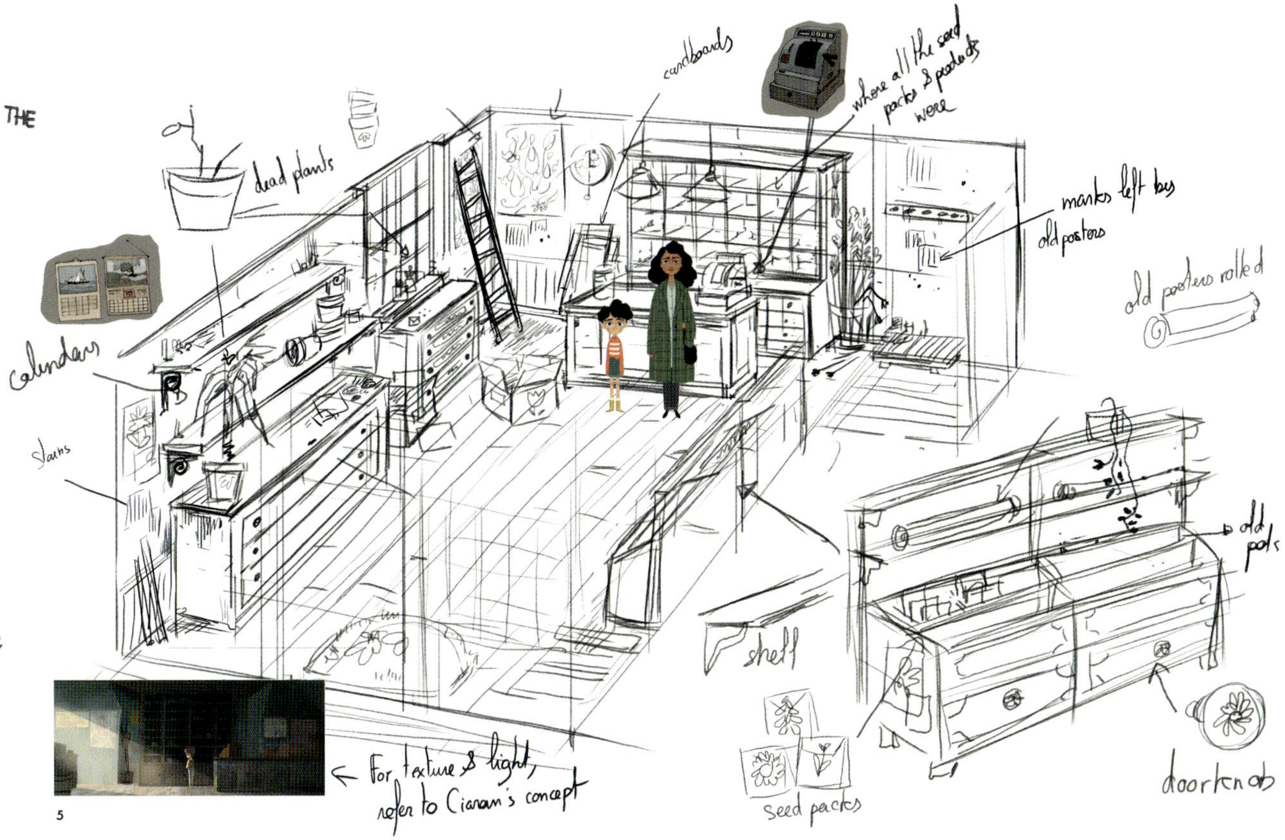
dead plants
calendars
stairs
cardboards
where all the seed packs & packets were
marks left by old posters
old posters rolled
old pots
shelf
seed packs
doorknob
← For texture & light, refer to Cianan's concept

5

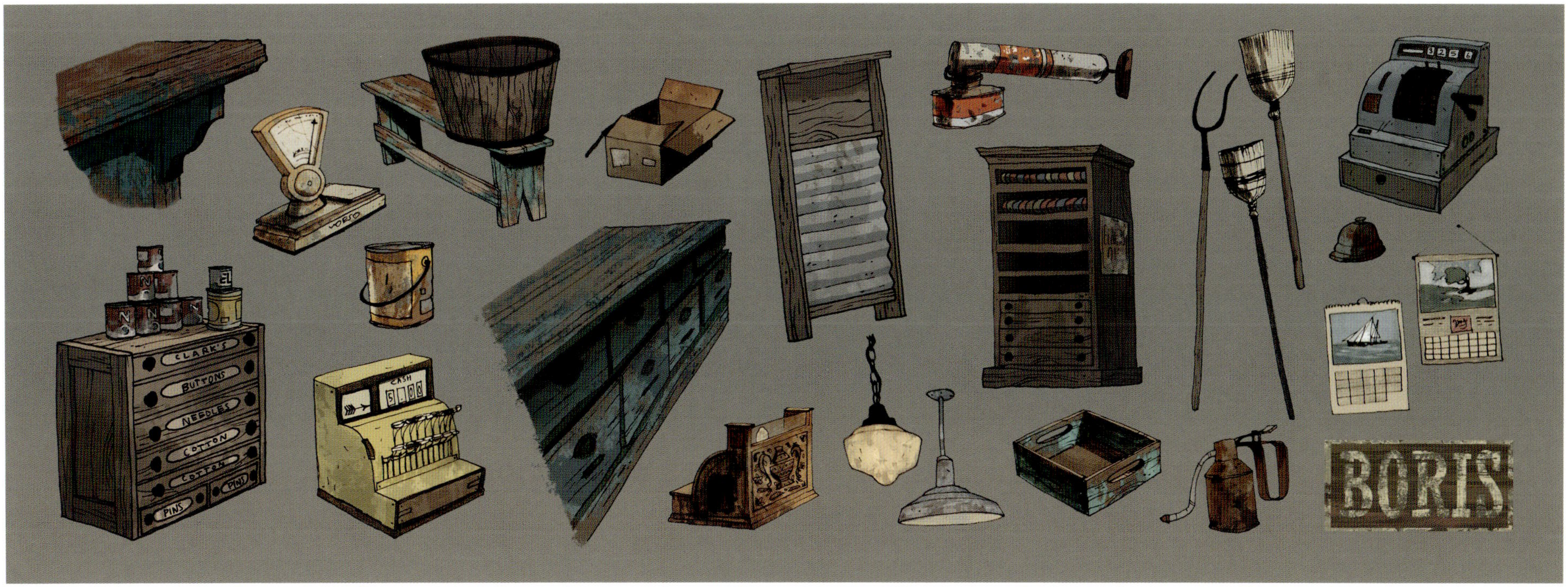
CLARKS
BUTTONS
NEEDLES
COTTON
COTTON
PINS
PINS
CASH
BORIS

6

LOCATIONS

1 Ciarán Duffy
2 Emilie Bach Nielsen

OPPOSITE Colour script by Ciarán Duffy, Martí Furgber Morales, Alice Dieudonné, and Emilie Bach Nielsen

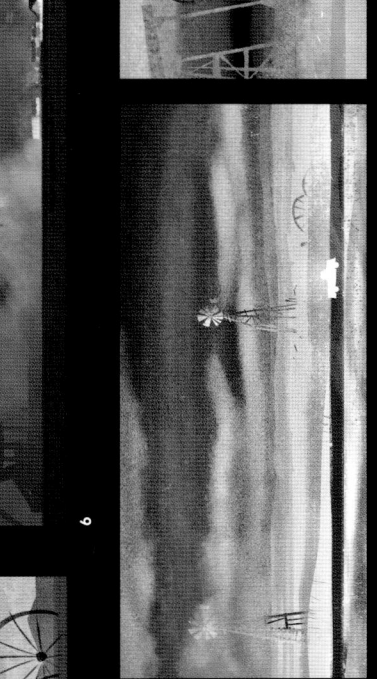
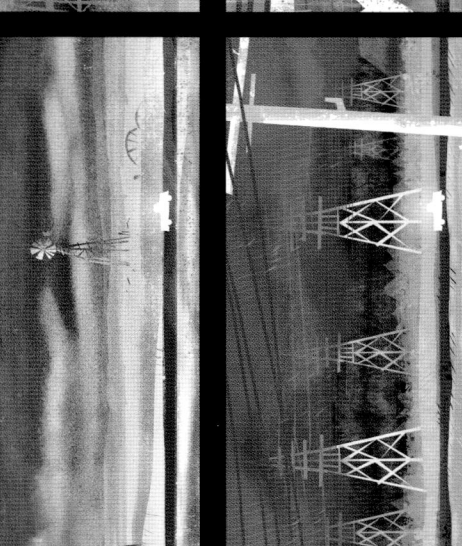

Colour script by Ciarán Duffy, Martí Furgber Morales, Alice Dieudonné, and Emilie Bach Nielsen

Lily Bernard

Scene illustration by Clara

4 Alice Dieudonné
5 Lily Bernard
6 Ciarán Duffy
7 Lily Bernard

Nevergreen City

Inspired by classic noir favorites like *The Night of the Hunter*, the film's artistic team set out to create a darker world that stands in complete contrast with the colourful world of the Dust Town central store. The objective was to show how much of an outsider Elmer feels in a city that feels strange to him; we see it from his perspective. The dominant colours in this world are dark blues and grays, and the sky is covered with clouds, and it's pouring rain when they first arrive in the city. The background design team looked at photographs of New York City in the 1940s, as well as famous movies set in New York, for inspiration. Later, when Elmer returns, the city becomes golden and warm in its "magic hour."

"[When we first see Nevergreen] we wanted to express how much Elmer is overwhelmed and taken out of his comfort zone," says Mc Guinness. "This sequence is dominated by big vertical structures and tall, oppressive buildings. There is a lived-in feeling about this city. There are cracks in the buildings and some of the buildings are a little wonky, and nothing is perfect. That was all very intentional."

Twomey also mentions the big influence of *The Wizard of Oz* in terms of how the beginning black-and-white act of that film stands in sharp contrast to the colourful world that surrounds Dorothy once she arrives in Oz. Viewers can sense the same shock to the system once Elmer leaves Dust Town and then, later when he enters the magical world of Wild Island.

Senior scene illustrator Almu Redondo mentions that the team sought to bring a surreal touch to the sequences in Nevergeen as Elmer runs from home toward the docks. "After he has the fight with his mother, we wanted to emphasis how lost and terrified he feels. The buildings of the city look even more dark and imposing."

THIS SPREAD Alice Dieudonné

LOCATIONS 125

Nevergreen (main view)
Main references: New York/Manhattan during the great depression (1930's)

From Downtown

Garnett street
Down the disaffected harbour
(Fig 02: out of Garnett street. Beginning of the cat chase.)

The disaffected harbour would be this way. (Fig 01:)
→ harbour
⊕ Shanty town

Ocean → to wild island

The poorest areas are clustered on the bottom of the bigger and rich building
→ Ocean

Avoid too modern buildings with glass windows. Stay with the weird out-of-time metropolis look.

126 LOCATIONS

1 Concept art by Solène Chevaleyre
2–4 Concept art by Almu Redondo
OPPOSITE Concept art by Lily Bernard

LOCATIONS

THIS PAGE Sketches by Alice Dieudonné demonstrating the oppressively vertical and crowded buildings that would loom over Elmer

1 This art by Lily Bernard was one of the first images created for Nevergreen.

2 Colour script by Ciarán Duffy, Martí Furgber Morales, Alice Dieudonné, and Emilie Bach Nielsen

LOCATIONS 129

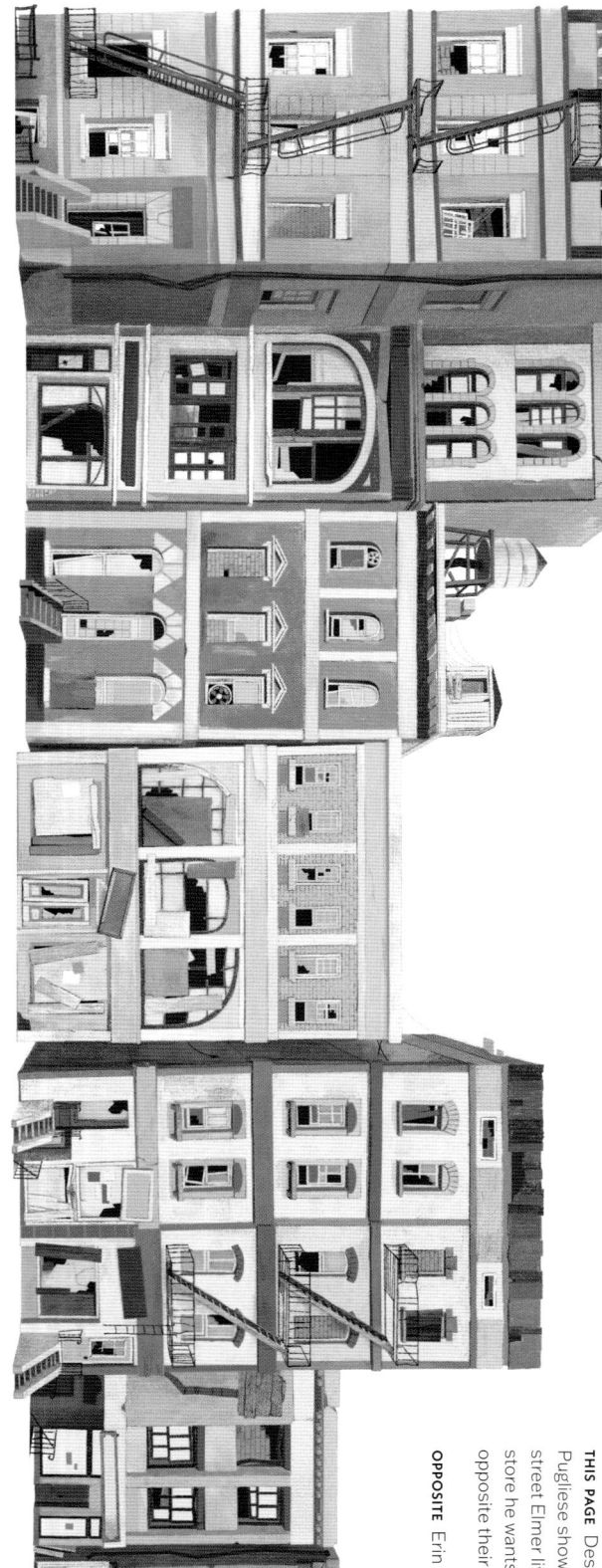

THIS PAGE Designs by Maria Cecilia Pugliese showing both sides of the street Elmer lives on, including the store he wants to open with his mom opposite their apartment

OPPOSITE Erin Overmann

considering the Apt floor PLAN
for size & window position
Attic
3RD
2ND
1st
Basement
*NO LINE
ELMER'S APT
Nevergreen

*would
Callie
decorate?
SHOP for Rent
Nevergreen

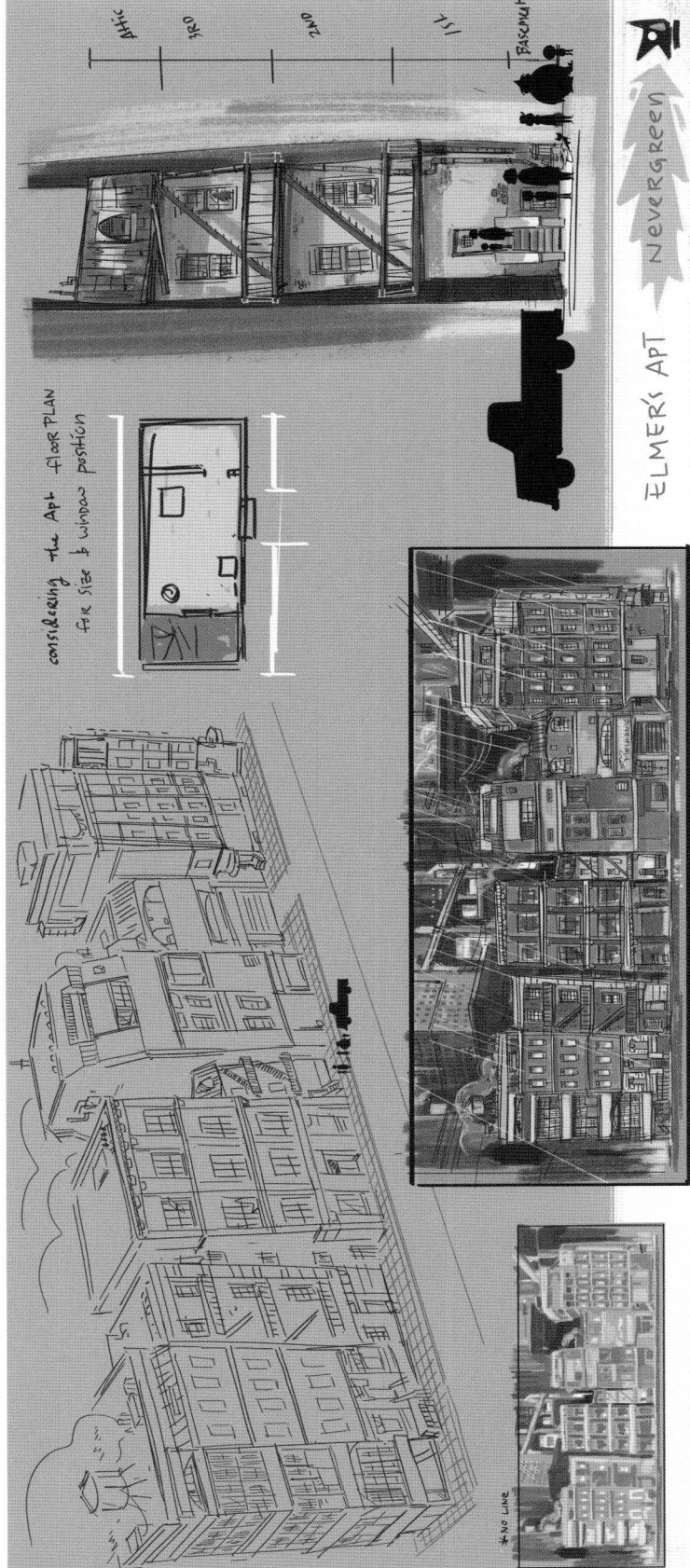

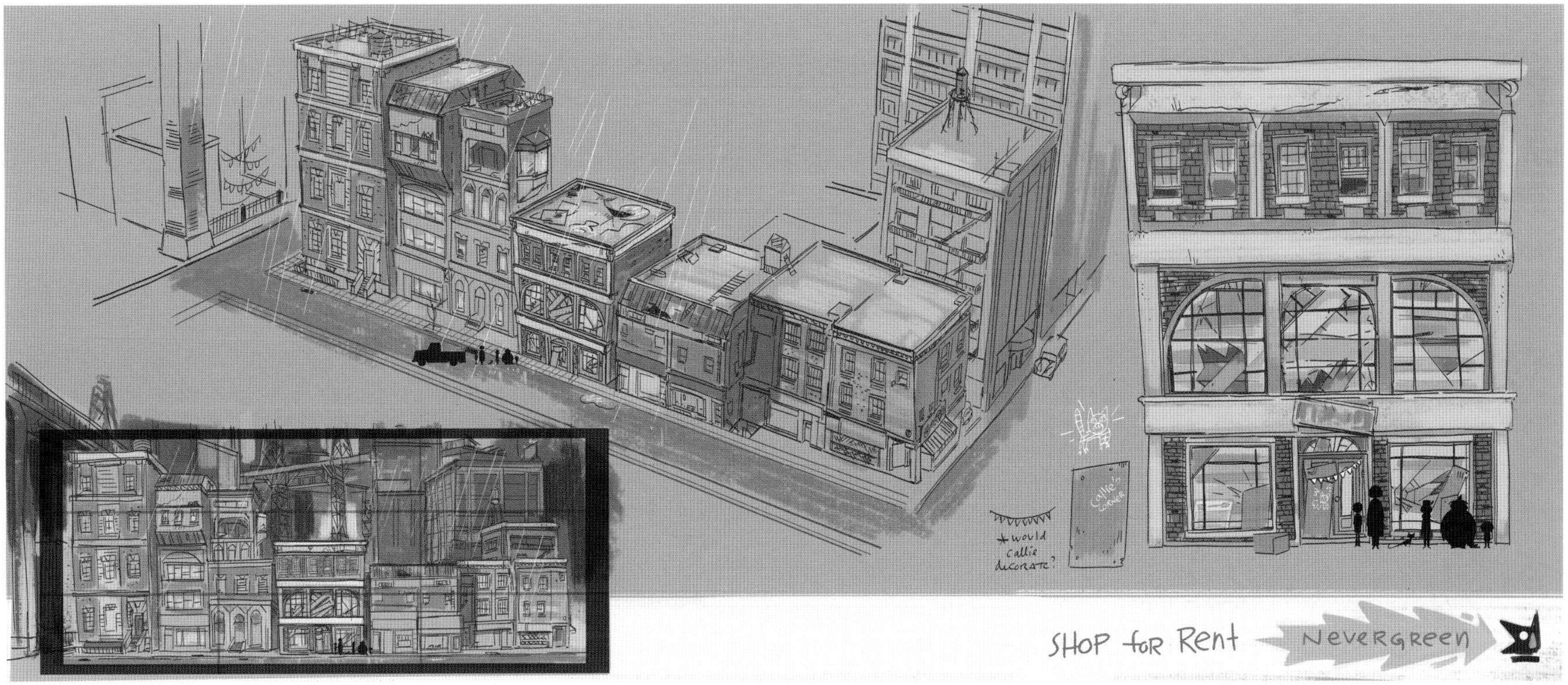

LOCATIONS

1 Location design by Erin Overmann
2 Concept art by Alice Dieudonné
3 Location design by Emilie Bach Nielsen
4 Location sketch by Erin Overmann
5 Location design by Lara Bentassil

LOCATIONS

The Apartment

The interior of the room was inspired by Ruth's barn and *Night of the Hunter*. The ceiling is covered in water pipes, the sound of which echoes in Wild Island's underwater roots. "We wanted it to look really modest but not dirty or neglected. We figured Mrs. McLaren didn't have much more than Elmer and his mom," says Twomey.

"The pipes are dark and oppressive, and link visually to the roots of the island, which we see later in the second act," says Mc Guinness. "Gradually through the film, the apartment becomes populated with their personal belongings and painted with personal touches so that by the end of the film, it feels really cosy and welcoming."

Interestingly enough, senior scene illustrator Almu Redondo recalls that she looked at many photographs of New York City apartments to get the details right, but the one reference that stayed with her was some of the flats seen in Martin Scorsese's 1976 movie *Taxi Driver*!

1 Ciarán Duffy

2 Background painting by Alice Dieudonné. Layout by Rory Conway and Léo Weiss

3–5 Erin Overmann

6–7 Location details and props by Lara Bentassil

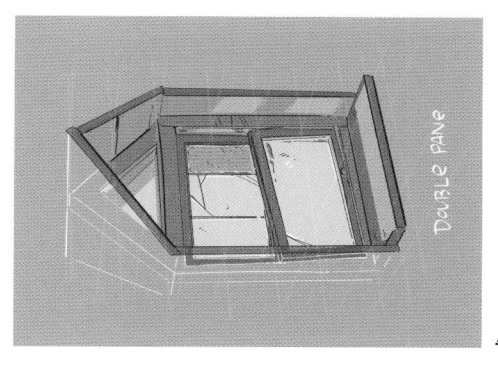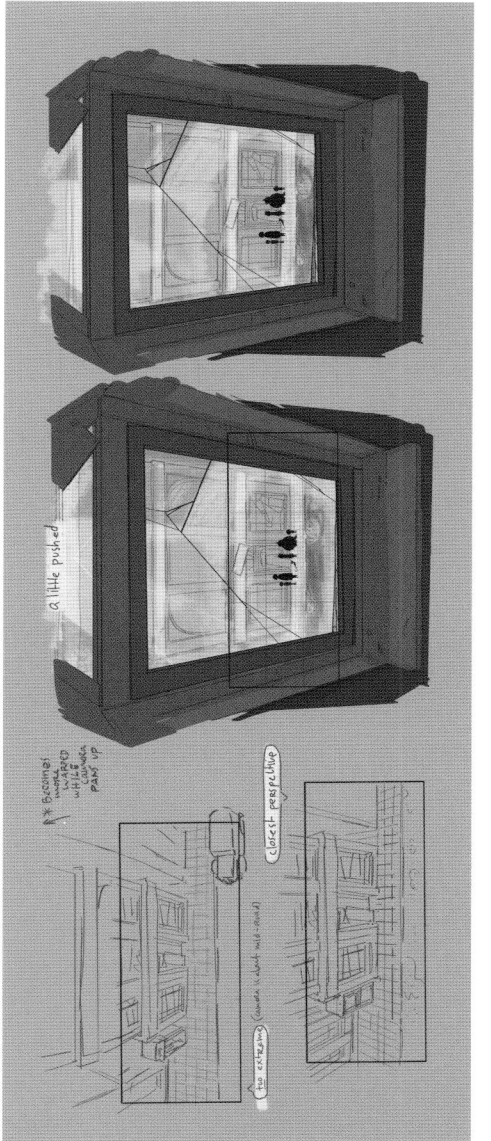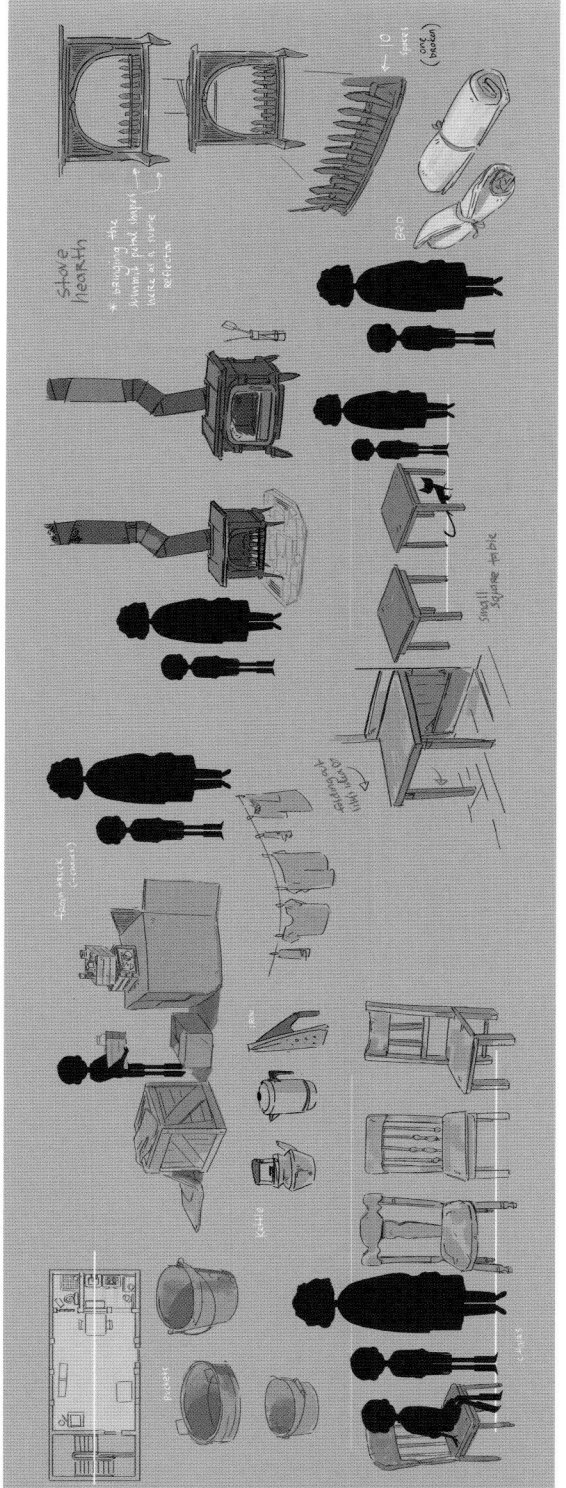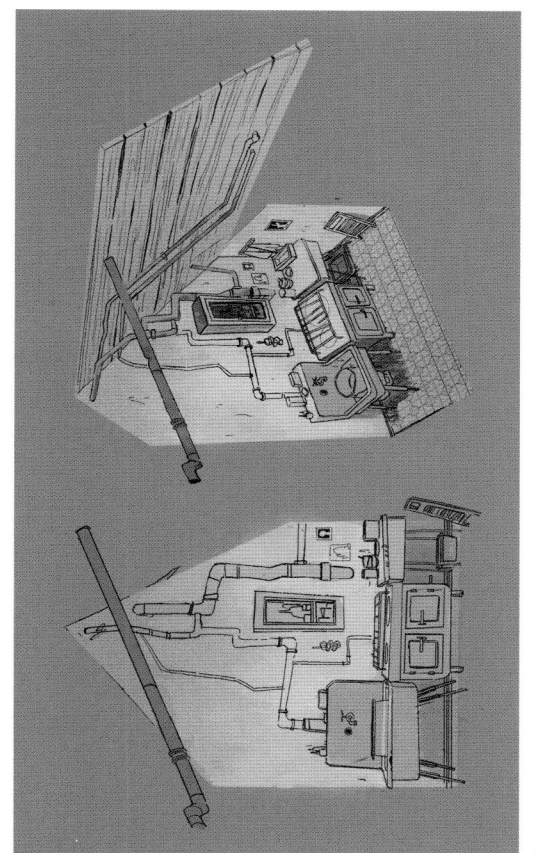

LOCATIONS

1

moving in

argument

epilogue

2

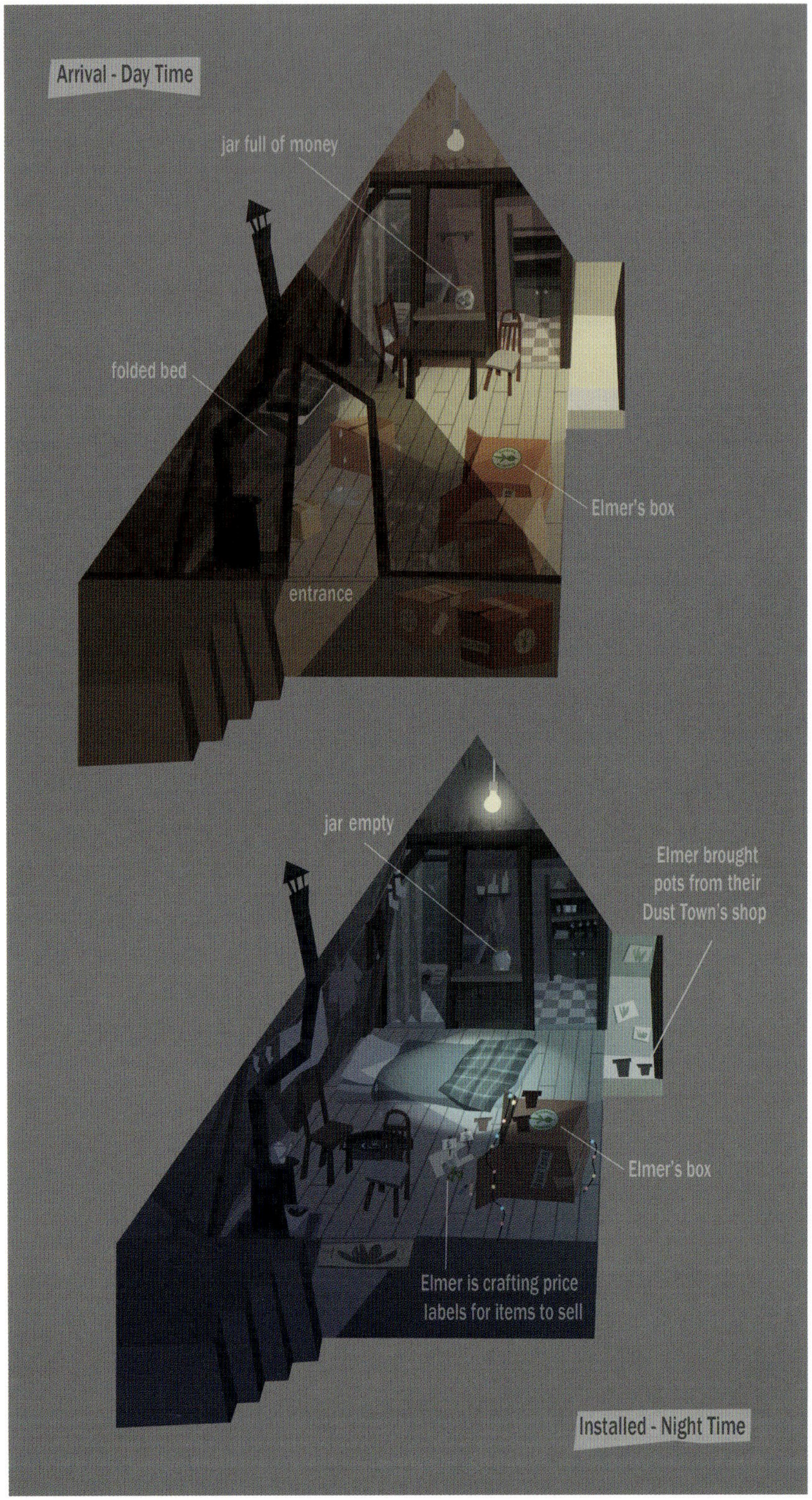

Arrival - Day Time
- folded bed
- jar full of money
- entrance
- Elmer's box

Installed - Night Time
- Elmer is crafting price labels for items to sell
- jar empty
- Elmer's box
- Elmer brought pots from their Dust Town's shop

3

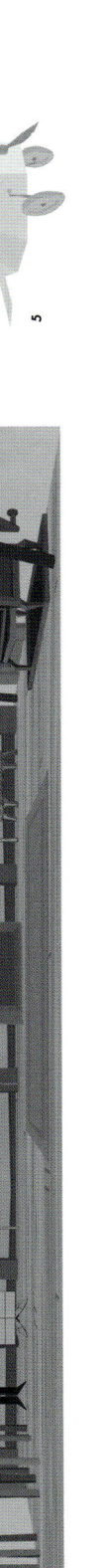

1 Lara Bentassil

2 Lily Bernard

3 Background painting by Tara Woods. Layout by Betsy Luk, based on location designs by Antonia Yordanova Gancheva

4 Apartment schematic by Antonia Yordanova Gancheva

5 Marco Manzoni

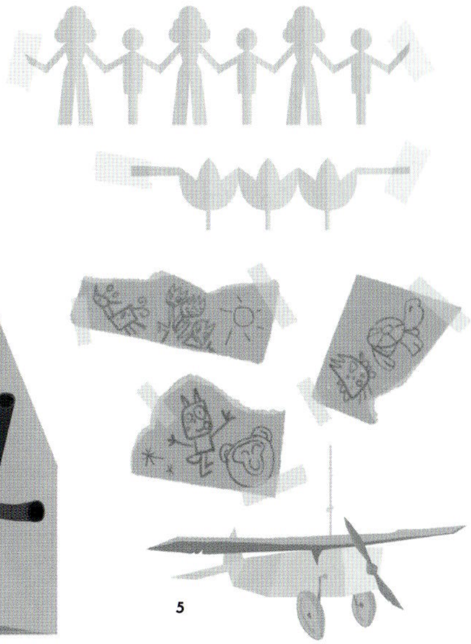

1 Colour script by Ciarán Duffy, Martí Furgber Morales, Alice Dieudonné, and Emilie Bach Nielsen

2–4 Early concept designs by Alice Dieudonné, featuring the constant diagonal descent of Elmer's run away from home

5–7 Julien Regnard

LOCATIONS 139

The Docks

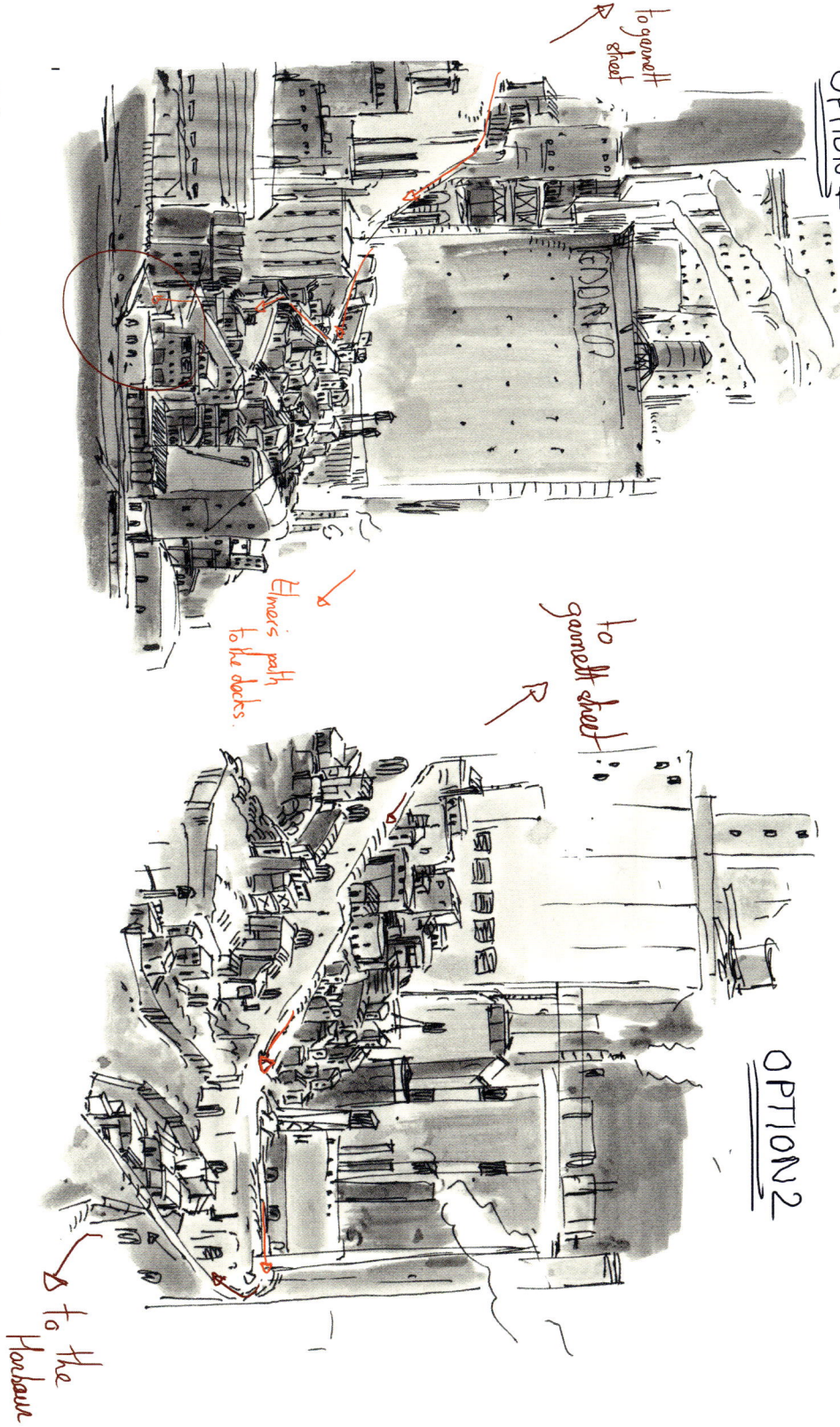

When Elmer runs away from home, he faces the dark, rainy streets of the city alone. We see the walls closing in on him as he tries to escape his reality. Then, as soon as he reaches the docks, we see the clouds part and blue skies shining through. That's where the cat talks to him and tells him about Wild Island and Soda the Whale and takes him to meet Boris. It's a magic-real space. When he reaches the docks we see, for the first time since the arrival in Nevergreen, a large, expansive sky with a more open composition. "We see the color palette changing in this sequence," says McGuinness. "The pink hues in the sky hint at something a little unusual, preparing the audience for a magical, talking cat. The sky sets the stage for Elmer's imagined dragon forming out of the city smoke. The elegant, flowing design and animation provide a brilliant contrast between Elmer's expectations of a dragon and the real dragon, Boris, whom we meet in the second act."

Redondo mentions that in addition to referencing New York City, she was inspired by Singapore's harbor, where she was living at the time. "As we were planning the city backgrounds, we decided that we wanted to have a scenic harbor, and I recall seeing these giant cranes from the window of my apartment there. So, I referenced them as I was designing the docks." She says she was also inspired by the works of Industrial Revolution artist William Hyde, and the painting *Isle of the Dead* by Swiss Symbolist artist Arnold Böcklin.

1 Concept sketches by Alice Dieudonné mapping Elmer's journey to the docks

2 Concept artwork by Ciarán Duffy

3–4 Concept sketches by Ciarán Duffy, Martí Furgber Morales, Alice Dieudonné, and Emilie Bach Nielsen

5 Colour script by Ciarán Duffy, Martí Furgber Morales, Alice Dieudonné, and Emilie Bach Nielsen

LOCATIONS

1 Scene illustration by Ciarán Duffy and Áine Mc Guinness, based on location design by Julien Regnard and Lara Bentassil
2 Background painting by Kaylee de Bruin. Layout by Raquel Fernan Largo
3 Scene illustration by Almu Redondo
4 Still frame from final film

Tangerina

Before reaching Wild Island, Soda takes Elmer to an isle known as Tangerina, because it's a very small space holding a few tangerine trees. As it's described in the script, it's basically a "strange cluster of trees, floating on little patches of land in the middle of water."

Elmer packs as many brightly coloured fruits as he can in his backpack, and he's able to use them wisely once he gets to the island. (In the book, he manages to fit thirty-one tangerines in his bag.) The designers referenced Ruth Christman Gannett's illustrated map of Tangerina and Wild Island from the original book and came up with a very stylized and graphic depiction of the charming location. In Gannett's version, Tangerina is much bigger and has a few houses and a very small town called Cranberry. A series of rocks join Tangerina to Wild Island in the original map in the book.

1 Early concept by Alice Dieudonné
2 Early concept by Solène Chevaleyre
3–4 Early concepts by Lily Bernard
5 Early concept by Alice Dieudonné

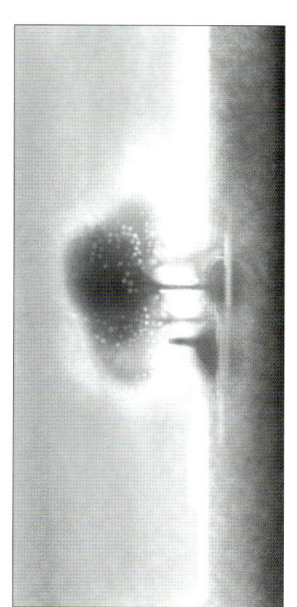
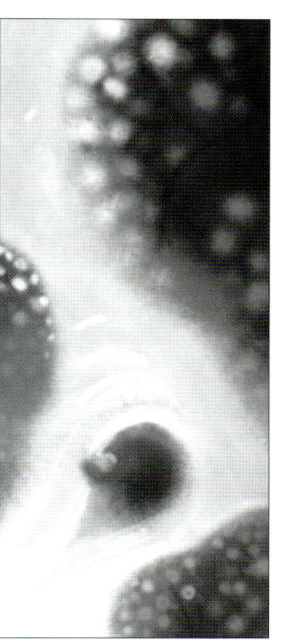
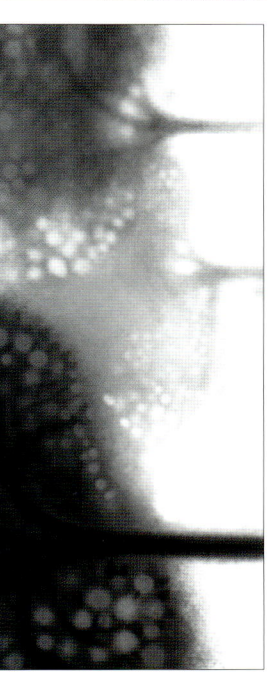

LOCATIONS

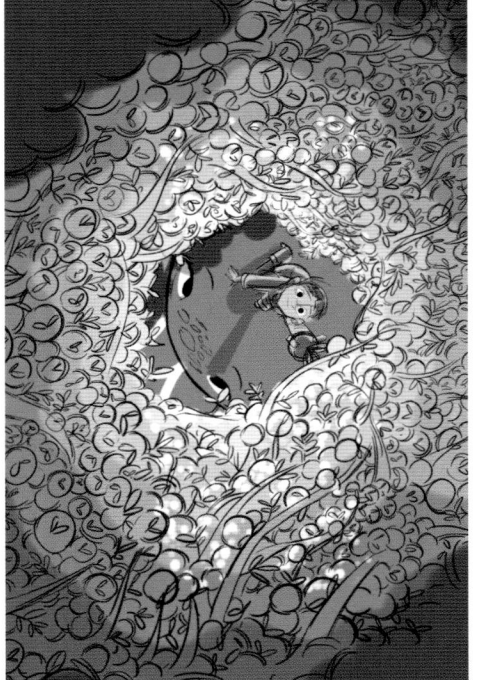

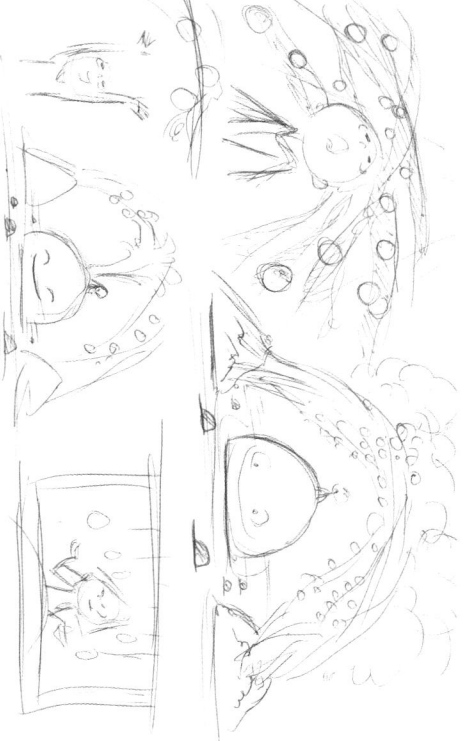

1 Concept art by Maria Kruse Gaardbo focusing on lighting and composition for Tangerina

2 Kayvon Darabi-Fard

3 Story team

4 Various artists

5 Background painting by Ulric Leprovost. Layout by Théo Prévost

Wild Island

Because a lot rested on the otherworldly and exotic look of Wild Island, the director and her design and animation team spent a lot of time coming up with just the right visual details and special physical landscapes of this location.

Twomey recalls, "The map which is included in the book is so beautiful, and I know that a lot of children love to look at it and figure out the location for each one of the animals. One of the key guiding influences was that the shape of the island needed to be driven by our need to see it sinking slowly. We wanted to make it feel like something that's in the pit of your stomach, which you cannot control. So to me, it felt like a large mass rather than something that was flat shaped. We needed the island to feel like a ticking clock as it is sinking throughout the film. It's a living form and deeply connected with the dragons who visit it. We see the island getting smaller as it plunges lower in the water. We also had to show that Boris and Elmer were continuing to travel from left to right. That also dictated that the island wasn't something that they could double back on. So, we just continue around the curve of the island and all the way to the cave and then up to the summit. It all had to feel very heavy."

1 Concept art by Lily Bernard of Wild Island close to Tangerina, produced before Wild Island was made an organism that is not part of the seabed

2 Alice Dieudonné

OPPOSITE Alice Dieudonné

LOCATIONS

148

1 Background painting by Laura Dong. Layout by Antonia Yordanova Gancheva.
2 Colour script by Ciarán Duffy, Martí Furgber Morales, Alice Dieudonné, and Emilie Bach Nielsen

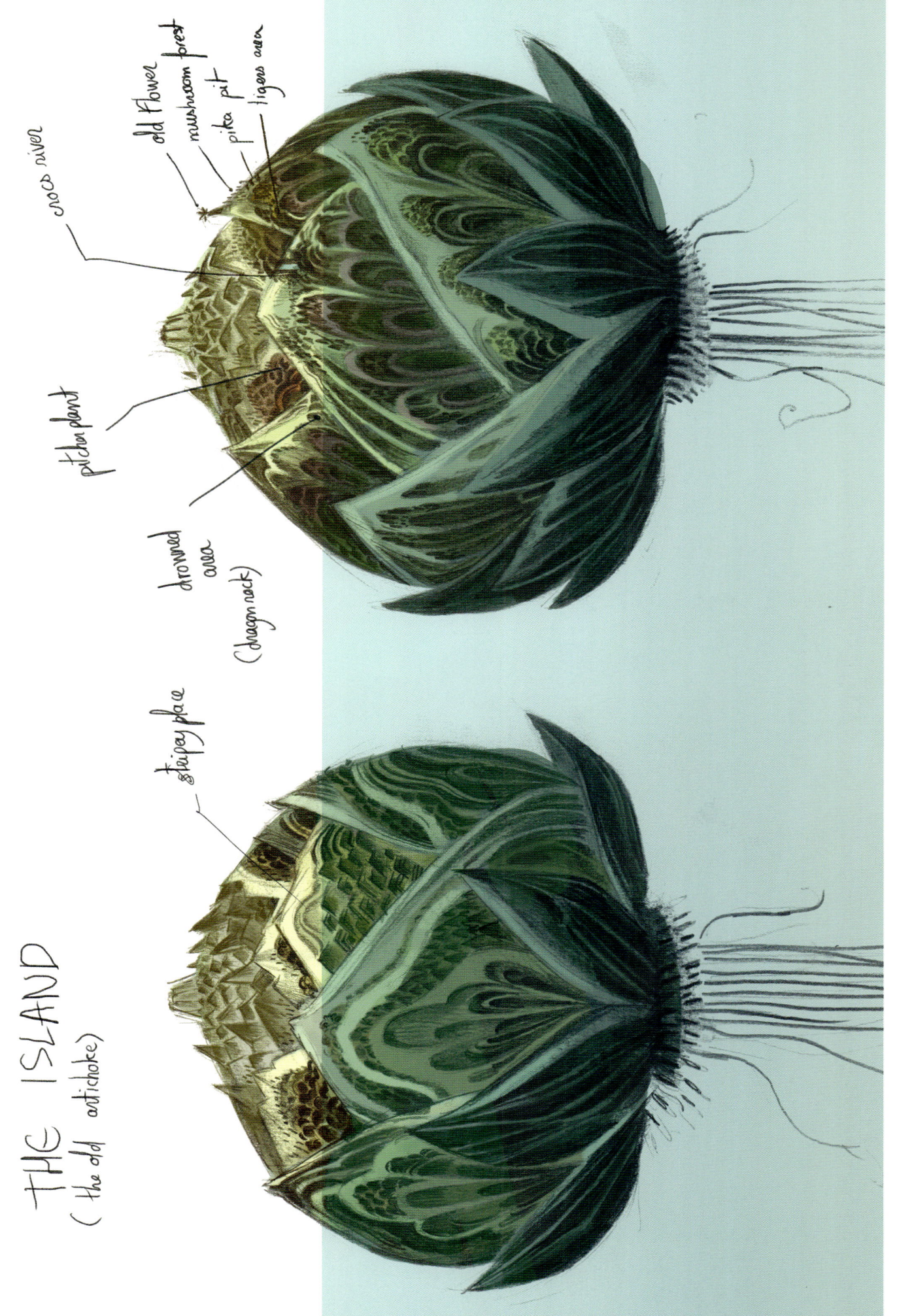

LOCATIONS

THIS PAGE A visual plan by director Nora Twomey illustrating the island's phases, the top row showing what transpired when Boris's brother visited Wild Island, the lower row illustrating Boris's interaction with the island throughout the film

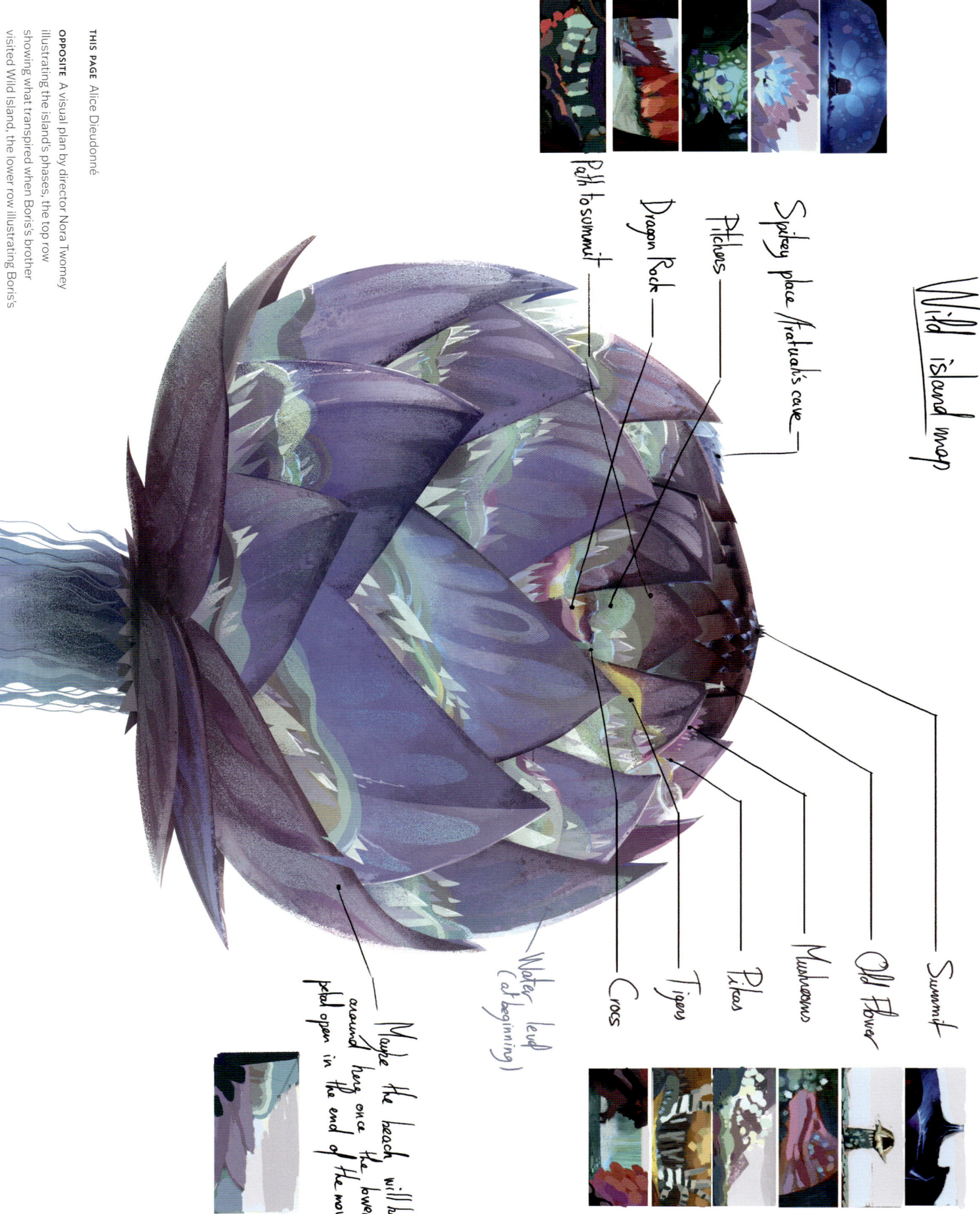

Wild Island map

- Path to summit
- Dragon Rock
- Pitchers
- Spikey place /Fratuah's cave
- Summit
- Old Flower
- Mushrooms
- Pikas
- Tigers
- Cross
- Water level (at beginning)

Maybe the beach will be around here once the lower petal open in the end of the movie.

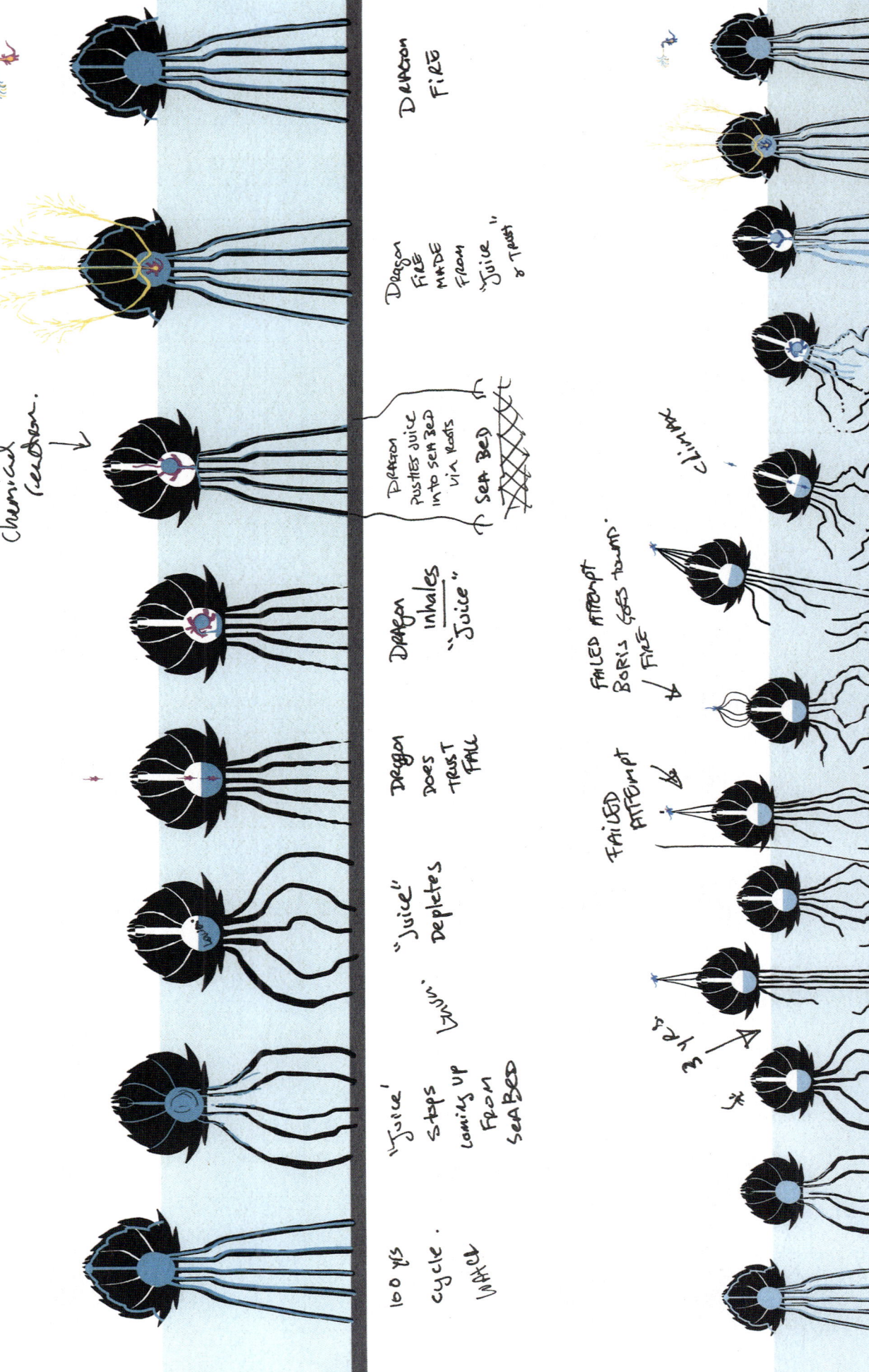

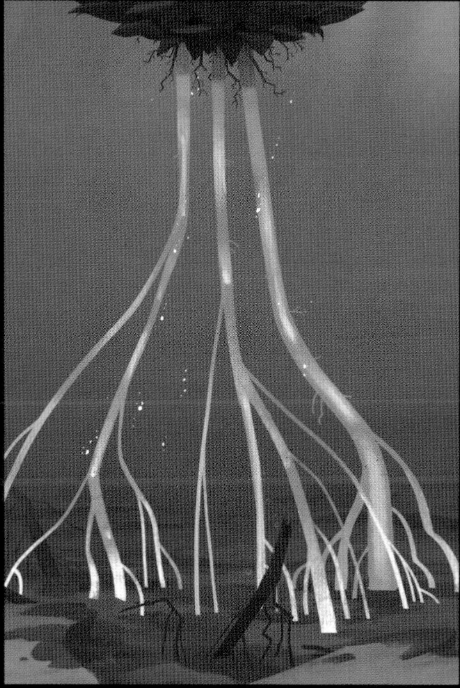

1–2 Early concept by Rosa Ballester Cabo of the island's roots

3–4 Erin Overmann

5 Art by Almu Redondo illustrating the evolution of the island's roots throughout the film

LOCATIONS

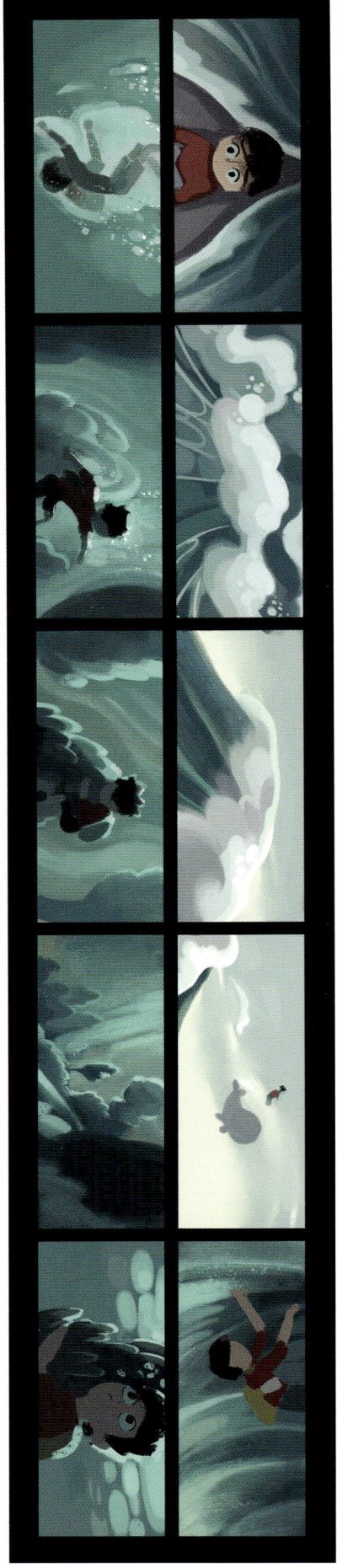

1 Colour script by Ciarán Duffy, Martí Furgber Morales, Alice Dieudonné, and Emilie Bach Nielsen

2 Location design by Erin Overmann, setting up how Elmer and the island summit could exist in one frame. The filmmakers went on to use these same camera angles in the final film.

3–4 Erin Overmann

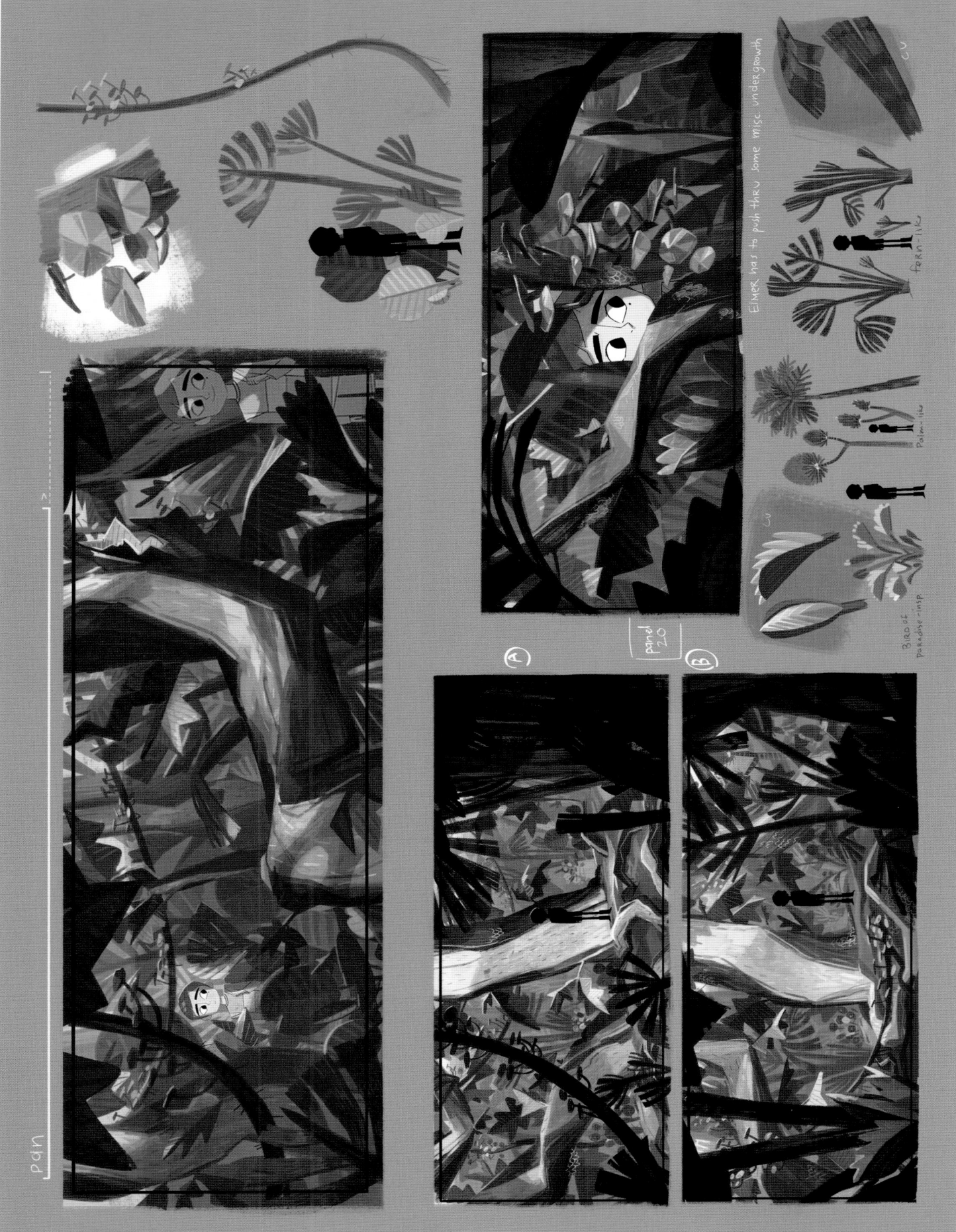

158 LOCATIONS

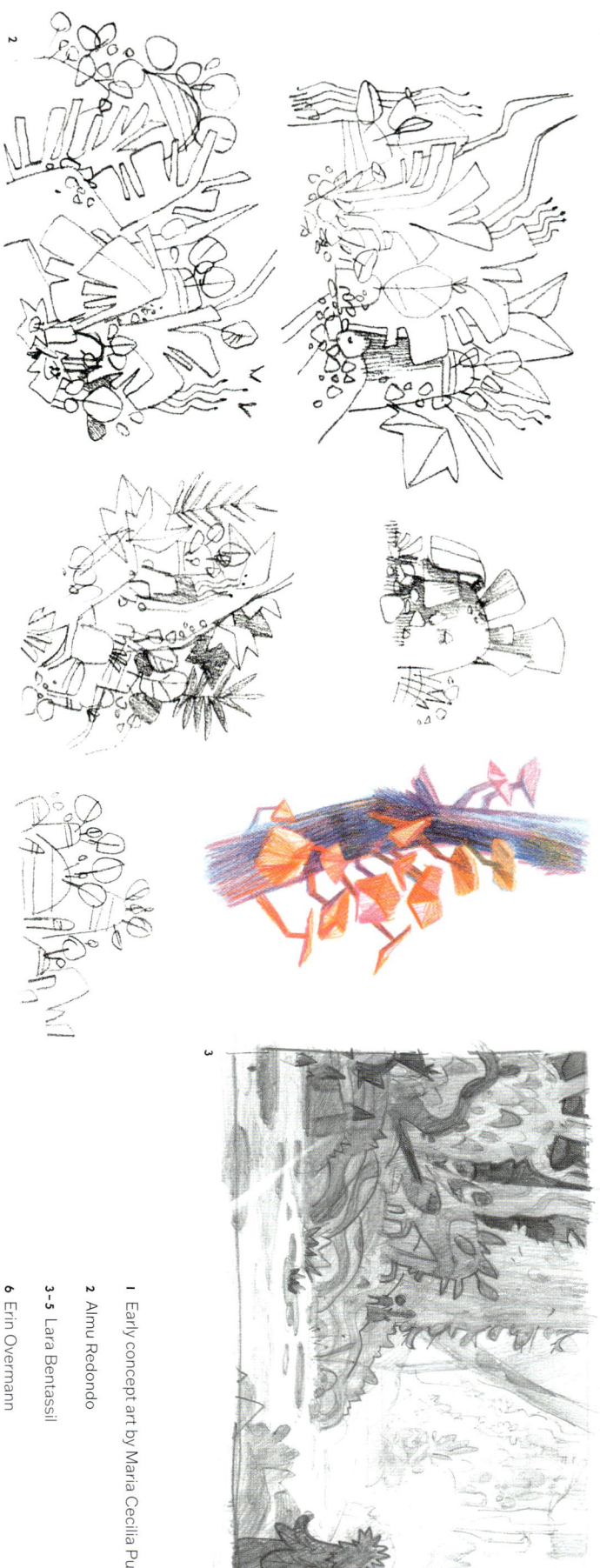

1 Early concept art by Maria Cecilia Pugliese
2 Almu Redondo
3–5 Lara Bentassil
6 Erin Overmann

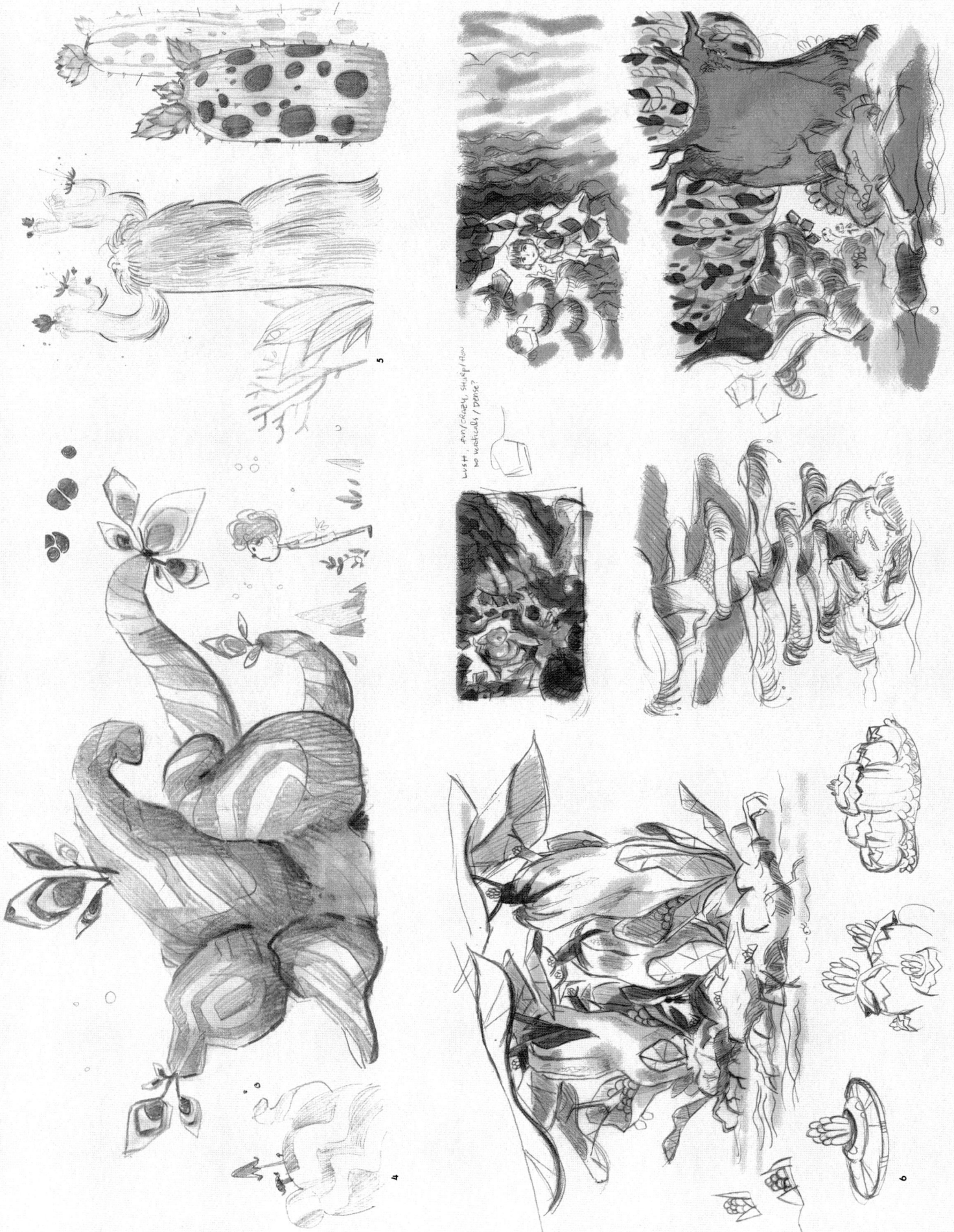

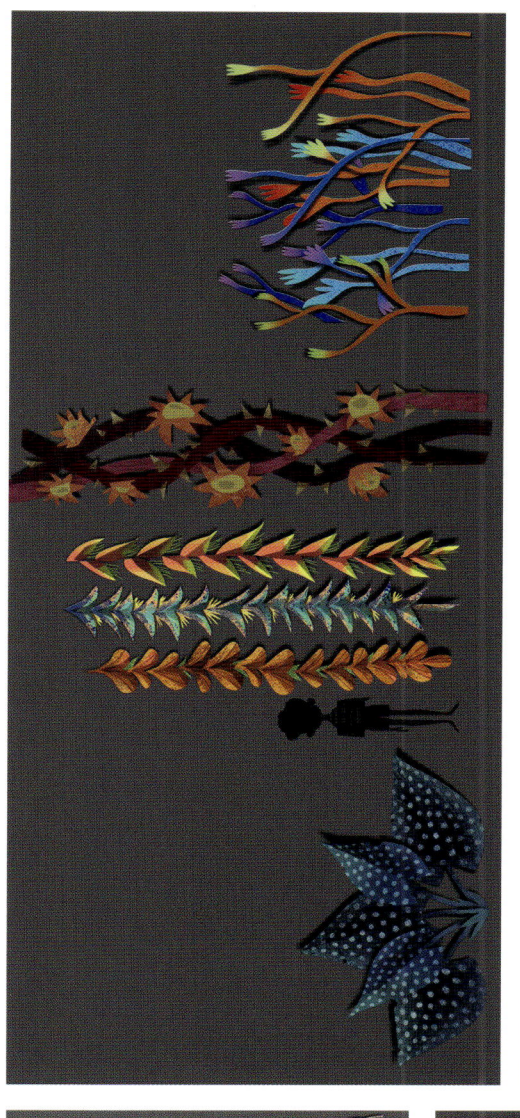

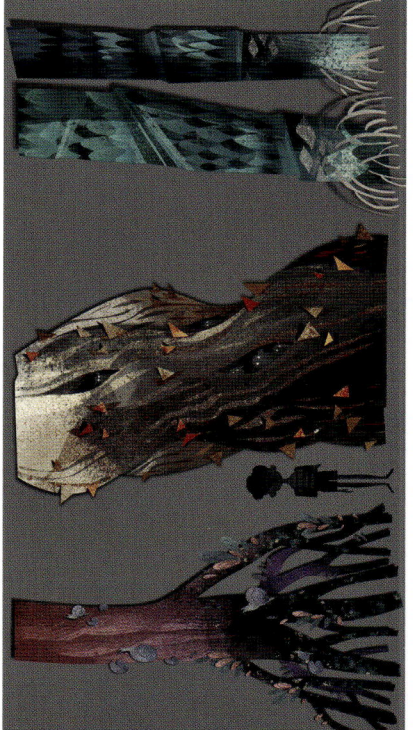

1 Early concept art by Rosa Ballester Cabo
2 Concept art by Lily Bernard of the island's transformation
3 Lily Bernard
4 Almu Redondo
5 Lily Bernard
6 Maria Cecilia Pugliese

LOCATIONS 161

LOCATIONS

pitcheR plant area

I made the lids round again

1–2 First concepts of the island summit by Lily Bernard
3–4 Alice Dieudonné
5–6 Rosa Ballester Cabo

164 LOCATIONS

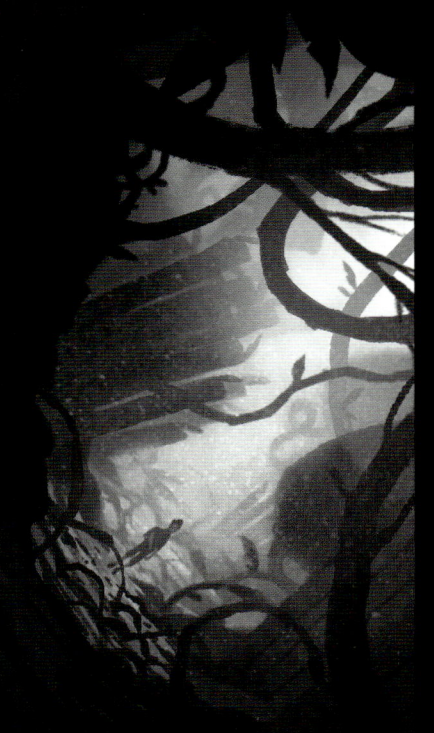

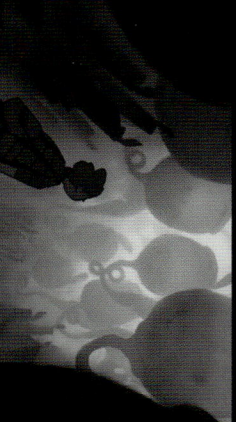

1 Production layout by Marco Manzoni
2–5 Lighting explorations by Ciarán Duffy
6 Colour script by Ciarán Duffy, Martí Furgber Morales, Alice Dieudonné, and Emilie Bach Nielsen
7 Scene illustration by Emilie Bach Nielsen
FOLLOWING SPREAD Emilie Bach Nielsen

Crocodile River

The Crocodile River was one of the most technically challenging locations in the movie. It's the backdrop for the action-packed sequence in which Boris and Elmer meet Cornelius the Crocodile and his babies as they try to escape Saiwa and the Howler Monkeys. Just like the tigers are camouflaged in the Tiger Forest, the crocs blend cleverly with the river designs. The blue shades of the graphic river waves stand out against the pinks and reds of the river shore and mountains and the striking purples of the island vines.

According to Mc Guinness, it required a lot of detailed planning early, at the layout stage, during which the team set up a massive "Before and After" as the river becomes flooded by the sea. Antonia Gancheva took on the location design of the whole area, planning its banks and how it could be sunk without the visual elements losing their compositional appeal. Mc Guinness explains, "This took a huge amount of collaboration across all our departments, especially our posing animation team, Moho [rig department], which was shaking and moving the riverbank and its vegetation, and the effects department, which was tackling two types of water animation: the freshwater and the dark, threatening seawater which comes in to flood the area. Like the tigers in Tiger Forest, we camouflaged the crocodiles carefully in their environment, so it has a big impact when we see them lose their home. It was very important to set this up carefully, as it is the audience's first encounter with animals who are coping with the sinking Island."

1-2 Concept art by Lily Bernard exploring how to treat the water in a way that could provide camouflage for the crocodiles

3 Alice Dieudonné

4 Lily Bernard

5 Scene Illustration by Maria Cecilia Pugliese showing the final look of Crocodile River

LOCATIONS

LOCATIONS

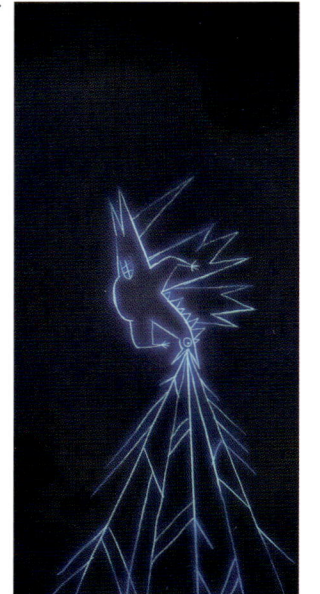

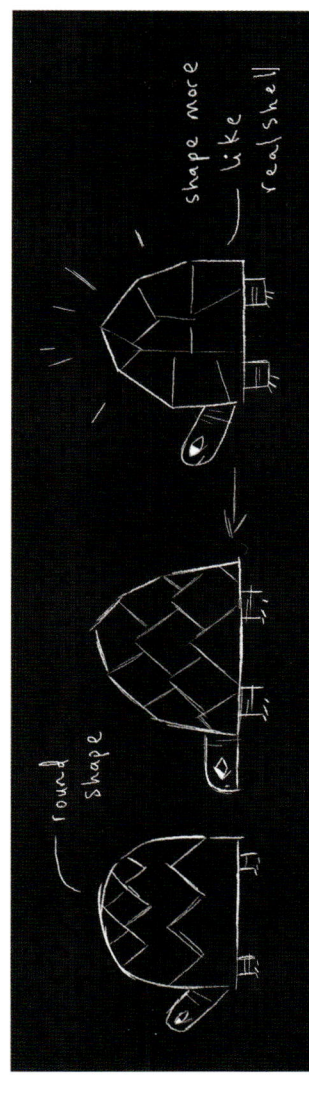

Dragon Rock

One of the most important aspects of the Dragon Rock location was its presentation as a stage. The rock itself is the darkest element in this background. "It's oppressive and dominates the compositions," says Mc Guinness. "The shoreline is littered with debris, evidence of the recent flood and rising sea. The design of the trees also reflects this, with their heavy and drooping canopies. The drawing on the rock was designed to give the impression it was drawn by Aratuah [the "rocks" are actually part of the island leaf structure but were referred to as rock throughout the production]. We see this drawing transform as we enter Elmer's imagination, and we were able to play with a more naive design and straight-ahead stand-alone piece of animation."

1 Maria Kruse Gaardbo
2 Erin Overmann
3 Rosa Ballester Cabo and Áine Mc Guinness
4 Rosa Ballester Cabo
5 Board panel by Nora Twomey
6 Background by Emilie Bach Nielsen with character by Rosa Ballester Cabo
7 Background painting by Hortense Mariano. Layout by Léo Weiss
8 Background painting by Enora le Luherne. Layout by Raquel Fernan Largo

LOCATIONS

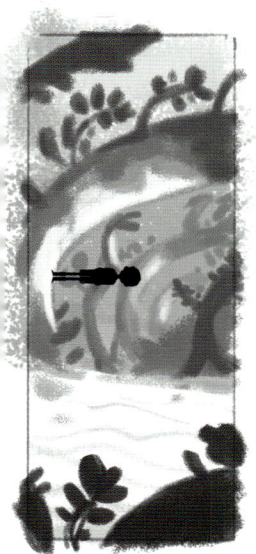
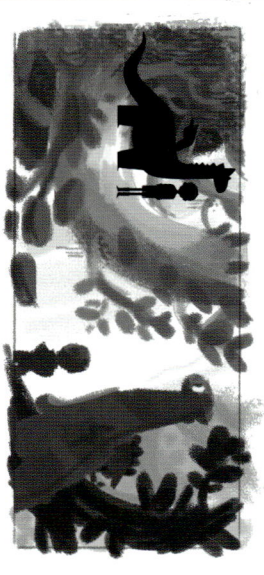

THIS SPREAD Erin Overmann's location design is serving storyboard needs and offering spatial solutions to script moments. Location design also adds visual information after storyboarding to give layout a consistent reference point.

ABOVE Schematic location plan by Erin Overmann

2 Background painting by Kaylee de Bruin and Tara Woods. Layout by Marco Manzoni

FOLLOWING SPREAD Background painting by Tara Woods. Layout by Paul Kavanagh

1 Background painting by Marina de Bustos Gonzales. Layout by Florencia Vasquez

LOCATIONS 175

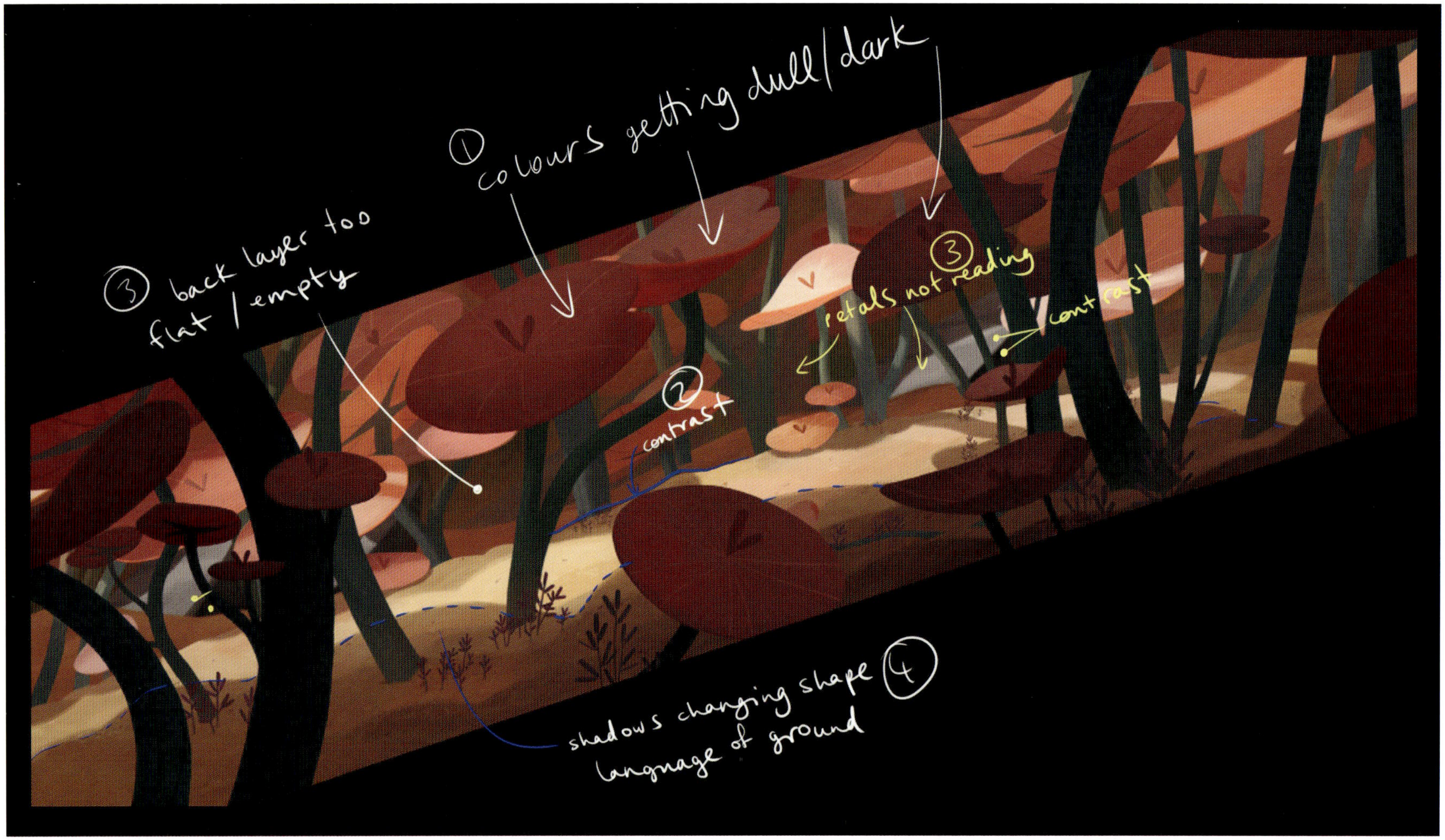

LOCATIONS

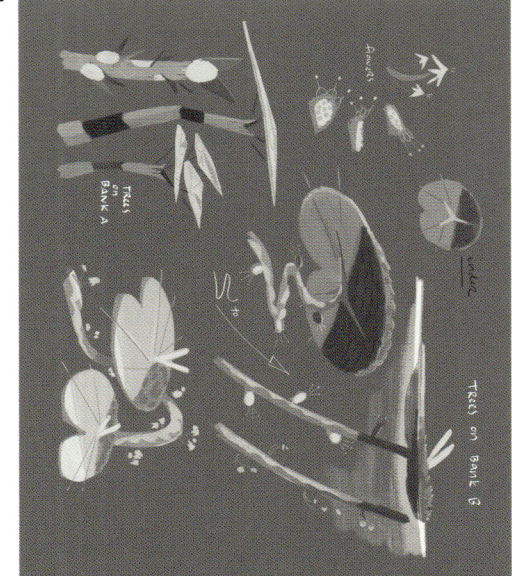

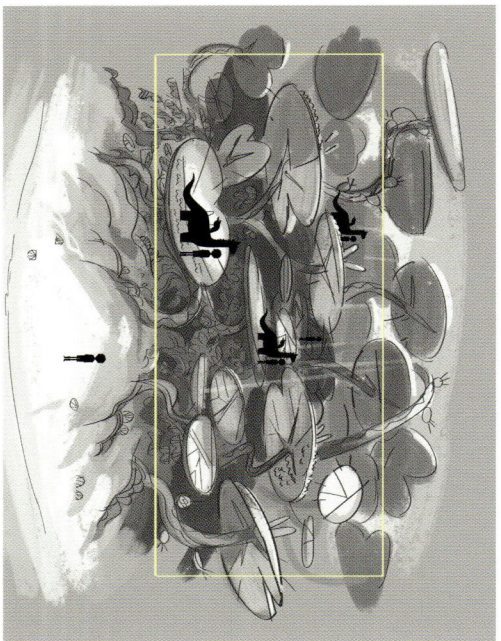

1 Background painting by Kaylee de Bruin. Art direction notes written by Áine Mc Guinness

2–3 Location plant design and location schematic by Erin Overmann

4–5 Background painting by Kaylee de Bruin. Layout by Léo Weiss

6 Colour key paintings by Emilie Bach Nielsen

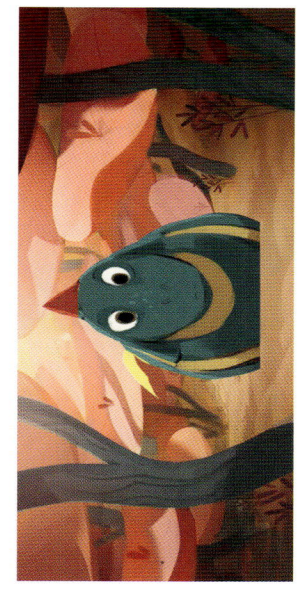

Tiger Forest

The Tiger Forest is described by the art and background team as one of the earliest locations that the production worked on, which helped unlock the distinct painting style of the movie. Early scene illustrations and background prototypes allowed the artists to explore textured brushwork and to play with the lighting.

"The tiger characters themselves were one of the first links made between children's imaginations and dealing with real fear," notes Mc Guinness. "So, the trees mimic tiger stripes, and in the earlier scenes, the tigers are camouflaged in their environment, which makes the location a little unsettling. The idea was that the audience wouldn't see the hidden tigers initially, but on the second or third viewing of the film, it would be fun for kids to see how many they could find!"

According to Mc Guinness, another unique aspect of the forest is the use of dappled lighting. The goal was to have the characters move in and out of the light and feel completely immersed in their environment, which is bright with strong light rays hitting the trees. "With comp, we applied light patches on the characters mimicking the light hitting the trees in the backgrounds," they say. "This was in addition to the characters' tonal colours so that we didn't flatten their volume. We also used a lot of effects-animated leaves to allow the characters to interact with, and feel immersed in, this visually striking location."

Background supervisor Eduardo Damasceno adds, "I love the fact that you feel the perfect balance between mood and style in this location. You actually feel the gravity of the situation. I remember that Nora wanted us to re-create the feeling of walking through a park that you've never been to. You are somewhere that you've never been before, and you're constantly trying to figure out what's going on."

1 Ciarán Duffy

2–4 Concept art by Rosa Ballester Cabo exploring trees with faces to camouflage the tigers

5 Alice Dieudonné

6 Lara Bentassil

7–8 Concept art by Maria Cecilia Pugliese

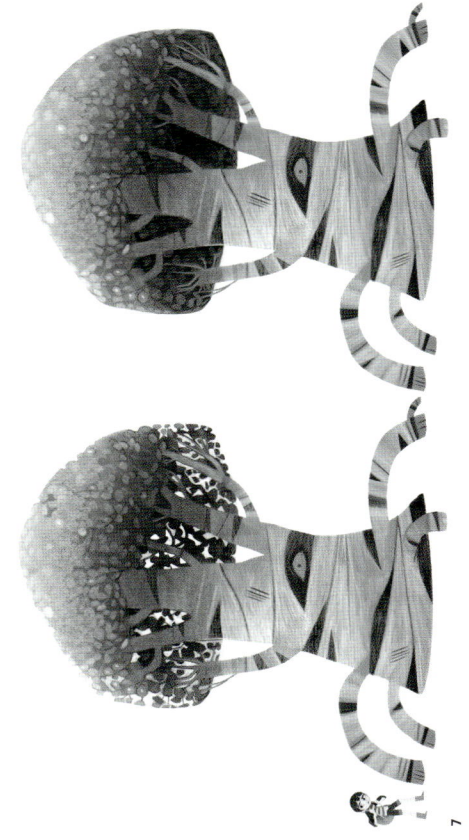

LOCATIONS

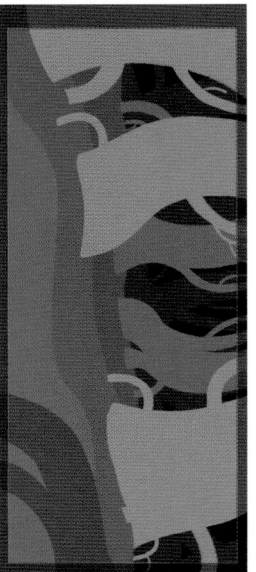

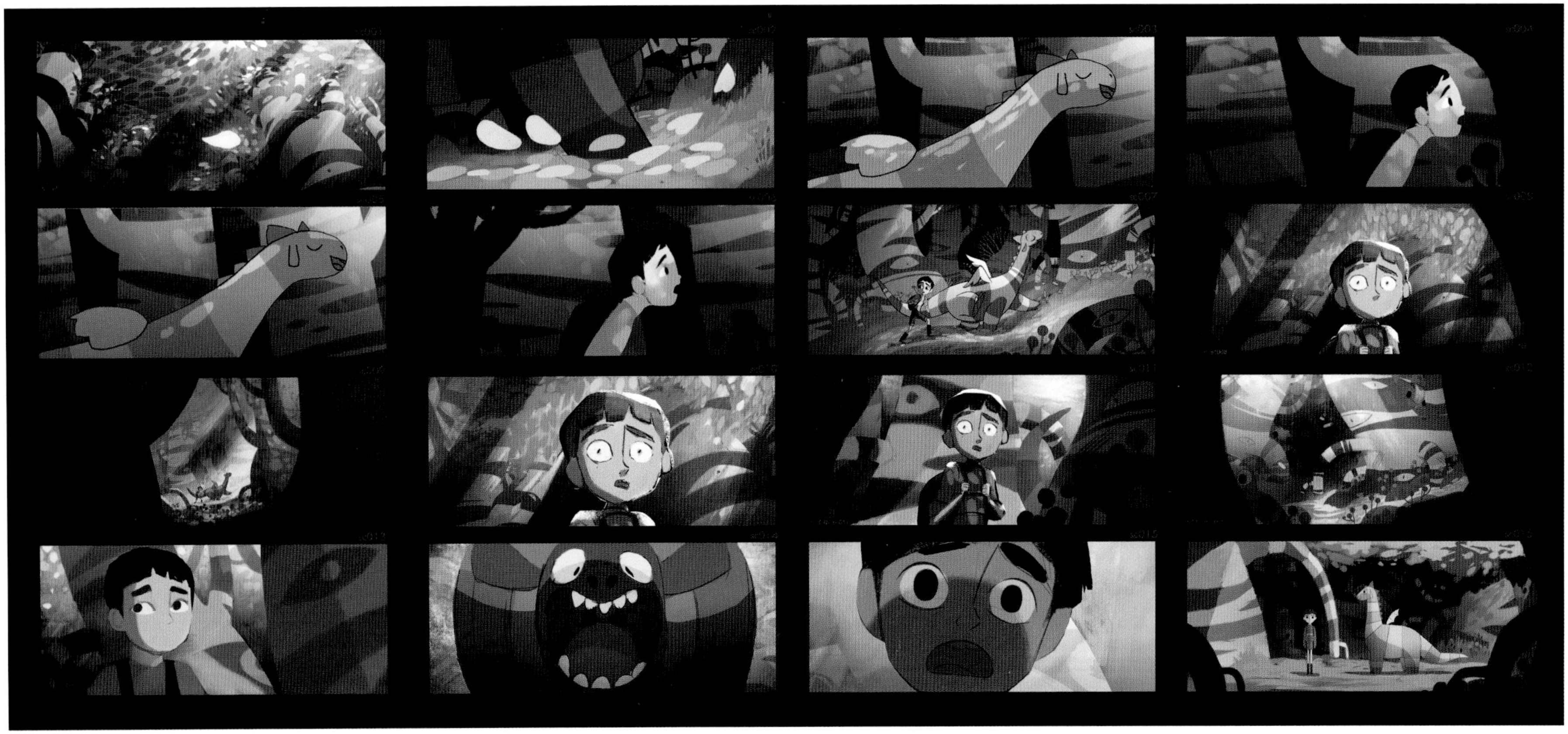

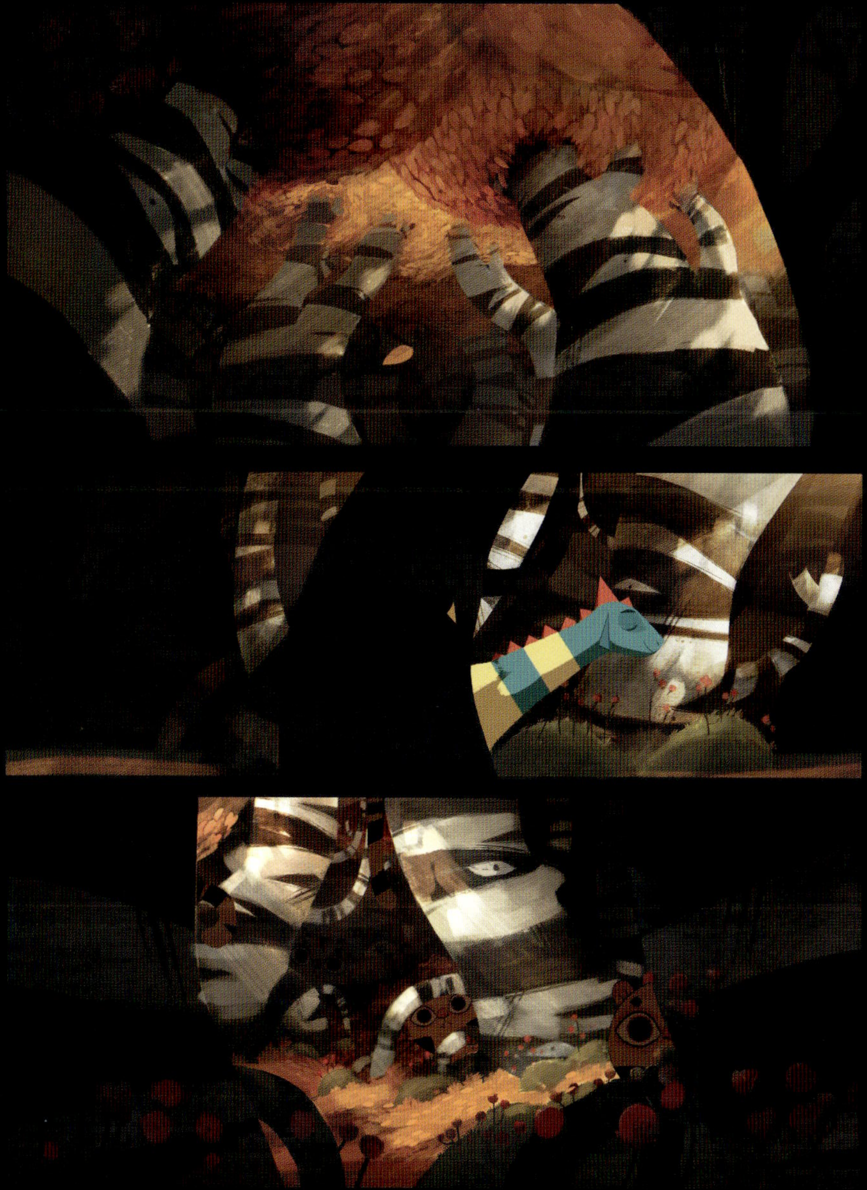

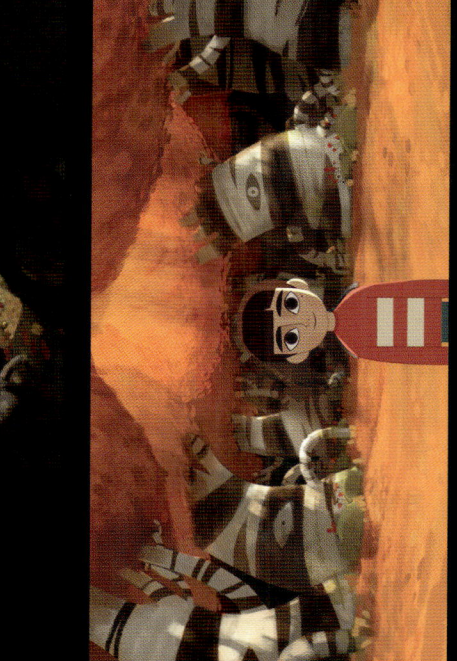

1. Layout breakdown by Léo Weiss. The first panel is by Giovanna Ferrari and Gaia Ruggenini.
2. Lighting pass for layout by Ciarán Duffy.

THIS PAGE
Emilie Bach Nielsen

LOCATIONS

Pika Place

The pika place is the home of the movie's very cute and unreliable lagomorphs. It's a bright, cotton-candy pink, airy spot, and you can see dandelion seeds floating in the wind. "The palette for this location is light and playful," explains Mc Guinness. "The fluffy pikas are adorable at first, but they set a trap for Boris. In contrast, the pit itself is very dark with dynamic, compositional, strong lighting to help build a sense of danger. Throughout these sequences we lose parts of the ceiling, which posed technical challenges for all our departments."

1 Location design by Erin Overmann exploring how far three-quarter down-shots could be pushed within the style language

2 Erin Overmann

3 Kaylee de Bruin

4 Erin Overmann

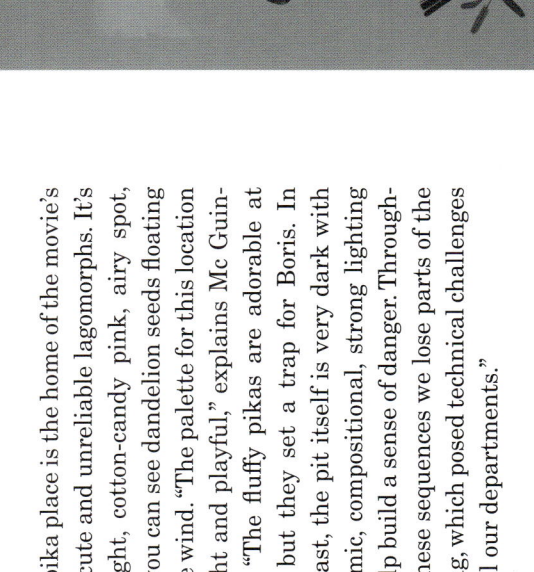

LOCATIONS

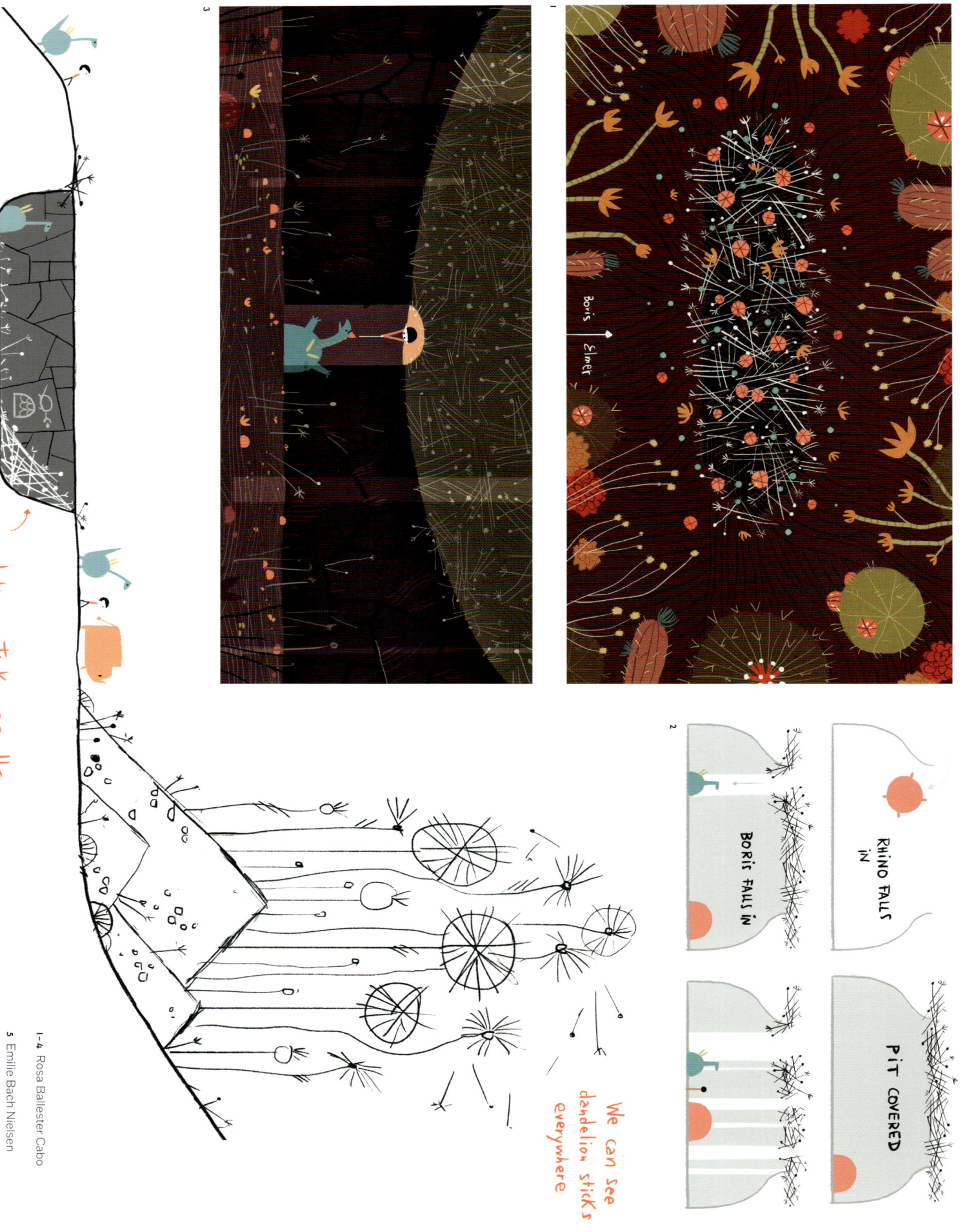

Dandelion sticks are thrown to make a ramp

We can see dandelion sticks everywhere

RHINO FALLS IN

BORIS FALLS IN

PIT COVERED

1–4 Rosa Ballester Cabo
5 Emilie Bach Nielsen
6 Lighting pass for layout by Ciarán Duffy

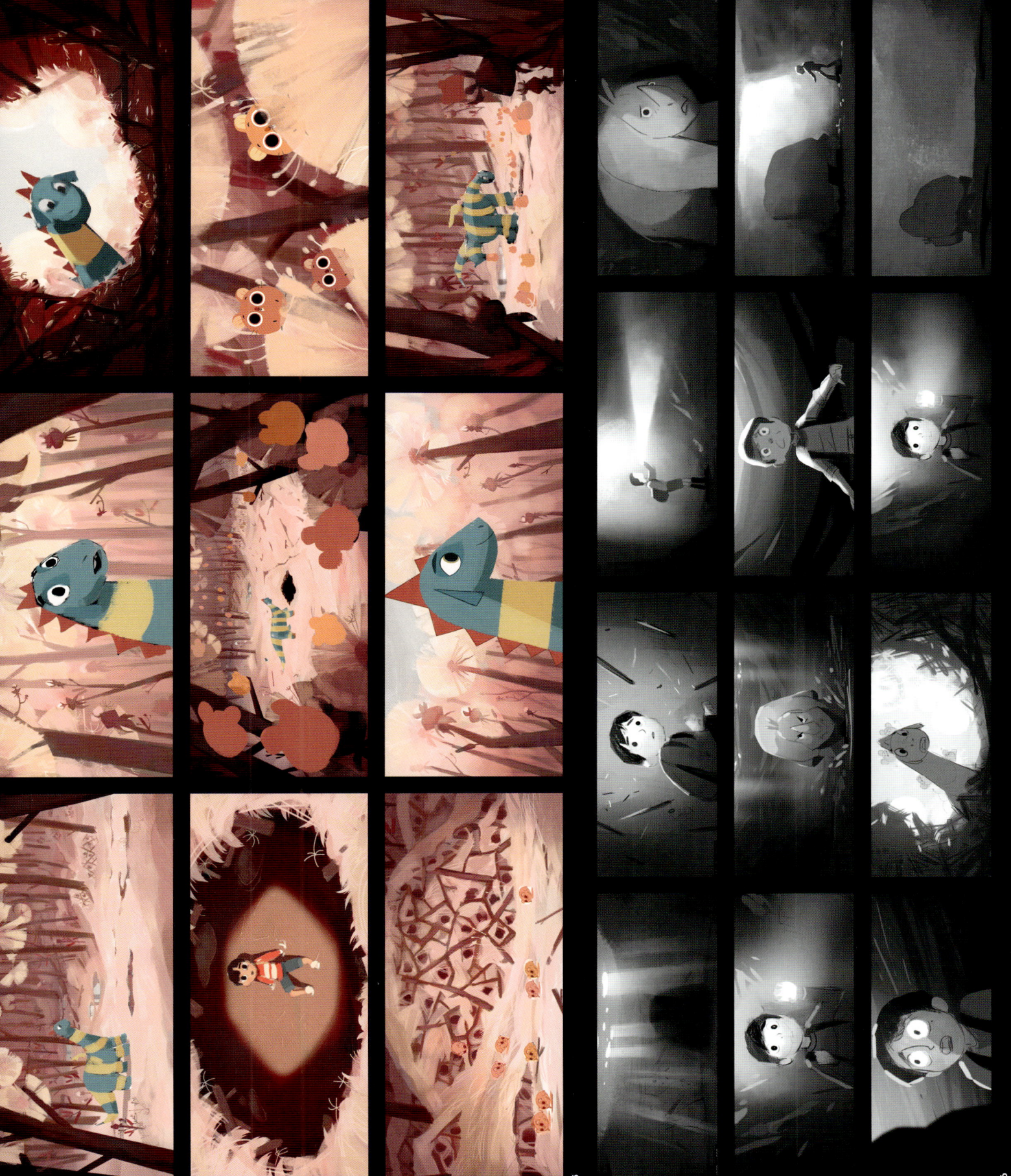

LOCATIONS • 187

Stripey Place

The stripey place location is a barren backdrop that has no vegetation apart from the organic patterns on the petals. "It's quite sparse and the palette is less vibrant compared to the other Wild Island locations," says Mc Guinness. "It is made up of the island petals, which in this location are slightly wilting and have areas that feel like they are starting to rot. We referenced dried-out succulent plants and apples which are starting to wither and rot."

1   Lara Bentassil
2–5 Ciarán Duffy
6   Alice Dieudonné
7   Colour script by Ciarán Duffy, Marti Furgber Morales, Alice Dieudonné, and Emilie Bach Nielsen
8   Still frame from final film

LOCATIONS

Aratuah's Cave

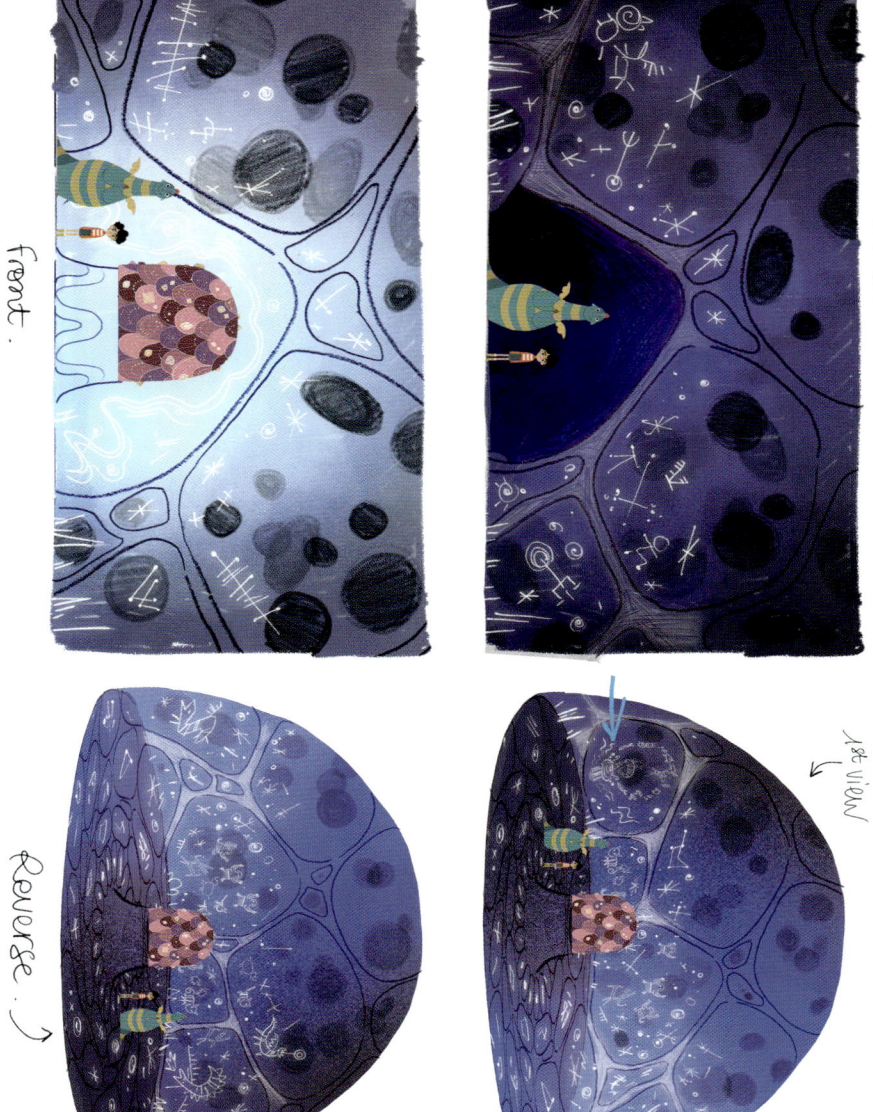

Just like Elmer and Boris, the audience has heightened expectations for Aratuah's Cave, a mystical destination that could hold the key to our duo's quest. "They are both nervous and full of expectations," says Mc Guinness. "We wanted the chamber to feel important and inspire reverence, so the main inspiration visually was for it to be cathedral- or mosque-like. The design of the shell itself was inspired by stained glass windows, so the shell has multiple reflective facets catching the bright green light in the cave. The walls are lit by bioluminescent vegetation, their stalks giving the cave a cathedral-like arch structure."

We did a lot of illustrations for this location," recalls background supervisor Eduardo Damasceno. "It underwent a lot of changes as we were trying to figure out the right number of reflections. We didn't want the walls to compete with the turtle shell. At one point, the whole cave was supposed to look like a cathedral, but we eventually brought it back to a simpler shell design. We also had to figure out how to depict the broken shells. We had to build the assets that could be broken and became background elements that needed to be animated."

1 Alice Dieudonné
2 Lara Bentassil
3–4 Ciarán Duffy
5 Lily Bernard
6 Alice Dieudonné
7 Ciarán Duffy

LOCATIONS

1 Colour script by Ciarán Duffy, Martí Furgber Morales, Alice Dieudonné, and Emilie Bach Nielsen

2 Background painting by Ulric Leprevost. Layout by Paul Kavanagh

RIGHT Background painting by Enora Le Luherne. Layout by Léo Weiss

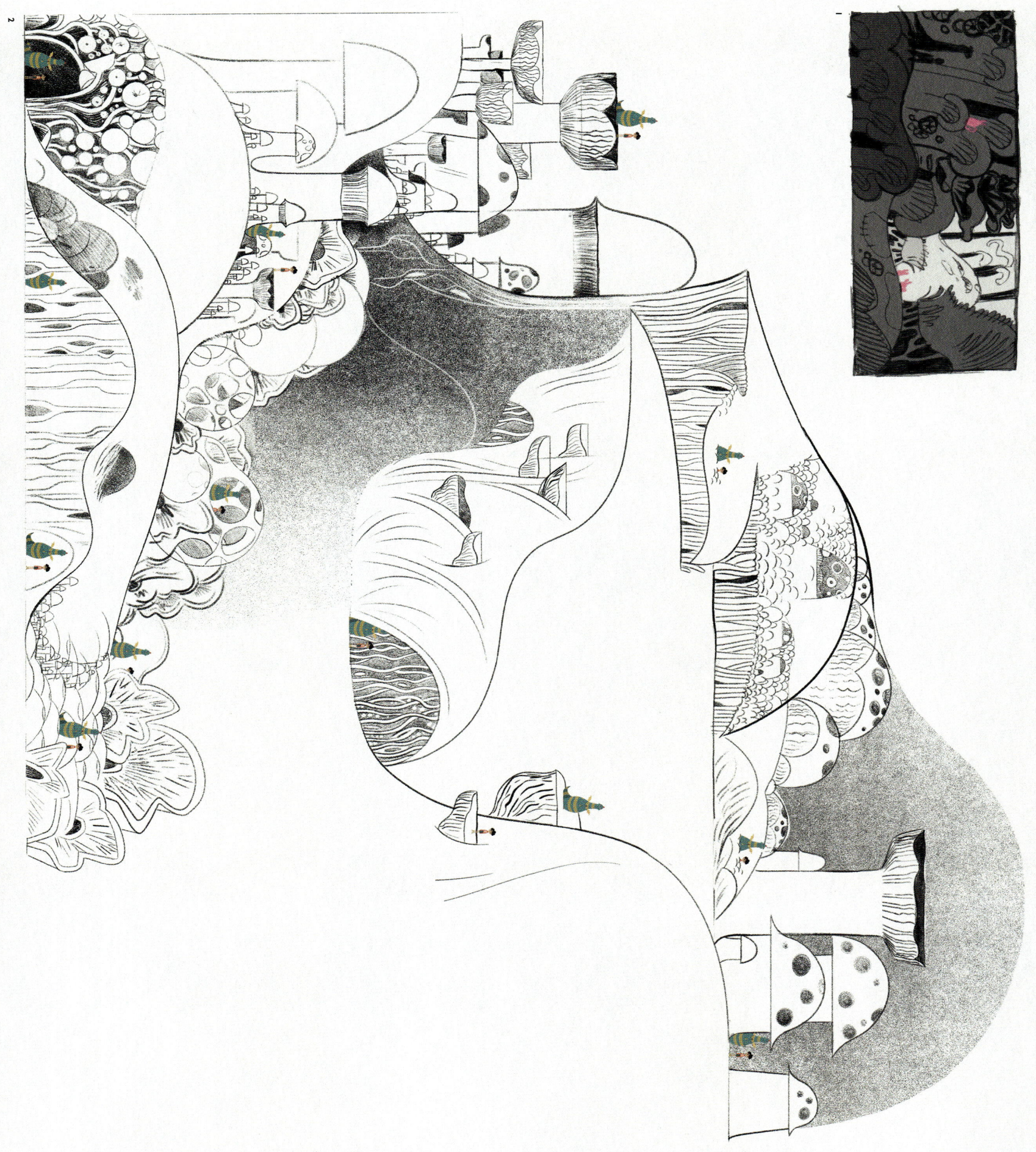

Mushroom Path

Elmer and Boris reach the Mushroom Path after realizing that Aratuah died some time ago, and they need to escape the flooded cave. The art team wanted the location to feel dank, but beautiful in order to keep the audience engaged during this low point in the protagonists' adventure.

"This sequence is one of the biggest mood pieces in the film," says Mc Guinness. "Luminous fungi and bead-like droplets of water on the mushrooms add an extra level of beauty, with mist and rain making the sequence really atmospheric. The palette consists mostly of browns, sprinkled with purple and green for contrast. It was important that there was no place to shelter here, as we lead the audience to the beautiful sunset vista in the next sequence when Boris and Elmer have their bonding moment on top of the old flower."

1 Tonal sketch by Marti Furgber Morales

2 Location design leading through the mushroom path by Maria Cecilia Pugliese, from an earlier draft of the script when rabbits lived in the mushrooms

3 Lily Bernard

4 Kayvon Darabi-Fard

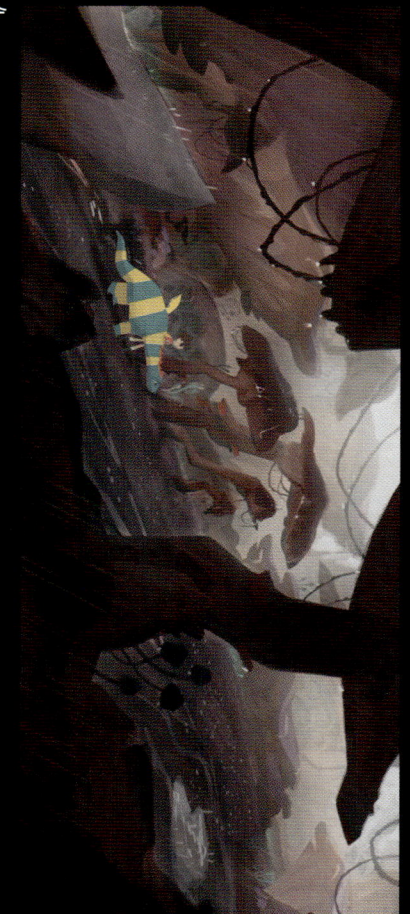
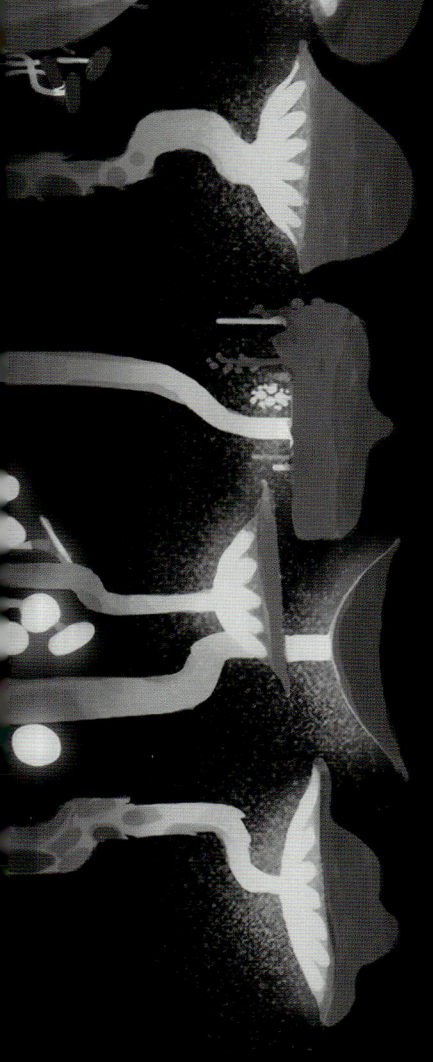

1–2 Lighting options for the clouded-over mushroom path by Ciarán Duffy

3–4 Colour key backgrounds by Emilie Bach Nielsen

5 Martí Furgber

OPPOSITE Background painting by Tara Woods. Layout by Marco Manzoni

LOCATIONS

a giant caterpillar did all that!

bit the petals

made a hole to get out

made his way through the trunk

made a hole to go in

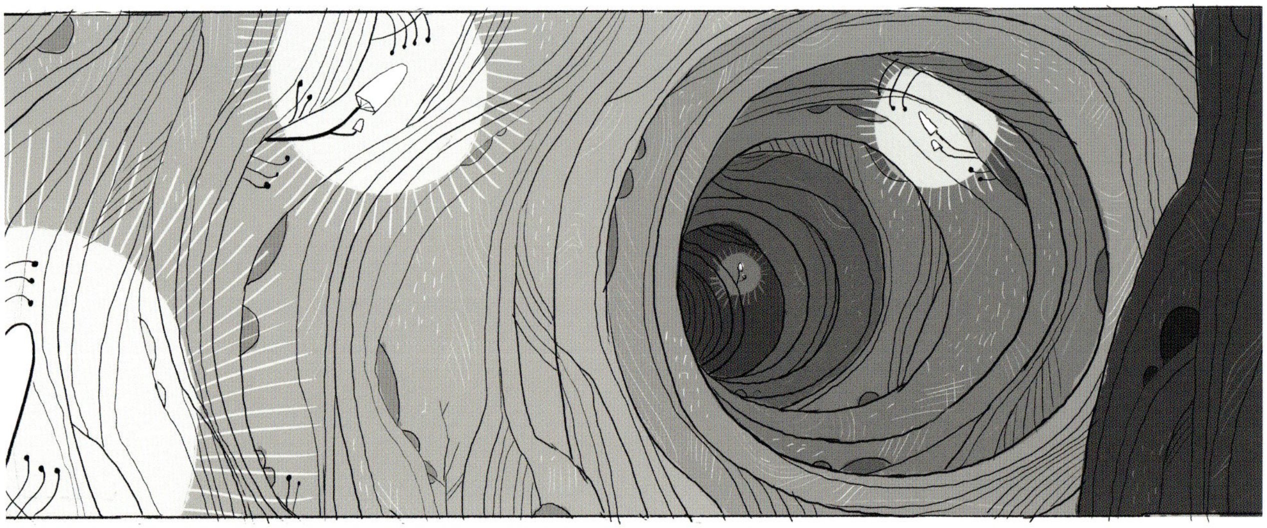

cave feeling

← dried out petals

stamens outside

- petals are losing life/color as they drop open
- Some petals have completely dried out (pointy/sharp)

Ground

Flower Top

The old flower is a shelter that offers safety and warmth to Boris and Elmer when they need rest. This is how the location is described in the script: "The top of the old flower is flat and sheltered. The petals open out at the front giving a spectacular view . . . Elmer looks out onto the sea: It's a beautiful sight, a calm sunset for a sinking island."

One of the interesting points about the flower top is that we see it in two very different conditions in the movie. "At first it is bathed in orange light in the magical hour after sunset," Mc Guinness points out. "This is a pivotal moment in the film during which Boris and Elmer have a big heart-to-heart, but it is the calm before the storm. The next morning we see it in the blue hour before sunrise. There's a big shift from the warm sunset to the colder blues of this early morning light. It is lit this way to make Kwan's torch dramatic and cold and to have a striking contrast between safety and danger. The island has also sunk during the night, so the sea has started to come in around the base of the flower. The inspiration for the design itself was a sunflower with the petals slightly drying out."

OPPOSITE Concept art by Rosa Ballester Cabo exploring the spiral tunnel to the top of the old flower, as it was a required location by an early draft of the script

1 Ciarán Duffy. Soft, warm lighting at the top of the old flower was made to reflect Elmer's sense of home.

2 Erin Overmann

LOCATIONS

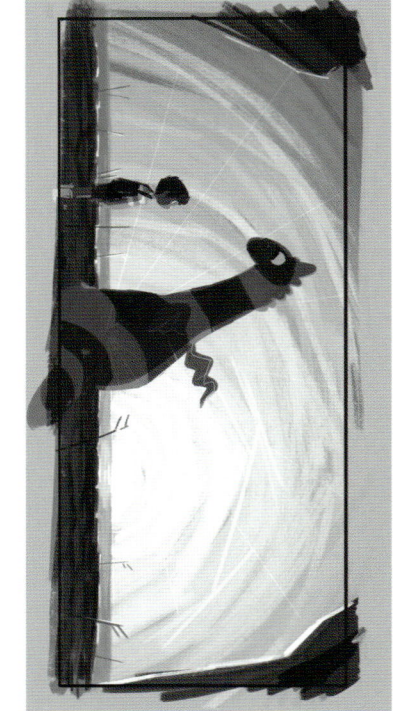
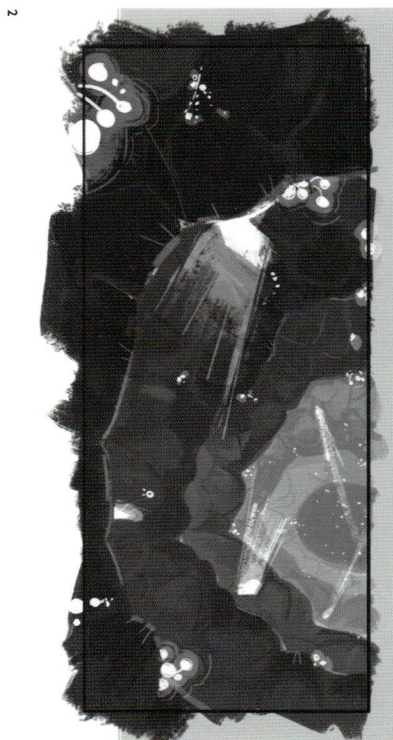

1   Location design by Maria Cecilia Pugliese
2–4 Erin Overmann
5   Alice Dieudonné
6–7 Rosa Ballester Cabo

LOCATIONS

1 Background painting by Florencia Vasquez. Layout by Léo Weiss

2–3 Emilie Bach Nielsen

OPPOSITE Background painting by Maria Kruse Gaardbo. Layout by Léo Weiss

LOCATIONS

Hmm...
Not very balanced,
but he can see everything

like a paraglider

Flap
Flap
Flap

ouch with the scales

Stry-surfer

Boris Riding options

1 Colour script by Ciarán Duffy, Martí Furgber Morales, Alice Dieudonné, and Emilie Bach Nielsen

2 Rosa Ballester Cabo and Alice Dieudonné

3 Background painting by Marco Manzoni. Layout by Paul Kavanagh

4 Background painting by Ulric Leprovost

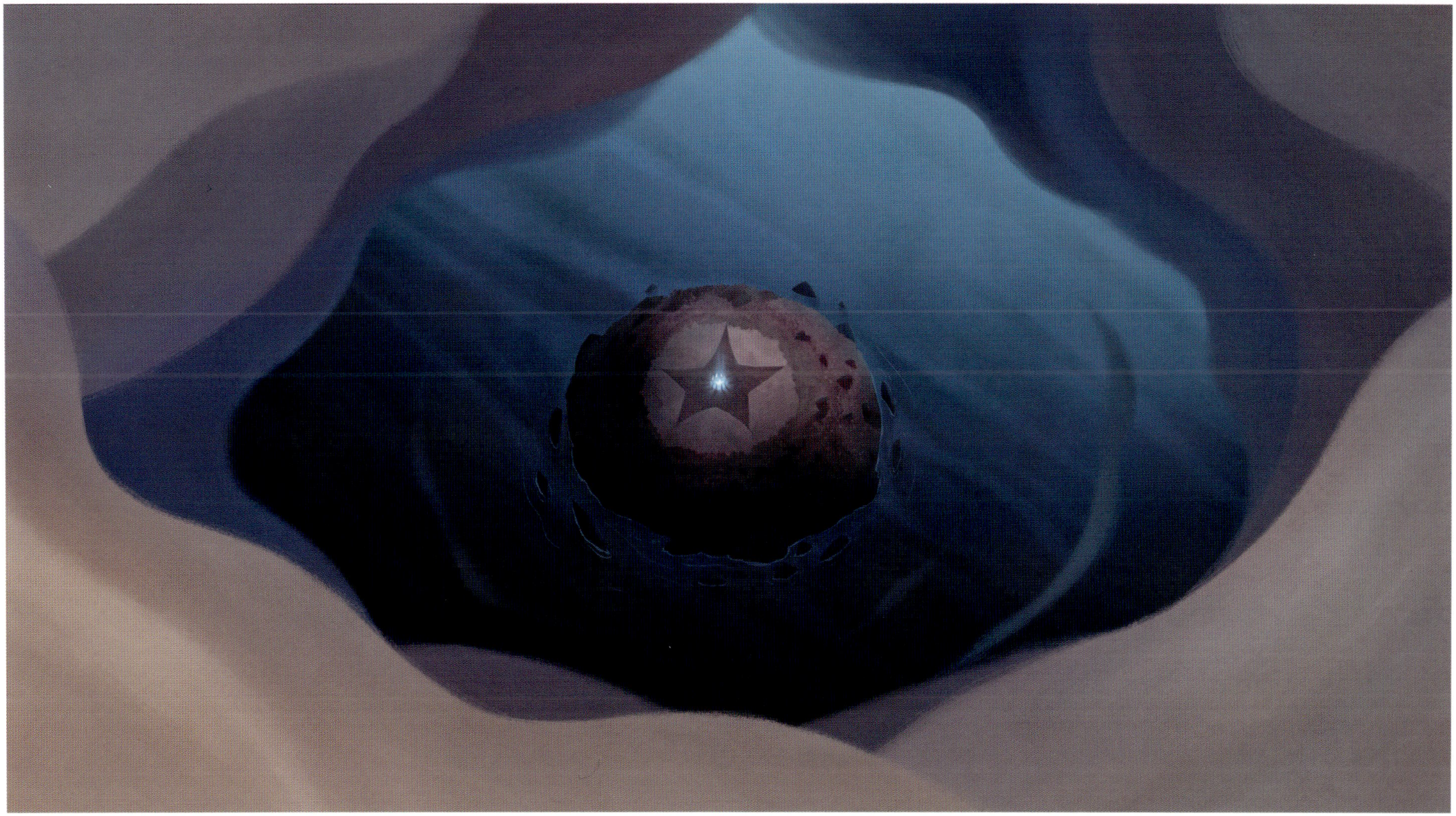

LOCATIONS 205

The Summit

The island's colourful summit is the site of many important developments and transformations in the story. As Twomey points out, "We knew going in that we needed to pare back our colour palette and make it 'dramatic.' But we didn't just do it for the sake of the art direction. The story dictated the visuals. Elmer and Boris come to the most dangerous place on the island to face the most dangerous task. That's why everything before the final climax leads to the summit and what happens there."

McGuinness explains that the viewers get to see the summit in four separate stages. "The idea is that the visuals evolve after the first time when we arrive and Boris is inside the volcano enclosure, and they're trying to save the island," they note. "As the island begins to submerge more, we see the opening of the volcano get wider. The palette here is stark, the lighting dramatic. Throughout the film we build up the intensity through the effects. Smoke, lighting, and embers billow out of the opening. This provides a really nice contrast for when Boris saves the island and we see a softening of the shape language, more vibrancy in the colours, and the effects quiet down to become friendlier and happier, to reflect the mood."

LEFT Concept art by Alice Dieudonné

OPPOSITE Maria Cecilia Pugliese

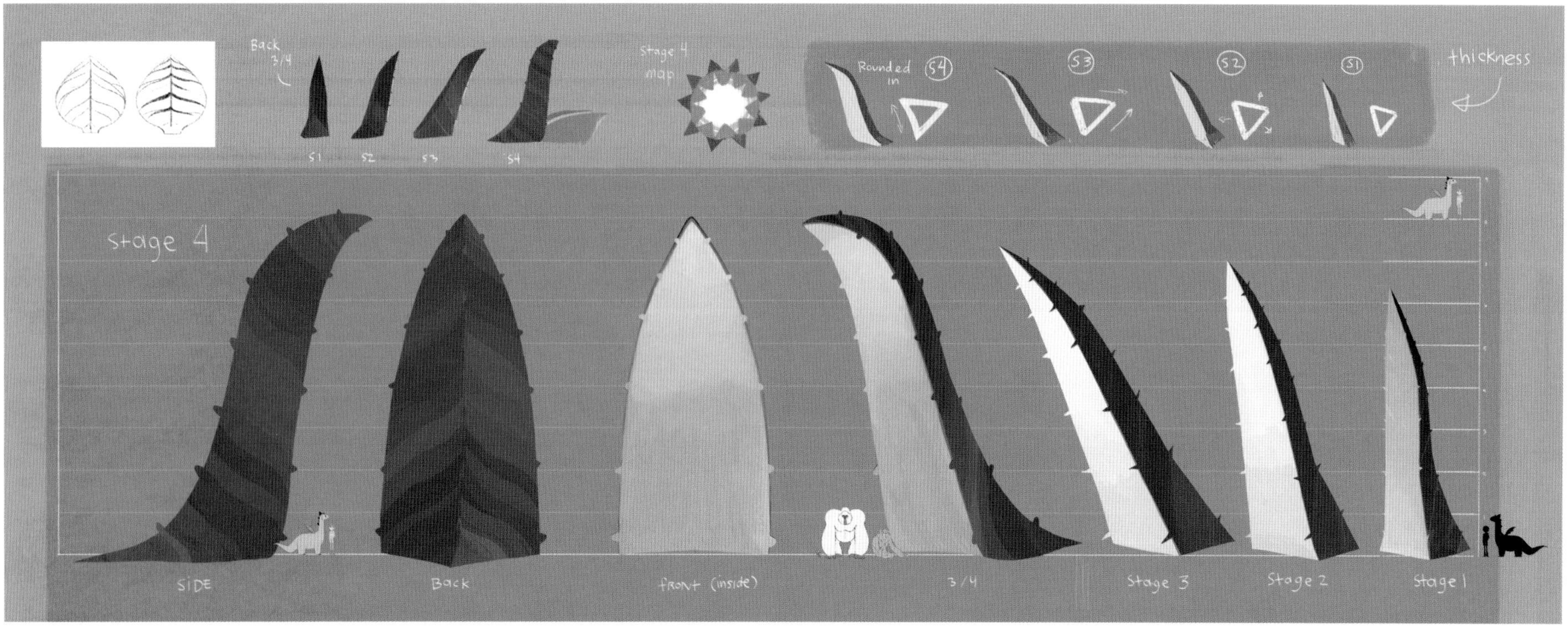

THIS PAGE
Erin Overmann

OPPOSITE Exploration of scale and camera elevation within the art direction parameters by Julien Regnard

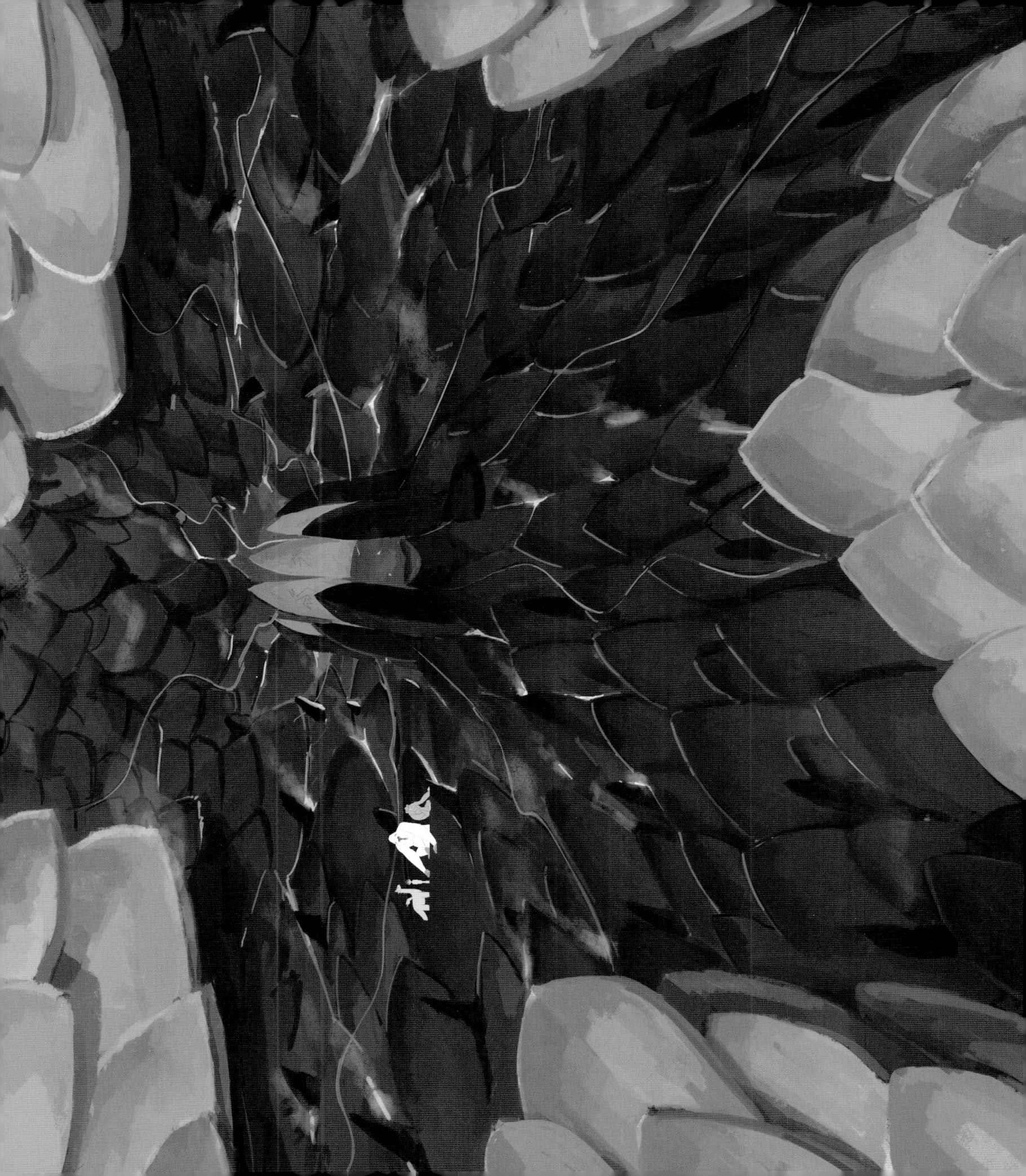

LOCATIONS

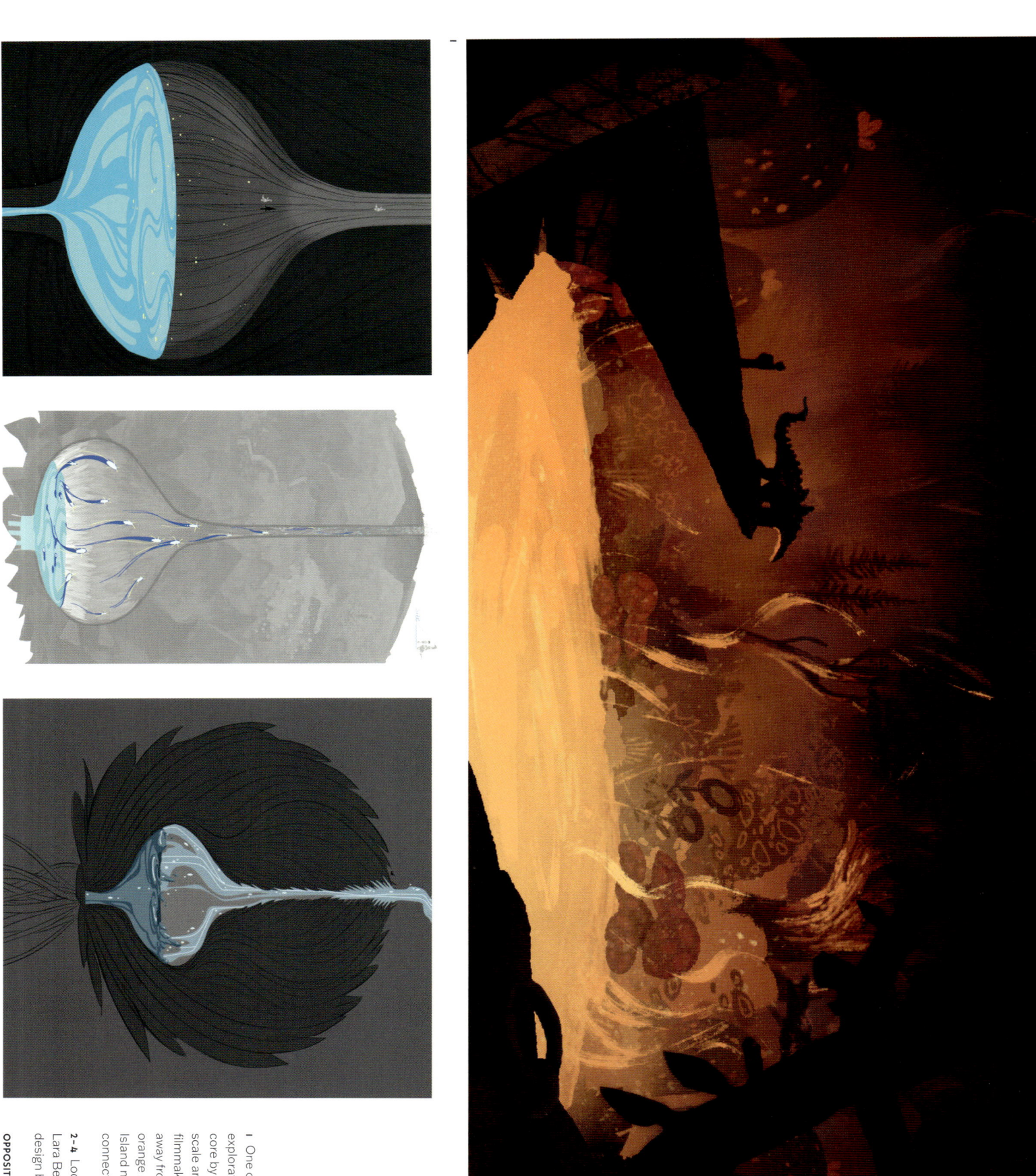

1 One of the first explorations of the island core by Ciarán Duffy, evoking scale and danger. The filmmakers soon moved away from the volcanic orange color to make Wild Island not have an expected connection with the seabed.

2–4 Location design by Lara Bentassil. Effects design by Narissa Schander.

OPPOSITE Marco Manzoni

LOCATIONS

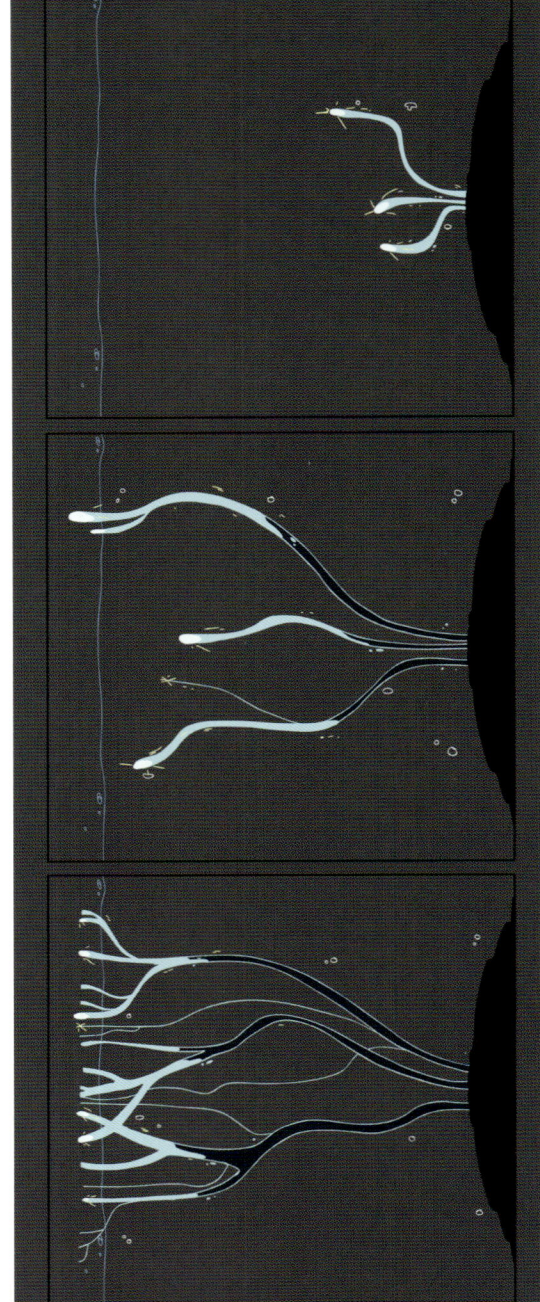

1 Location design by Lara Bentassil exploring Wild Island's connection with the seabed. Scale and cinematographic values are taken into consideration at the earliest stages of location design.

2 Location design by Lara Bentassil. Effects design by Narissa Schander.

3 Location design by Erin Overmann. Effects design by Narissa Schander.

Far – Detailed (shot example)

ANATOMY OF A SCENE
The Crocodile River Crossing

One of the most challenging and exciting sequences of *My Father's Dragon* takes place about forty-two minutes into the movie. We see Elmer and Boris trying to get across the river as they are chased by Kwan, Saiwa, and the rest of the animals, while the island continues to sink into the ocean. "It's probably the biggest action set piece of the film in terms of all the different characters and the number of elements they're interacting with, as well as the effects and the environments," says editor Richie Cody. "It was a sequence that used to play a lot differently in the previous versions. Originally, the crocodiles built a bridge out of their own bodies for them. Boris and Elmer climbed up to a cliff to escape and it was all very fantastical, and the changing motivations for some of the characters were hard to explain."

Cody points out that as the sequence changed and evolved, the creative team realized that it was simpler and clearer to have the story's lead characters get themselves out of the situation without the help of the crocodiles. Elmer motivates Boris with a strawberry lollipop and keeps him moving across a giant vine to the other side of the river. "This new shift also helped show the strengthening of the bond between the two main characters, as well as illustrating the changing power dynamics between Saiwa, Kwan, and the duo. We also learn more about Cornelius and how he is constrained by the other crocodiles. There were many changing dynamics to track, while making sure the scene seemed believable without getting bogged down by all the details."

Assistant director Mark Mullery says a sequence this elaborate required the creative team to have faith in the process. "Work-in-progress versions of these shots will never quite have the intensity and dynamism that you know will come together in the final picture, but it's a mistake to force that dynamism in the wrong place with the wrong team on every given shot," he offers. "If the purpose of a shot is to read Elmer's thinking expression or Boris's sense of panic, then you need to let the animators draw that emotion carefully on a simple canvas instead of demanding that they have the characters shake about on-screen trying to steady themselves, stumbling in every given shot."

Mullery also brings up the fact that a little camera shake and some expert sound design marry together Boris's and Elmer's simply rendered emotion with the dynamism of the broader sequence. "It's important to remember that you have experts and specialists on hand for every task, and a lot of filmmaking is knowing what part of the puzzle to give each artist and when, as well as having faith that the missing pieces will come together," he adds.

Background supervisor Eduardo Damasceno remembers that he and his team knew this particular sequence would be a challenge as soon as they had a director's pass. The movable background elements and a generous

```
The RIVER STARTS PULLING APART! Filling with sea water.
Saiwa, Howlers, Cornelius and the baby crocs are swept away.

             CORNELIUS CROCODILE
                (in distress)
             Oh HELP!
             (mumbling through closed
             beak)
        Oh - careful with my - Look here,
        watch out, watch out!

More waves come crashing up the river. Saiwa is barely able
to hold on to the vine AND Cornelius. The chain breaks.
Babies are lost in the gap, chirping loudly.

             SAIWA
        I've got you!

Saiwa holds on to a vine. He grabs Cornelius' tail, trying to
form a barrier to stop baby crocs from being swept out to sea
as the root dam is submerged.

On the riverbank edge Kwan grabs Boris' tail pulling him back
down the bank-- but then:

Kwan has closed in on Boris. He manages to grab the end of
his tail.

             TAMIR
        Saiwa?
```

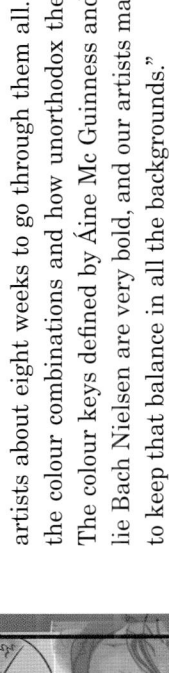

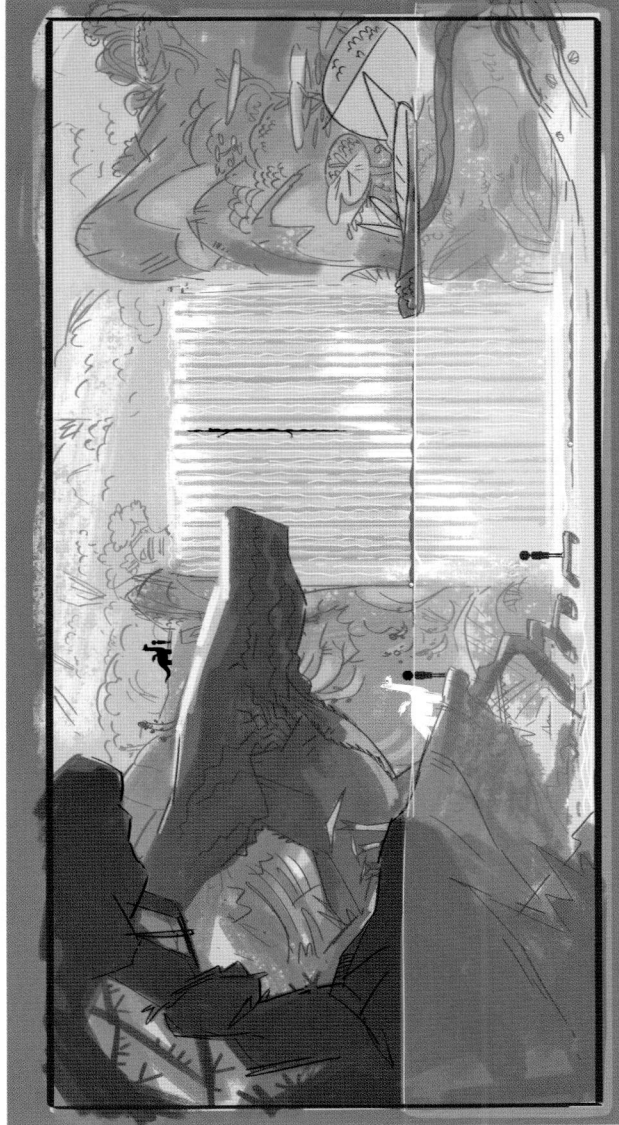

artists about eight weeks to go through them all. I love the colour combinations and how unorthodox they are: The colour keys defined by Áine Mc Guinness and Emilie Bach Nielsen are very bold, and our artists managed to keep that balance in all the backgrounds."

Twomey elaborates: "Once location design and layout had set up the moving pieces, each subsequent department had to make sure nothing got broken along the way. Croc River was a massive accomplishment in the service of raising the stakes from a narrative perspective. It's a miracle of teamwork, given a lot of this work was done from artists' homes rather than a physical collaborative room."

According to the film's technical director, Fergal Brennan, the sequence is a great example of how to rely on a nonstandard pipeline successfully. "You have two main characters trying to cross the river, but the island is starting to sink at the same time," he notes. "We ended up in a situation where Boris and Elmer are crossing the river using Moho-animated vines. You have the Moho backgrounds shaking, the effects-created water, Moho crocodiles in the effects water, and seawater rushing on top of the river water. A lot of the shots had everything moving at once, and all the departments working on them at the same time, which led to some very complicated setups."

Brennan further explains that what made this pipeline nonstandard is that the team had to first focus on the primary action of the scene. "If the island is moving so much that it's affecting the characters, you have to move the island before the character, so that you'd have Moho come before the animation. Then if the effects are rushing in, all of a sudden, you have another prime reaction. It's possible that you could jump back and forth between departments, so you could start in

number of effects complicated the process to a certain degree. "From the start we knew we would use the ground colours and the waterfall backdrop to help keep the focus on the characters," he says.

Since the backgrounds were created to have as close of a final frame mock-up as possible for the review, the team painted haze, water droplets, water splashes, and suggested character tints for each one of them. "A big challenge was the technicalities for the work files," notes Damasceno. "A lot of elements on this sequence are animated background elements, and in order for them to work we needed not just to keep everything separated and organized, but also to make sure we had lit and dark versions for a lot of them, so light could behave more naturally throughout the sequence."

Because this sequence arrived late in the filmmaking process, the design teams were very familiar with the overall style and knew how to set up the files quite well by then. "We created a guide specifically for the location with direction on how to deal with each element," says the background supervisor. "We worked the five sequences, from when they arrive at croc river to when they leave, as one big block of backgrounds, since we're on the same location. We had about sixty between those five sequences, and it took our team of fourteen

1 Script by Meg LeFauve

2 Location design by Erin Overmann. Based on the scene illustration, the designer worked out the script requirements for the rising water and moving elements.

3 Storyboard by Federico Chericoni

animation, then go to effects, then go back to Moho to do the characters. It was incredibly complicated, but now that we are done with it, I can tell you that everyone did an amazing job!"

Effects supervisor Narissa Schander also considers the sequence one of her toughest assignments. "The interaction with the moving background elements and the characters which are being washed by the water and pulled around was a challenge," she says. "We were also cutting quickly from one scene to the next and had to be very consistent. However, something that should have been difficult ended up flowing smoothly because we had been very good about communicating about all the little details."

Damasceno agrees. "I loved that this was such a great collaborative work between every department. There was a lot going on, and we still managed to preserve the emotions of the scene. To watch everything come together in such a beautiful way was very satisfying for all of us."

1 Master layout by Antonia Yordanova Gancheva, Maria Cecilia Pugliese, Álvaro Ramírez, and Paul Kavanagh
2 Posing by Myra Hild and Lamberto Anderloni
3 Background element rigged animation by Victor Paredes
4 Hand-drawn water effects by Paulo Passaro
5 Rough, hand-drawn character animation by Bryony Evans
6 Rigged character animation by Régis Rodríguez
7 Hand-drawn water ripples by Paulo Passaro
8 Pre-comp by Damien Bayard and Anushka Deedwania
9 Compositing by Valerie Guichard

Final Words

From the early days of cinema, beloved children's books have inspired beautiful and memorable animated movies that build upon the legacy and themes of their source material.

Cartoon Saloon follows in the footsteps of classics such as *Dumbo*, *Bambi*, and *Pinocchio* as it brings its charming take on Ruth Stiles Gannett's Newbery Medal–winning book *My Father's Dragon* to the screen.

This lovingly crafted feature follows in the footsteps of the Kilkenny-based studio's four previous gems (*The Secret of Kells*, *Song of the Sea*, *The Breadwinner*, and *WolfWalkers*) and offers audiences a colorful adventure that explores the possibilities of the art form. Students of animation would be wise to study the movie as a brilliant way to expand upon a brief (eighty-seven-page) book and create a unique, magical world of its own while staying true to the unforgettable characters and themes of the original property.

What the film's gifted director, Nora Twomey, and her dedicated team of artists, writers, visual-effects gurus, and animators have given us is a chance to revisit a childhood where simply imagining a faraway place and magical creatures could make them come alive. They have used the latest achievements in animation technology without straying from the handcrafted and artisanal origins of 2-D animation. In addition, they have paid homage to some of their favorite classics while exploring Elmer and Boris's complicated friendship and the importance of banishing fear to achieve greatness. There's no doubt that we will all want to revisit Wild Island again and again to spend more time with our resourceful hero and his kindhearted dragon friend with the long tail and yellow stripes.

OPPOSITE Colour key by Emilie Bach Nielsen

THIS PAGE Early character concept scale lineup by Rosa Ballester Cabo

Acknowledgments

It's not every day that you get to fly away with a boy and his dragon to a magical island. It has been a true pleasure and an honor to go behind the scenes of *My Father's Dragon* with the brilliant and kind Nora Twomey and her fantastic team at Cartoon Saloon. I am forever grateful to Nora and everyone at the studio for their precious time, generosity, and insights into the process of making this wonderful movie. A huge thank-you to my three friends at Cartoon Saloon, Gerry Shirren, Paul Young, and Tomm Moore. A big thank-you to Rosa Ballester and Áine Mc Guinness for being especially kind and accommodating as I went back to them again and again! Warm dragon hugs to the rest of the amazing crew of the movie, including (alphabetically) Sandra Norup Andersen, Louise Bagnall, Helga Kristjana Bjarnadóttir, Fergal Brennan, Richie Cody, Bonnie Curtis, Eduardo Damasceno, Jeff and Mychael Danna, Justin Davey, Fabian Erlinghäuser, Giovanna Ferrari, Morgan Fontana, Julie Lynn, Meg LeFauve, Cal McLoughlin, Esther Morales Sanchez, Mark Mullery, Emilie Bach Nielsen, Narissa Schander, Zach Seivers, Brian Tyrrell, John Walsh, and Léo Weiss. Dear Desirée Meade, you will always have my gratitude for patiently scheduling all those interviews. And a huge thanks to designer Liam Flanagan, and my captain at Abrams Books, the brilliant Eric Klopfer, who saves me constantly from all the island's pikas.
—**Ramin Zahed**

ABOVE Early concept art by Solene Chevaleyre exploring Boris's stripes and their relationship to Wild Island's patterns, inspired by the book and illustrations of the era

Editor Eric Klopfer
Designer Liam Flanagan
Managing Editor Lisa Silverman
Production Manager Denise LaCongo
Asset Manager for Cartoon Saloon Cal McLoughlin

Library of Congress Control Number: 2022938582

ISBN: 978-1-4197-6700-5
eISBN: 979-8-88707-121-3

Copyright © 2023 Cartoon Saloon

Published in 2023 by Abrams, an imprint of ABRAMS. All rights reserved. No portion of this book may be reproduced, stored in a retrieval system, or transmitted in any form or by any means, mechanical, electronic, photocopying, recording, or otherwise, without written permission from the publisher.

Printed and bound in the United States
10 9 8 7 6 5 4 3 2 1

Abrams books are available at special discounts when purchased in quantity for premiums and promotions as well as fundraising or educational use. Special editions can also be created to specification. For details, contact specialsales@abramsbooks.com or the address below.

Abrams® is a registered trademark of Harry N. Abrams, Inc.

ABRAMS The Art of Books
195 Broadway, New York, NY 10007
abramsbooks.com

BELOW Sandra Norup Andersen
FRONT ENDPAPERS Concept art by Almu Redondo
FOLLOWING PAGE Colour key by Almu Redondo
BACK ENDPAPERS Alice Dieudonné
CASE Áine Mc Guinness